Audience Feedback in the News Media

"Bill Reader traces a remarkable history of reader comment and feedback, bringing the phenomenon full circle from anonymity and partisanship through balance and restraint to today's faceless, nameless and full-throated digital free-for-all."
—*Frederick Blevens, Florida International University, USA*

"This book provides a revealing look at the public's conversation shared via the press. It lets readers know that even though technology has changed, today's ability for the individual to reach a mass audience has much more in common with the press before the 20th century than we might imagine."
—*David Copeland, Elon University, USA*

As long as there has been news media, there has been audience feedback. This book provides the first definitive history of the evolution of audience feedback, from the early newsbooks of the 16th century to the rough-and-tumble online forums of the modern age. In addition to tracing the historical development of audience feedback, the book considers how news media has changed its approach to accommodating audience participation, and explores how audience feedback can serve the needs of both individuals and collectives in democratic society. Bill Reader writes from a position of authority, having worked as a "letters to the editor" editor and having written numerous research articles and professional essays on the topic over the past 15 years.

Bill Reader is Associate Professor in the E.W. Scripps School of Journalism at Ohio University, USA. He is the co-author of two other books, *Moral Reasoning for Journalists* (2007) and *Foundations of Community Journalism* (2012).

Routledge Research in Journalism

Audience Feedback in the News Media

Bill Reader

Routledge
Taylor & Francis Group

LONDON AND NEW YORK

First published 2015 by Routledge

2 Park Square, Milton Park, Abingdon, Oxfordshire OX14 4RN
711 Third Avenue, New York, NY 10017

*Routledge is an imprint of the Taylor & Francis Group,
an informa business*

First issued in paperback 2018

Library of Congress Cataloging-in-Publication Data

Reader, Bill, 1970–
   Audience feedback in the news media / by Bill Reader.
     pages cm
   Includes index.
  1. Mass media—Public opinion. 2. Press—Public opinion.
3. Journalism—Public opinion. I. Title.
   P96.P83R425   2015
   302.23—dc23
   2014036835

ISBN: 978-1-138-77533-6 (hbk)
ISBN: 978-1-138-54865-7 (pbk)

Typeset in Sabon
by Apex CoVantage, LLC

Contents

Acknowledgements

In many parts of this book, I make the (somewhat unpopular) argument in defense of anonymity. But my 15-year journey to write this book has been assisted by many people, and I would be ungrateful to not mention them here by name.

My few years in the newsroom of the *Centre Daily Times*, especially my two years as opinion page editor, set the stage. I remain deeply grateful to John Winn Miller, then the editor, for hiring me; to Lou Heldman, then the publisher, for promoting me; to Becky Bennett, then the managing editor, for supporting me; and to Kakie Urch, then the assistant editor, for encouraging me.

I graduated from The Pennsylvania State University twice, and both times there were several professors who helped me to first become an award-winning journalist and later to become a relatively successful professor and researcher. Among my mentors from Penn State are Jock Lauterer, currently director of the Carolina Community Media Project at the University of North Carolina-Chapel Hill; Steven Knowlton, currently a professor at Dublin City University in Ireland; Shyam Sundar, Mary Beth Oliver, and Ford Risley, all senior faculty members of distinction at Penn State's College of Communication; and especially Richard Barton, who chaired my thesis committee and, as such, oversaw my first in-depth study of audience feedback in the news media.

My first academic job was at the University of Wisconsin-Milwaukee, and from my time there I'd like to thank my former colleague David Allen for his integrity and insights over the years. I am especially grateful to my former UWM colleague Tasha Oren and her husband, Stewart David Ikeda, who have been and remain steadfast friends.

At Ohio University, I have had many excellent colleagues who have since moved on to more success. They include the person who first hired me at Ohio, Michael Bugeja, now director of the Greenlee School of Journalism at Iowa State University; his successor, Jan Slater, who at the time of this writing is dean of the College of Media at the University of Illinois; Diana Knott Martinelli, associate dean of the P.I. Reed School of Media at West Virginia University; Deborah Gump, visiting professor at the University of South

Carolina School of Journalism and Mass Communications; and Dan Riffe, currently Richard Cole Eminent Professor in the School of Journalism and Mass Communication at the University of North Carolina at Chapel Hill.

I still have many excellent colleagues at Ohio University's E.W. Scripps School of Journalism, and I am grateful to my close friends and colleagues Eddith Dashiell, Mary Rogus, Carson Wagner, Aimee Edmondson, Mike Sweeney, and Yusuf Kalyango for their personal as well as professional generosity. Scripps Howard Visiting Professional Andy Alexander, professor Bernhard Debatin, and associate professor Hans Meyer also have been helpful colleagues over the years. I am especially grateful to school director Bob Stewart and to dean of the Scripps College of Communication, Scott Titsworth, for the sabbatical in the spring of 2013 during which the bulk of this project took shape.

At Routledge, I am thankful to Felisa Salvago-Keyes, editor, and Nancy Chen, editorial assistant. Their patience and support has been invaluable throughout this process; Routledge's excellent reputation is certainly owing to its having such excellent people on its staff.

Many of the "best practices" ideas describe in later chapters originated from excellent conversations via the International Society of Weekly Newspaper Editors, run by Chad Stebbins at Missouri Southern State University in Joplin. The ISWNE members who agreed to have their ideas included in this book include Andrew Schotz, Melissa Hale-Spencer, Bill Tubbs, Vernon Oickle, John Derby, and Erika Neldner. Other journalists who contributed include Cleveland's Tom Kelly, host of "Kelly and Company" on WHK radio, and Jim Ryan, who was editor of the Ohio University student newspaper, *The Post*, as this book went to press.

I cannot imagine having been in a position to tackle this kind of project without close friends and family. Bill and Elinor Reader raised me to work hard and not back down from a challenge, and so my parents get much of this thanks. My old friends Chris Curley and Kevin Moist are always there as philosophical sounding boards—they both have made me a better and deeper thinker. My neighbor and friend in Coolville, Ohio, is Walt Dowler, who, along with his Jack Russell terrier, "Jack," arrived at my door just in time for much-needed mid-afternoon breaks over the years (and while on the topic of faithful dogs, dear old Malcolm and frisky young Maggie deserve shout-outs as well). Finally, the last big push to get this project finished relied very much on the loving support, kindness, and patient compassion of my confidante and sweetheart, Sarah Harmelink.

Introduction

Turn to the index of any major book focused on the news media. Flip to the
L's. Look for the entry named "letters to the editor."

Most likely, you will not find much, if anything.

"Letters to the editor" is not listed in the index of Leonard Levy's *Emergence of a Free Press*,[1] nor in that of *Voices of a Nation* by Jean Folkerts
and Dwight L. Teeter Jr.,[2] nor in the index of *The Press and America* by
Michael Emery, Edwin Emery, and Nancy L. Roberts.[3] It is not in the indices
of David Halberstam's *The Powers That Be*,[4] in George Seldes's *Lords of
the Press*,[5] nor in *The Press* by Geneva Overholser and Kathleen Hall Jamieson (the latter does, however, have a listing for "Letterman, David," in the
space where "letters to the editor" would have appeared).[6] David Nord's
Communities of Journalism mentions letters to the editor in the body of the
text, but not in the index.[7] Gaye Talese had just three references to "letters
to the editor" in the index of *The Kingdom and the Power*, each only a brief
statement acknowledging that *The New York Times* received and published
letters.[8] The collected memoirs of renowned CBS News president Richard
Salant, interestingly enough, has a multi-item entry for "letters to the editor" in its index,[9] an unusual thing for a book about broadcast news. It is
also a bit disconcerting that one of the most elemental parts of journalism in
Western democracies—the publication of comments from the audience—is
not an indexed term in *The Elements of Journalism*, either, although they
are certainly mentioned (albeit briefly and superficially) in various parts of
that important treatise.[10]

Such collective oversight in such major works is both surprising and disappointing. The oversight is surprising, because of all of the modern practices of journalism, audience feedback is the one with the longest unbroken
tradition. News media have published opinions and objections from the
reading public since the 17th century at least; in fact, the early newsbooks
and newspapers were filled with them. The oversight is disappointing,
because if it hadn't been for the publication of opinions from the public, it is
doubtful that freedom of public expression would have achieved its status as
an inherent human right. Historically, the public arguments in the late 17th
and early 18th centuries calling for an end to government control of the

media were essentially letters to the editor. Some were signed but most were not, and instead were written under pseudonyms, such as "Cato," "Publius," and "Junius." Many of those pseudonyms belonged to noted statesmen, particularly in the British colonies in North America—John Dickinson as "A Farmer from Pennsylvania," James Madison and Alexander Hamilton as "Publius," John Adams under a variety of pen names including "Novanglus," "Humphrey Ploughjogger," and "U." Many of those pseudonyms were not revealed until years later, sometimes even after the writers had died.

At the time "freedom of the press" was first written into constitutions and laws, and long before the Internet age would expand those freedoms to some of the most repressed societies of the world, letters to the editor were the principle source of public discourse. For example, the First Amendment to the U.S. Constitution was written primarily to protect the rights of people to have their letters published in newspapers of the time, and less to set the stage for journalism to become a profession dominated by trained authors, powerful editors, and wealthy media corporations. Even discounting the role of audience comments in establishing the free press, it is hard to ignore that untold millions of letters to the editor have been published over the centuries, and that many more millions of unpublished letters, phone calls, and digital missives have been submitted to newspapers, magazines, radio "talkback" shows, and other media. Many news outlets created special positions to handle feedback starting in the mid-20th century, first "letters-to-the-editor editors" and, eventually, "community engagement editors," who deal with all manner of feedback today. The size and scope of the practice is simply too colossal to overlook by accident. The omission of "letters to the editor" in major works of journalism history and practice must have been either intentional or dismissive.

I am not suggesting that the authors of those important books have been wholly ignorant toward the existence of audience feedback, only toward audience feedback's importance. The lack of attention to the topic in such works does suggest, however, that the authors, their editors, and their publishers collectively have not considered audience feedback to be significant enough to even be indexed, let alone discussed in any deep or meaningful way as a significant part of the phenomenon of "freedom of the press."

Many who work within or for the big tent we call "journalism" tend to take the "forum function" of news media for granted, especially in the big leagues of the news business where audience feedback arrives in huge volumes, sometimes thousands of submissions daily. Before computer-mediated communication, dealing with feedback at huge media had been laborious and time consuming; today, those procedures have become largely automated and impersonal in nature via Web-based applications: submission forms, automated replies, server-side language filters, and online registration systems for writers, as well as various ranking-and-reporting buttons that readers can use to praise or condemn specific comments, or even to flag them for removal. And, on balance, many large media companies expend quite a bit of money and staff time to develop and manage those systems. But in the end, much of that effort seems only like so much traffic control. Large, mainstream media outlets might pretend that they are providing "community engagement," but their audiences are far too large and diverse to constitute discernable communities, and much of the engagement is an impersonal and abstract process of selection and rejection.

At the far more numerous mid-sized and small news outlets, however, the volume of feedback tends to be much more manageable: a few dozen submissions daily on particularly busy days, sometimes only a handful of submissions, and on some days none at all. Although not as well known or respected within the elite circles of the media industry or the academy, such small news organizations overwhelmingly dominate the journalism industry. In the United States, for example, the average newspaper is a weekly with a circulation of about 7,500; about 95 percent of all U.S. newspapers have circulations below 50,000; and small newspapers make up about 75 percent of total newspaper circulation in the country.[11] Small, community-focused publications also far outnumber the prestige press titles in England, Australia, Germany, Japan, and much of the industrialized world—the community press has been described as the "bottom of the iceberg" of journalism, much larger in size and scope than the prestige media outlets that are easier to see.[12] Small-media journalists tend to be far more accessible to their small audiences, allowing them to deal personally and individually with submissions from their readers or listeners.

For just one example, consider Melissa Hale-Spencer, editor of the weekly *Altamont Enterprise & Albany County Post* in upstate New York. Hale-Spencer is quite passionate about her newspaper's role as a forum for public debate in her community, and about her role in managing that forum. She edits and publishes several pages of letters for each edition of the weekly newspaper, often four to six pages of LTEs each week. The newspaper publishes a fairly typical "letters policy," which stipulates the newspaper's guidelines for letter-writers—no anonymous letters, no letters that have been published elsewhere, deadline information, and so forth. Large media outlets run similar policies too, but very few use them as anything other than a tool for rejection. The process used to prepare LTEs at the *Enterprise* is far more involved than merely rejecting and sorting according to those criteria—Hale-Spencer calls every letter-writer, including those whose letters are not suitable for publication to explain why and to offer suggestions for improvement.

"I usually chat, on average, five minutes with each writer, because I want to know who they are and why they're writing," she explained in a telephone interview.[13] In addition, all factual claims made in submitted letters are fact-checked by Hale-Spencer or one of her staff members: "We stick to the saying 'You're entitled to your own opinions, but not to your own facts,'" she said. If a fact error is discovered, the letter is not simply discarded, but usually sent back to the writer for correction or clarification, what academics usually call a "revise and resubmit," with clear guidance for acceptable revision. Hale-Spencer also will (rarely) agree to withhold the name of a writer if the person's safety or job could be adversely affected—an example she gave was when an employee of a local public school district complained about the district administration's budget priorities. Such individual attention toward writers has made the letters section of the *Enterprise* a vibrant and essential public forum in that community.

A three-hour drive to the south of Altamont, the headquarters of *The New York Times* does not provide anything close to that kind of individual response to the vast majority of its letter-writers. Starting in 2004, Letters-to-the-Editor editor Thomas Feyer explained it this way in an online message to readers (still online at this writing, more than 10 years later): "Thanks largely to the ease and ubiquity of e-mail, letters submissions (and a lot besides) come in relentlessly, round the clock, from around the country and around the world, at a rate of roughly a thousand a day. My small staff and I try to read them all, but we can publish only about 15 letters a day."[14] That number was reduced in 2007, when space for LTEs in the print edition of the *Times* was cut by a third, though more letters were published only on the *Times'* website.[15] Such paucity of accommodation leads to very thin odds of getting a letter published in the *Times*, except for letters penned by celebrities, power brokers, and those who play the law of averages. In early 2014, there was a bit of attention paid to one letter-writer who has had more than 200 letters published in the *Times* since 1987. That writer was interviewed on the public-radio program "On the Media," during which Feyer also was interviewed, and he admitted that the episode was the first time he and that prolific writer had spoken.[16]

In 2013, any reader who submitted a letter via *The New York Times* website received an automated reply, blandly titled "Automated Reply," that began with this paragraph:

> "Thank you for your letter to *The New York Times*.
> If your letter is selected for publication—in all editions (print and online) or only online—we will contact you within a week. We regret that because of the volume of letters received, we are not able to respond to all submissions, other than by this automated reply. . . ."[17]

Much can be inferred from comparing the feedback-management practices of those two very different newspapers. *The New York Times* recommends letters not exceed 150 words; *The Altamont Enterprise* gives writers up to 1,000 words to make their cases. The *Times* has an editor and staff devoted to handling feedback, but publishes only a tiny fraction of all submissions; the *Enterprise*'s top editor handles those duties in addition to all other newsroom management duties, and publishes nearly all LTEs that meet publication guidelines. Writers to the *Times* get an impersonal form letter that basically says the letter is unlikely to be published; writers to the *Enterprise* get a personal phone call from the editor, and, if the letter is rejected, a chance to rehabilitate the comment and try again. From all of the letters it receives, the *Times* constructs a relatively superficial capsule narrative about what some of its readers are thinking and saying; Hale-Spencer will publish every letter that fits the *Enterprise*'s criteria, providing a far more robust and representative narrative about the discourse in and near her community. The *Times* shifts most of the audience feedback it gets to its largely automated, chaotic online discussion forums; at this writing, the *Enterprise* does not provide online forums, preferring that readers express their views via the printed LTE forum.

AUTHORSHIP VS. WRITING

The alternate approaches of those two newspapers illustrate the differences between "authorship" and "writing," and how society applies different values and considerations to each. "Authorship" and "authority" share a common etymology, and in fact the latter is derived from the former as a reflection of the cultural power of scriptures and legal codes. A person can write an opinion or an idea, and even share it, but it has no inherent authority unless the person starts from a position of power and influence. Likewise, anything written by a person of power or prestige can absorb and transmit that authority, regardless of what is written—even if it is merely a signature, which is called an "autograph" if it is scribbled by a person of cultural import.

Consider an example from the autumn of 2012. Thousands of people write letters to the editor to *The New York Times* each day, and very few of them get published, let alone mentioned in other media, but when comedian Jerry Seinfeld wrote one in 2012 defending the popular use of the word "really" (that is, the letter was essentially about nothing), it was published and became news on a variety of mainstream media outlets, from Entertainment Weekly[18] to *The Daily Mail* in London,[19] to the entertainment section of "The Today Show."[20] Media blogger Jim Romenesko reported that Feyer, the *Times*' LTE editor, said the letter was the first LTE to be the most viewed item on the newspaper's website: "I've never seen anything like this," Feyer wrote to Romenesko.[21] The letter's popularity and newsworthiness was not based on its content, only on the popularity of Seinfeld—who was not just a "letter-writer," but an author writing a letter.

The privileging of authors over writers is a centuries-old phenomenon that began shortly after the development of the printing press and the expansion of public literacy that followed. Social theorist Walter Benjamin noted in 1936 that "[w]ith the increasing extension of the press . . . an increasing number of readers became writers—at first, occasional ones. It began with the daily press opening to its readers space for 'letters to the editor.' . . . At any moment the reader is ready to turn into a writer."[22] That observation, in Benjamin's celebrated essay "The Work of Art in the Age of Mechanical Reproduction," is tied to Benjamin's overall argument that an original work of art has an "aura of authenticity" lacking in even the most perfect reproductions. In the context of journalistic work, that "aura of authenticity" appears not in the original manuscript of an article or essay, obviously, but rather in the byline, the masthead, and the copyright—the marks of journalistic authorship that combine creation, control, and ownership.

Journalism is primarily an editor-driven enterprise, and most editors are themselves former authors, and so they perhaps are best described as "author-editors" whose value judgments are rooted in both practices. Author-editors seek and reward works that are specifically meant to be mass produced and widely distributed, and those works contain ideas, observations and, quite often, aesthetically pleasing prose, all of which are distributed to inform and influence the audience. Author-editors generally encourage members of the audience to further distribute those works via sharing the "original" (e.g., passing off the newspaper or magazine to a friend, or in the Internet age posting the link to one's Facebook wall or Twitter feed). The "aura of authenticity" of journalistic work is not lost in the reproductions unless they are stripped of the byline of the author, the control of the editor, and (most importantly) the copyright of the publisher.

Author-editors are often loath to share their authority, even if with the loyal audiences they rely upon. From the early 20th century forward, advances in publishing coupled with a professionalization of journalism initiated the news media to protect that authority by creating segregated, heavily managed spaces for such "readers-turned-writers." But even the segregation of audience feedback did not prevent many editors and scholars from judging that feedback from a detached, elite perspective. Not only were writers purged from the news columns, but their writing was screened according to the biases of author-editors. By the late 20th century, news media seemed only interested in publishing feedback that met the trappings of authorship—with poignant opinions, clear and engaging prose, and a valid signature from the writer—but without sharing the benefits of authorship: remuneration, artistic control, and professional advancement. The only benefit to such writers was to be allowed into the forums at all.

The distinction between "author" and "writer" is not just a differentiation of power, however. It is a distinction between numerous discrete and overlapping factors: intent and motives, technique, and expected outcomes. Twentieth-century philosophers Michel Foucault and Roland Barthes each considered the differences in various essays. Both essentially argued that "writing" is the common, everyday expression of thought, whereas "authoring" is a more professional endeavor that results in prestige and preferential consideration. Barthes was especially blunt in that regard: "The author performs a function, the writer an activity."[23] To Barthes, an author is a practiced hand (if not a professional) who blends technical mastery of the craft of writing with the aesthetic considerations of art. A writer, however, is someone who is merely trying to communicate something, Barthes argued. He further suggested that society places much higher value on the former, to the point that authored works become "a merchandise offered through traditional channels," whereas "the writer's language, on the contrary, can be produced and consumed only in the shadow of institutions."[24] Such institutions certainly include the professional press itself, and the authority it exercises over public participation in their self-described "public" forums.

Michel Foucault also considered the historical process by which writing was overpowered in culture by authoring. Foucault focused in large part on the value placed not on the authored work, but merely on an author's name. One example he gave was that mundane writings by a recognized author, such as a disorganized notebook, a memo, or even a laundry list by Friedrich Nietzsche, could be considered significant.[25] He wrote, "As a result, we could say that in a civilization like our own there are a certain number of discourses that are endowed with the 'author function,' while others are deprived of it. A private letter may well have a signer—it does not have an author . . . An anonymous text posted on a wall probably has a writer—but not an author."[26] Modern news media are likewise ensorcelled by prestige and fame, as evidenced by the aforementioned LTE by comedian Jerry Seinfeld. Many author-editors consider their audiences to be amorphous conglomerates to be managed and contained rather than as collectives of distinct individuals with whom to build distinct relationships. Whereas the news media began as collections of individual letters from a variety of writers (many of them purely anonymous), over time the professionalized press gave its best spaces to authors—bylined reporters and photographers, celebrated columnists, and op-eds penned by notable people. It shifted the nuggets of individual expression from audience members into confined spaces and segments, and then, by the late 20th century, into precious, exclusive spaces available only to the select few. The Web 2.0 era saw a tepid restoration of broader, egalitarian access to untrained and unsophisticated writers, but those online-only forums have for the most part been poorly managed and under-resourced ghettos of public discourse.

One problem with applying the standards of authorship to works of lay writing is that author-editors often don't appreciate negative criticism, and of course audience feedback is predominantly negative—complaints, objections, harsh rhetoric, and opinions of opposition and dissent. That can become wearying for even the most libertarian comments editor. A number of studies have shown, however, that readers of the forums tend to be more tolerant of such negativity (including unpleasant rhetoric or offensive opinions) than editors and journalists themselves.[27] Another common phenomenon is the predominance of the educated middle class to become "successful" feedback writers—"successful" in having their submissions selected and published. Studies of published LTE writers have consistently found that they are better educated and better off financially than the average person, and as such the aggregate opinions in such forums are rarely good indicators of broader public opinion.[28] That also means that such forums really are not utilized by a true cross-section of the community—they are not really "public" forums at all. That is especially true when media outlets require submissions to be signed, which is a primary marker of "authorship." Such "must-sign" policies can have a disproportionate deterrent effect on traditionally marginalized writers, such as women, racial minorities, the poor, and both young adults and senior citizens.[29] Even in essentially anonymous forums, such as the oft-maligned "online comment forums" found on most news websites, participants tend not to be representative of the general public (specifically, participants in such forums tend to be better educated and younger than average).[30] And, with regard to anonymity, many journalists make rather broad (and largely inaccurate) assumptions about both the motives of anonymous writers and the role of anonymity in modern rhetoric. Many journalists view anonymity as anti-democratic and inherently unethical, yet considerable research shows that anonymous discourse online is far more dynamic and communitarian than many journalists assume, despite the "bad apples" who post rude or disruptive comments.[31] Anti-anonymity sentiments in the journalism community are largely based on journalists' personal disdain toward anonymity rather than empirical evidence of the historical, legal, and ethical dimensions involved—in fact, many journalists reject and attack pro-anonymity arguments with visceral, dogmatic zeal, even when presented with evidence that casts serious doubts on their beliefs.[32] Still, even the most thoughtful author-editors are prone to make broad assumptions about their feedback forums, often with little understanding (or even awareness) of nearly a century of scholarly research focused specifically upon those very issues.

THE UNEXPLORED DEPTHS OF AUDIENCE FEEDBACK

The slow, long evolution of author-editor power in society reached its apex in the late 20th century, and that may be the overwhelming reason why the authors of so many works about journalism history and practice have made so little mention of audience feedback. Well-known journalists and scholars of the 2010s, most of them veterans of the newsrooms of the mid-to-late 20th century, carry with them many of the myths, ideals, and assumptions about journalism that were formed and propagated in that bygone era. When experienced journalists become teachers and researchers, many of those outdated beliefs and ideas go with them into the academy. Those beliefs and ideas invariably put an emphasis on the value of authorship in journalism, and give little consideration to the importance of the forum tradition. How many journalism schools offer courses in feedback management, for example, or even one or two units devoted to the practice? That may explain why so many of the most important anthologies of journalism history and practice published over the past several decades have given little to no attention to audience comments, and why more reference works devoted to the topic are needed.

There are a few such collections that exist—so few, in fact, that they can be enumerated in just a few paragraphs. But all told, the amount of serious scholarship devoted to the history of the "forum function" of journalism is woefully lacking. That dearth of information does a disservice to one of the most important roles of the news media.

One of the most significant scholarly contributions to date is from Karin Wahl-Jorgensen of Cardiff University, who arguably produced the first scholarly book on the subject with *Journalists and the Public: Newsroom Culture, Letters to the Editor, and Democracy* (2007: Hampton Press). The theoretical exploration of the editing process stems from her doctoral dissertation when she was at Stanford University. The book is primarily focused on Wahl-Jorgensen's discoveries while observing how letters editors at dailies in the San Francisco Bay area handled their duties—the result is an eye-opening account of how well-meaning and devoted journalists can become detached from and cynical toward the very audiences they try to serve. The forums constructed by those journalists can become heavily managed spaces that are not really all that democratic or representative of their communities. Wahl-Jorgensen's analysis of what she terms "the idiom of insanity" (an assumption among some journalists that many letter-writers are mentally unstable) and "hating the public" (the evolution of journalistic disdain toward feedback writers) were particularly helpful in many parts of this book.

Another prolific LTE scholar is Brian Thornton, currently at the University of North Florida, who has written more than a half dozen studies regarding the history of audience feedback in magazines and the ethnic press. Two studies by Thornton, "Disappearing Media Ethics Debate in Letters to the Editor"[33] (1998) and "The Moon Hoax: Debates about Journalistic Ethics in Four New York Newspapers in 1835"[34] (2000), helped me to develop my own line of research in this area while I was a full-time opinion-page editor and part-time graduate student in the late 1990s. Compiled together, Thornton's various "letters" studies would in the aggregate make a book-length contribution to understanding the role of feedback forums in media criticism and journalistic accountability, particularly in the 19th century.

There have been a few dozen peer-reviewed research articles produced on the topic by other scholars, but even then "letters to the editor" research is relatively scarce. A complication is that most research databases do not do a very good job of parsing "letters to the editor" as a research topic versus "letters to the editor" as an article format—used as a search term, the phrase is more likely to return actual letters to the editor than to gather only research articles about them. "Comments" can be an even more difficult search term in those databases, especially given the popularity of "online comments" as a research topic in the 2010s. There are surely some feedback studies that get overlooked as a result (and this author apologizes to those scholars whose works may not be mentioned herein).

The issue of "how to manage forums" does come up sometimes in news media or in journalism trade publications, usually as personal essays from editors or scholars or as decidedly unscientific bits of reportage and anecdote. For example, over the past decade, a number of very high-profile journalists have used their publications or trade journals to denounce anonymous comment forums based on anecdotes and unverifiable claims. In the mid-20th century, *The Masthead* (a trade magazine for editorial-page journalists, published by a professional organization since renamed Association of Opinion Journalists) published a few special issues devoted entirely to the issue of handling "letters to the editor," but those essays were dominated by anecdotes and were decidedly lacking in empirical rigor. Although such works cannot be considered "research" in any legitimate sense, they are nonetheless useful contributions that illustrate how professional attitudes have changed toward audience feedback, particularly through the 20th century and into the early 21st century. Many such essays and articles are referenced throughout this book as examples.

Devotees of audience feedback also can benefit from some of the better compilations of letters to the editor that have been published over the years. Although many are long out of print, copies should be available via university libraries or good used-book sellers. One of the best collections is *Letters to the Editor: Two Hundred Years in the Life of an American Town*,[35] compiled in the mid-1990s by several members of The Bloomsburg Theatre Ensemble in Bloomsburg, Pennsylvania. The book stemmed from an original stage play of the same name, in which the small-town theater troupe "performed" real letters that had been published since the 1700s in the Central Susquehanna River Valley of Pennsylvania. I was a daily newspaper reporter in the region at the time, and got to cover a full dress rehearsal of the performance before its premiere. I went back to see the full performance at least three times during its initial run. It was a mesmerizing performance, start to finish, and that stage play, and the book that followed, was perhaps the single most important inspiration for me to seriously study LTEs as a journalism scholar.

There are a few other LTE collections from the mid-20th century that could be of some interest to devotees. A series of books edited by Kenneth Gregory compiled letters from *The Times* of London, starting in 1976 with *Your Obedient Servant: A Selection of the Most Witty, Amusing and Memorable Letters to The Times of London, 1900–1975*.[36] Four more volumes followed, each using "Cuckoo" in the title (*The First Cuckoo, The Second Cuckoo, The Third Cuckoo*, and *The Last Cuckoo*). Another world-famous *Times* newspaper, *The New York Times*, was the source for another anthology of note, Kalman Seigel's *Talking Back to The New York Times: Letters to the Editor, 1851–1971*.[37] Both *Your Obedient Servant* and *Talking Back* to *The New York Times* include forewords and introductions that provide some insight into what editors at those newspapers thought about audience feedback at the time. The prolific compiler of letters to the famous and powerful, Bill Adler, also produced an LTEs anthology during that era, a slim and poorly referenced book titled simply *Letters to the Editor*,[38] which, because of a lack of attribution for individual letters, is of little utility beyond its entertainment value. Conversely, a fascinating and very useful collection published in 1992, *Dear Comrade Editor: Reader's Letters to the Soviet Press Under Perestroika*,[39] provides an important perspective for those who assume that "letters to the editor" and freedom of expression has only been a phenomenon of Western democracy.

Via the auspices of the vanity press, there also have been quite a few collections of letters to the editor that were compiled by the letter-writers themselves. Examples can be found from the mid-1700s through modern times, but of course such collections are of limited utility to most journalists and scholars beyond being artifacts of the self-importance (even narcissism) some "regular" letter-writers feel toward themselves.

And, of course, most modern news media have online archives that can be useful for those who want to search audience comments themselves and sort them by topic, date, and so on, to create their own customized collections. A few high-end databases, usually available only through university or public libraries, also make it far easier to find pre-Internet comments than was previously possible via faded-and-scratched microfilm and crumbling bound volumes (although not all digital scans of old print media are of readable quality). Digitized archives of very old publications are especially useful, as they not only provide the text of those comments, but also show them as they appeared and in the context of the rest of the publication, something that most online news archives do not do at all.

In closing, the reader should know that I have been actively researching audience feedback since 1997, and like most scholars I have my own packrat's nest of clippings, trade-journal articles, PDFs saved from websites, emails, etc., devoted to this particular topic of interest. I also have collected many thousands of audience comments, from original handwritten letters sent to me when I was a "letters editor" to raw examples shared with me by editors who share my passion for audience feedback. That personal collection is very much the skeleton of this book. But the flesh of the text is owed greatly to the scores of journalists who took the time and effort to share their thoughts and experiences with me over the years, sometimes in fierce debate but almost always in the spirit of collegiality. In many ways, this book is also a forum, constructed from uncountable contributions from the community of letter-writers and comment editors, past through present. Without such dutiful champions of audience feedback, modern journalism would be very, very different—and probably much, much worse.

NOTES

1. Leonard W. Levy, *Emergence of a Free Press* (Chicago: Ivan R. Dee, Publisher, 2004), 378.
2. Jean Folkerts and Dwight L. Teeter Jr., *Voices of a Nation: A History of Mass Media in the United States* (Boston: Allyn & Bacon, 2002), 577.
3. Michael Emery, Edwin Emery, and Nancy L. Roberts, *The Press and America: An Interpretive History of the Mass Media* (Boston: Allyn & Bacon, 1996), 717.
4. David Halberstam, *The Powers That Be* (New York: Alfred A. Knopf, 1979), 758.
5. George Seldes, *The Lords of the Press* (New York: Blue Ribbon Books, 1941).
6. Geneva Overholser and Kathleen Hall Jamieson, *The Institutions of American Democracy: The Press* (New York: Oxford University Press, 2005), 458.
7. David Paul Nord, *Communities of Journalism: A History of American Newspapers and Their Readers* (Urbana, Ill.: University of Illinois Press, 2001), 290
8. Gay Talese, *The Kingdom and the Power* (New York: The World Publishing Co., 1969) 100, 104, and 163.
9. Susan Buzenberg and Bill Buzenberg, *Salant, CBS, and the Battle for the Soul of Broadcast Journalism* (Boulder, Colo.: Westview Press, 1999), 319.
10. Bill Kovach and Tom Rosenstiel, *The Elements of Journalism* (New York: Three Rivers Press, 2007), 263.
11. Jock Lauterer, *Community Journalism: Relentlessly Local* (Chapel Hill, N.C.: University of North Carolina Press, 2006), 5–7.
12. Bill Reader and John Hatcher, *Foundations of Community Journalism* (Thousand Oaks, California: SAGE Publishers, 2012), xiv–xv.
13. Personal communication, March 22, 2013.
14. Thomas Feyer, "Our Compact, Updated," *The New York Times*, May 23, 2004. Accessed March 27, 2013, from www.nytimes.com/2004/05/23/opinion/23READ.html.
15. *The New York Times*, "To Our Readers," *The New York Times*, August 6, 2007. Accessed April 9, 2013, from www.nytimes.com/2007/08/06/opinion/l06note-web.html?_r=0.
16. On the Media, "Dear Editor," Radio show segment, April 25, 2014. Accessed May 26, 2014, from www.onthemedia.org/people/felicia-nimue-ackerman/.
17. *The New York Times*, "Automated Reply," Email to author, April 9, 2013.
18. Maane Khatchatourian, "Jerry Seinfeld Pens 'Really' Fuming Letter to the Editor," *Entertainment Weekly*, October 3, 2012. Accessed August 21, 2014, from http://popwatch.ew.com/2012/10/03/jerry-seinfeld-really-letter-new-york-times/.
19. *Daily Mail*, "Really? Jerry Seinfeld's Attack on New York Times Columnist for Rubbishing One of His Favourite Words," *The Daily Mail*, October 2, 2012. Accessed August 21, 2014, from www.dailymail.co.uk/news/article-2212088/Jerry-Seinfeld-defends-word-really-letter-editor-New-York-Times-columnist-rants-loathsome-trend-undoing-2–000-years-worth-human-progress.html.
20. Courtney Hazlett, "Jerry Seinfeld Really Defends the Word Really in Letter to New York Times," *Today.com*, October 3, 2012. Accessed August 21, 2014, from www.today.com/entertainment/jerry-seinfeld-really-defends-word-really-letter-new-york-times-6261013.
21. Jim Romenesko, "Jerry Seinfeld's Letter is #1—Really!," *JimRomenesko.com*, October 3, 2012. Accessed August 21, 2014, from http://jimromenesko.com/2012/10/03/seinfeld-letter-is-1-really/.
22. Walter Benjamin, "The Work of Art in the Age of Mechanical Reproduction," in Hannah Arendt, ed., *Illuminations: Essays and Reflections* (New York: Schocken Books, 1969), 217–52.

23. Roland Barthes, "Authors and Writers," in Susan Sontag, ed., *A Barthes Reader* (New York: Hill & Wang, 1982), 185–93: 186.
24. Barthes, "Authors and Writers," 190.
25. Michel Foucault, "What is an Author?," in Paul Rabinow, ed., *The Foucault Reader* (New York: Pantheon Books, 1984), 101–29: 103.
26. Foucault, "What is an Author?," 107–108.
27. Jack Rosenberry, "Users Support Online Anonymity Despite Increasing Negativity," *Newspaper Research Journal* 32, 2 (2011), 6–19; Bill Reader and Daniel Riffe, "Survey Supports Publication of Controversial Letters," *Newspaper Research Journal* 27, 1 (2006), 74–90.
28. Sidney A. Forsythe, "An Exploratory Study of Letters to the Editor and Their Contributors," *Public Opinion Quarterly* 14, 1 (1950), 143–44; H. Schuyler Foster Jr. and Carl J Friedrich, "Letters to the Editor as a Means of Measuring the Effectiveness of Propaganda," *The American Political Science Review* 31 (February 1937), 71–79; David L. Grey and Trevor Brown, "Letters to the Editor: Hazy Reflections of Public Opinion," *Journalism Quarterly* 47, 3 (1970), 450–56, 471; David B. Hill, "Letter Opinion on ERA: A Test of the Newspaper Bias Hypothesis," *Public Opinion Quarterly* 45, 2 (1981), 384–92; Ernest C. Hynds, "Editorial Page Editors Discuss Use of Letters," *Newspaper Research Journal* 13, 1&2 (1991), 124–37; Bill Reader, Guido Stempel, and Douglass Daniel, "Age, Wealth, Education Predict Letters to the Editor," *Newspaper Research Journal* 25, 4 (2004), 55–66.
29. Reader et al., "Age, Wealth, Education Predict Letters to the Editor."
30. Hans Meyer and Clay Carey, "In Moderation: Examining How Journalists' Attitudes Towards Online Comments Affect the Creation of Community," *Journalism Practice* 8, 2 (2013), 213–228.
31. Terry Connolly, Leonard Jessup, and Joseph Valacich, "Effects of Anonymity and Evaluative Tone on Idea Generation," *Management Science* 36, 6 (1990), 689–703; Rob Kling, Ya-ching Lee, Al Teich, and Mark Frankel, "Assessing Anonymous Communication on the Internet: Policy Deliberations," *The Information Society* 15, 2 (1999), 79–90; Adam N. Joinson, "Self-Disclosure in Computer-Mediated Communication: The Role of Self Awareness and Visual Anonymity," *European Journal of Social Psychology* 31, 2 (2001), 177–92; Boris Baltes, Marcus Dickson, Michael Sherman, Caroline Bauer, and Jacqueline LaGanke, "Computer-Mediated Communication and Group Decision Making: A Meta-Analysis," *Organizational Behavior and Human Decision Processes* 87, 1 (2002), 156–79; A. Christie Hurrell, "Civility in Online Discussion: The Case of the Foreign Policy Dialogue," *Canadian Journal of Communication* 30, 4 (2005), 633–48; Helen Kennedy, "Beyond Anonymity, or Future Directions for Internet Identity Research," *New Media & Society* 8, 6 (2006), 859–76; Stephen Rains and Craig R. Scott, "To Identify or Not to Identify: A Theoretical Model of Receiver Responses to Anonymous Communication," *Communication Theory* 17, 1 (2007), 61–91; Hiroaki Morio and Christopher Buchholz, "How Anonymous Are You Online? Examining Online Social Behaviors from a Cross-Cultural Perspective," *AI & Society* 23, 2 (2009), 297–307.
32. James Aucoin, "Does Newspaper Call-In-Line Expand Public Conversation?" *Newspaper Research Journal* 18, 3&4 (1997), 122–40; Bill Reader, "Should 'A Citizen' Have His Say? A Historical Argument for the Publication of Unsigned Commentary in 'Letters to the Editor' Forums," paper presented at the AEJMC Convention, History Division (Washington, D.C., August 2001); Bill Reader, "An Ethical 'Blind Spot': Problems of Anonymous Letters to the Editor," *Journal of Mass Media Ethics* 20, 1 (2005) 63–78; Bill Reader, "Free Press vs. Free Speech? The Rhetoric of 'Civility' in Regard to Anonymous Online Comments," *Journalism & Mass Communication Quarterly* 89, 3 (2012), 495–513.

33. Brian Thornton, "Disappearing Media Ethics Debate in Letters to the Editor," *Journal of Mass Media Ethics* 13, 1 (1998), 40–55.
34. Brian Thornton, "The Moon Hoax: Debates About Journalism Ethics in Four New York Newspapers in 1835," *Journal of Mass Media Ethics* 15, 2 (2002), 89–100.
35. Gerard Stropnicky, Tom Byrn, James Goode, and Jerry Matheny, *Letters to the Editor: Two Hundred Years in the Life of an American Town* (New York: Simon & Schuster, 1998).
36. Kenneth Gregory, *Your Obedient Servant: A Selection of the Most Witty, Amusing and Memorable Letters to The Times of London, 1900–1975* (New York: Methuen, 1976).
37. Kalman Seigel, *Talking Back to The New York Times: Letters to the Editor, 1851–1971* (New York: Quadrangle Books, 1972).
38. Bill Adler, *Letters to the Editor* (New York: Doubleday, 1967).
39. Jim Riordan and Sue Bridger, *Dear Comrade Editor: Reader's Letters to the Soviet Press Under Perestroika* (Bloomington, Ind.: Indiana University Press, 1992).

1 Audience Comments, the Spice of History

Historical research of news media often focuses on big headlines about relatively major events involving influential people. The better works also sprinkle in details from the smaller print of the inside pages—news briefs, legal announcements, advertisements, etc., that teach us about the vagaries of life in the previous century, or how much more our money would have been worth fifty years ago. Those little details provide a subtle but powerful context through which we can better understand significant historical events and people, but many times those small items are considered as little more than rhetorical ornaments.

The same holds true for letters to the editor and other forms of audience feedback. Based on how letters have been treated in major works of media history, one might be inclined to find such items interesting, even amusing, but not terribly important. Scholars, students, and journalists themselves too often skim past the letters to the editor that are ubiquitous in source materials in search of big headlines and famous bylines. Which is (if you'll forgive a food metaphor) like making a stew with only major ingredients and leaving out the pinches of this and dashes of that. Ignoring audience feedback in media history is like cooking without herbs and seasoning.

Even a single letter to the editor can be a fascinating and illuminating artifact. Independent of the opinion expressed therein, one can learn a lot from studying a unique piece of feedback. An LTE can reveal a lot about the writer and about the culture of that time and place, and it also can reveal a lot about the author-editor who allowed it to be published. Consider the following analysis of an LTE by "Delia" from the late 19th century. By most standards of modern scholarship, the letter itself is not "significant." It was published nearly five generations ago in a long-defunct, essentially forgotten small newspaper from a rural, small town. It was written by an unknown person, likely someone of little importance in that small town at the time. It was printed on a date of little historical note. The writer makes a common complaint about a common issue, all within a decidedly local context that wouldn't matter much to someone living a day's drive away (either a drive by motor vehicle or a drive by horse-drawn carriage). The prose is clean, but not necessarily poignant. The letter does not have significance by extension, either—it does not refer to an important event, an important date, or any important people. The letter to the editor is about as "typical" as it gets, all things considered. And yet from that small item, the only letter published in the May 31, 1877, edition of the weekly, four-page *Montour American* of Danville, Pennsylvania, we can construct a better sense of that time and place, and of the person who wrote that letter.

'DELIA'

She was born into an age of lingering oppression, in the last days of American slavery and the earliest days of the women's suffrage movement. She entered the world after the ratification of the U.S. Constitution and lived through the U.S. Civil War. Her central-Pennsylvania town was thriving in 1877 thanks to the bustling iron mills just inland from the north branch of the broad Susquehanna River. The previous year, the first-ever World's Fair was held outside of Philadelphia, less than 150 miles to the southeast via the Reading Railroad. Maybe she went; more likely she read about it in one of the local newspapers, such as *The Intelligencer* or *The Montour American*. She read *The Montour American* at least enough to be familiar with its unpublished policies regarding submissions intended for publication, which is why she submitted her own letter to the editor.[1]

The Seneca Falls Convention had been held 30 years earlier, and it would be 40 years more before the Nineteenth Amendment to the U.S. Constitution gave women the constitutional right to vote in that country. Clearly aware of the smoldering women's rights movement across the post-Civil War nation, she felt the need to at least mention it in the opening of her letter: "I am not what men call a 'woman's rights woman,'" she began. "I have never asked to preach, to lecture or to vote. . . . I do not aspire to be a justice of the peace or a school director. I am willing to confine my influence and my enjoyments mainly to my own home."

"Still," she continued, "I have some rights outside my home. God gives some things to the human family without distinction of age or sex. Among these are pure air and pure water." For an example, she discussed her farm's spring-fed well, which her family had excavated and "walled up with stones, and there is the living water, as pure as crystal bubbling up and over those stones."

"Now I think I have a right to that water pure as it is, and no one can rightfully put anything into that spring which will pollute it," she wrote. "The same would apply, even more strongly, to a public fountain. So also God gives us the pure air and fit for breathing and no one has the right to render it impure and unfit for breathing, yet this is done and done in a manner very offensive."

She explained that she often goes into town to shop and run errands, "and in walking, often get behind two or three men with pipes or cigars in their mouths filling the air with the stench of burning tobacco and making it entirely unfit to breath," she complained. "I often turn and cross the street to get rid of the nuisance only to fall into the snare again. I go into a store and find one or two men smoking there. I go to the post office and generally find it filled with a cloud of smoke which I can scarcely endure long enough to get my mail."

"In carriages and places of amusement," she continued, "even in the vestibule of the church, everywhere, I am exposed to the nuisance."

Tobacco use itself did not offend her to the point that she would want to ban it entirely. Nor was she inclined to use her letter to tell people what they should or should not do in their own homes or solitude. She was just asking for certain residents of her community (mostly men) to show some consideration toward non-smokers (mostly women). "Let smokers understand that tobacco smoke is offensive to all but smokers and that very few ladies are smokers," she stated. "Let common courtesy teach them not to pollute the air on the streets and in places of common resort. Ladies and others who do not smoke have some rights which smokers ought to respect. If they must smoke out of their house or some room set apart for such a purpose, do let them be on some by-streets and not in the public thoroughfare, and, when they enter the post office or a store or any other place of business, do let them leave their pipe or cigar outside."

She made one final request in her essay distinct from the issue of public smoking: "I suppose it is your rule that correspondents shall give their names, but, if you can suspend that rule for the present, you will much oblige, DELIA, Danville, Pennsylvania."

Delia's letter, like many comments published in the news media over the past four centuries, is not just a statement of opinion. Nor is it simply a historical artifact. It is an extension of the writer's personality, a public avatar of the private self. Not all letters provide those glimpses directly, but even the most impersonal prose can reveal something about the writer, or at least the writer's state of mind at the time of composition. Polite people tend to write polite comments; passionate people tend to write passionate comments; people who are angry write angry prose; people who are hateful write hateful prose, and so forth. It is not difficult to also identify from the rhetoric they employ that writers can be zealots and partisans, optimists or pessimists, playful or humorless, etc. Minor rhetorical clues often can help the reader to discern the writer's gender, relative age, educational background, social status, and, of course, ideological and political leanings. Considered against the context in which the feedback is produced, a single letter can tell us a lot about a writer.

In the case of Delia's letter, we can clearly tell that she was an adult woman, and the clarity of the prose suggests she had formal education. Was "Delia" really her name? It wouldn't matter if it hadn't been. The publication of her real name might have contributed little to readers' reactions to her opinion regardless, except perhaps among those who would have either known her or known of her. From today's perspective, she was and remains relatively anonymous anyway—even if I were to spend years trying to identify who she was and profile her biography, it is doubtful that such information would significantly enhance our interpretation of Delia's prescient anti-smoking message. Some might question the veracity of anonymous claims, and indeed many media professionals and scholars have clear and unwavering disdain toward anonymous or pseudonymous comments. But in the case of Delia's letter, residents of Danville, Pennsylvania, in 1877 could have easily assessed the veracity of her claims with their own senses—either the public's air was fouled by smokers, as she claimed, or it was not.

The flimsy authorship of the letter also raises questions of identity and accountability in regard to audience feedback. "Delia's" letter to the local newspaper could just as well have been signed "Dolly," or "Abigail," or even simply "A Local Farmer." And yet there are many clues that help us construct an idea of who Delia might have really been. She mentioned her family's farm, which in 1877, in that part of Pennsylvania, suggested a relatively middle-class lifestyle—many of the stately, well-appointed farmhouses built in that era near Danville remain to this day, along with their massive post-and-beam barns standing on robust stone foundations—elegant and expensive structures in their day, and many of them painstakingly maintained to this day by relatively affluent owners, few of them farmers. Delia also seems to have been ideologically moderate, evident from the core of her argument recognizing that individuals have certain liberties (such as smoking in public if they choose) but also have responsibilities to the community (such as not smoking on crowded streets or in public buildings). She also rather presciently predicted the anti-smoking campaigns that would curb such public smoking more than a century later, suggesting she was a deep, forward-thinking individual. To the community, at least, she clearly did not want to be known as a "women's rights woman," but she also demanded that she had certain rights nonetheless—to drink clean water, to breath clean air, and, obviously, to have her opinion heard and considered via the pages of a community newspaper.

Although Delia was the only person to have a letter published in that edition of the *Montour American*, she was not the only person to exercise that right on that day, or to provide examples of how individual LTEs can be important texts worthy of study.

MAY 31, 1877. UNITED STATES OF AMERICA

In the rapidly growing Midwestern state of Indiana, the imagery of tobacco smoke was invoked in another anonymous letter to the editor, although that letter was not nearly so demure or polite as the one by Delia. The Indiana letter concerned the results of an unusual local election. A board had been assembled to oversee the design and construction of a new statehouse for the Indiana state legislature, and an election was held for the position of "Secretary of the Board of State House Commissioners"—basically, the leader of the statehouse-construction committee. The election was won by John S. Tarkington, a prominent Indiana lawyer, military captain, and state legislator (and father of novelist Booth Tarkington, who was six years old at the time). One of the unsuccessful candidates for the position, or at least someone claiming to be one, submitted a letter to the *Indianapolis Sentinel* newspaper issuing a backhanded congratulations to "Captain Tarkington":

> "How happy the thought to the gallant captain as bright visions flit before him of an office, in the near future, over which he has absolute control; where he can procure his own Bogardus-kicker and smash the demnition sharks—of which there will of course be a plentiful supply—into eternal smithereens. . . . Never again will it be required of him to be surrounded by courts, juries, litigants and witnesses, among the fumes of tobacco, bad breath generated by foul stomachs, filthy mouths, too much scorpion juice, and lunching on garlic and onions, enough in itself to make one transferred from such a place to a small pox hospital, cry out: 'Mein Got in himmel, surely I am in a manufactory of attar roses!'
>
> "Happy, thrice happy Captain Tarkington, you are now in a position where you can join the Y.M.C.A., the red ribbons of anything else to your liking, and be a Christian, something no individual can attain as a deputy clerk, and in the hope that you may live long and prosper, and finally having left this vale of steers, if you should enjoy a higher seat on the other side, you will look down with pity and consideration on the brave little band of thirty-eight loyal and true patriots you so ingloriously defeated. I bid you bon voyage.
>
> ONE OF THEM, Greencastle."[2]

It is doubtful that "ONE OF THEM" was unknown to Captain Tarkington, or even to other contenders for the ad hoc position. It may never be known whether the writer's true identity was known to the *Sentinel*'s editor, though it was relatively common practice of that time for editors to ask for writers' names and addresses as a "sign of good faith," even if such information often was not for publication. The seething irony and sharp wit in the letter is indicative of the same traits one would find in a living, breathing person with the same personality, perhaps someone who either identified with (or mocked) Americans of German ancestry who might still use the expletive "Mein Got in himmel" ("My God in heaven"). The writer's anonymity was limited by his self-identification as one of about three dozen others who sought the same office. Likewise, the letter exudes an aura of petty jealousy and righteous indignation, neither of which are much flattering to the writer. A reader of the *Sentinel* that day did not need a name to identify "ONE OF THEM" as a sore loser, and a cowardly one at that.

In New York City, however, "ONE OF THEM" might not have been able to hide his name from James Gordon Bennett Jr., the second-generation publisher of the venerated *New York Herald*. The *Herald*'s popular column, "Our Complaint Book," was happy to publish harsh criticisms of local officials and biting sarcasm, but the column began with this notice: "Letters intended for this column must be accompanied by writer's full name and address to insure attention. Complainants who are unwilling to comply with this rule simply waste time in writing."[3] The rule did not apply, however, to publishing those names—only one of the eleven "complaints" published that May 31 included a credible name. The other ten were signed only with initials or labels, including "One of the Residents," "The Conductors, Third Avenue Railroad," and "Coelebs (Not) in Search of a Wife." The latter was lamenting the lax grammar of wedding announcements in the newspaper: "To state that Mr. Brown was married 'to' Miss White by the Rev. Dr. Black constructively indicates that the former only was married, the use of the preposition 'to' being, I think, altogether wrong; whereas, instead of it the conjunction 'and' would more correctly state the absolute fact. Am I right?"[4]

The *Boston Daily Advertiser* also published letters without names, although its letters policy in 1877 suggested that writers had to identify themselves to the editor as well: "We do not read anonymous letters and communications. The name and address of the writer are in all cases indispensable as a guaranty of good faith."[5] It was under that rule that the *Advertiser* gave space in its May 31 edition to a letter signed "A Russian," whose scathing rebuke of a local stage play called "The Dani-Sheffs" suggested the actors "slaughter the Russian language every night (besides matinees) in a merciless manner, and the cries of the tortured call forth no avenger."[6] "A Russian" also used the letter to object to the play's alleged misuse of titles when referencing Russian aristocracy, to suggest that a Russian serf could not credibly "monologize *á la* Hamlet about love, friendship, duty, sacrifice, &c.," and to dispute the story's characterization of a "typical" liquor merchant in that country ("a pure creation of imagination, since a liquor-seller in Russia is never worth 100,000 rubles, is never found in good society, and is never approached by a powerful princess with respect."). The writer was willing to pardon those offenses as "poetical (?) license," but concluded that "Even this crime against truth could be overlooked; but my tortured mother tongue appeals to me for relief, and I herewith make my protest."

The publication of a letter-writer's true name may have been optional in 1877 newspapers, but not if the goal of the letter was to defend one's honor in the public eye. Such was the case of "M. N. Murray," who used that day's edition of *The Cincinnati Commercial* to provide his account about his role in a recent incident involving an employer-employee dispute, a handgun and "bowlders" (Mr. Murray's spelling of "boulder," which for him meant rocks that a person could reasonably throw):

> "My name having had some prominence before the public, in connection with a shooting affray, and in some instances carrying the impression that the same was the result of a quarrel between myself and a colored employee, it is perhaps pardonably proper to briefly state the

facts. Those who are acquainted with me need no assurance that I do not quarrel with my employee. My position was one of self-defense entirely against a most vicious and persistent assault with bowlders, thrown with evident determination to kill me, this desperado having followed me to the field after his discharge, to a point where such missiles were abundant. . . . This party had menaced me with bowlders, and threatened my life the preceding day, when, as usual, I was not armed. He was then requested to resort to peaceable means of adjusting his fancied grievances. On the day of the affray, however, heedless of repeated requests and warnings to keep away, he rushed upon me, and not until my life was in imminent jeopardy did I resort to my revolver to protect it."[7]

Far to the south and west, *The Galveston Daily News* in Texas published a letter to the editor that same day, signed only by "G." The letter contained news from Lancaster, Texas, located 200 miles to the north in still-rural Dallas County and 15 miles south of the county's namesake city.[8] Despite "G.'s" unwillingness to be fully identified, he or she apparently had no problems with sharing the names of others. "There is another desperado caught," the letter begins, and it goes on at some length detailing the exploits of "a young man calling himself Charles Warren" who, according to G., landed in the Corsicana jail (some 40 miles south of Lancaster) after a "drunken spree at Spring Hill." The young man's horse and saddle were sold to settle his fine, and he spent ten days in jail, G. reported. Upon Warren's release, he sought pity at "the house of a Mr. Leslie," who offered food and lodging. "Leaving the house some time during the night, Warren stole Mr. Leslie's fine dun mare and silver mounted saddle," the letter continues. A few hours behind Warren's flight to the north, Mr. Leslie passed through Lancaster, "his horse being about broken down. After making his statement, he was furnished with a fresh horse, and four of our young men, viz: Charlie George, Willie Taylor, James Lindsey and W. L. Grove, armed and mounting good horses, started with Leslie in pursuit. . . ." The vigilante posse caught up with Warren close to sundown that day, "and had him in town under a watchful guard by one o'clock the same night." The writer further explained that "[y]oung Lindsey recognized Warren as being one of the five prisoners who broke from the Weatherford jail some time ago," and noted that "[i]t is also said there is an indictment for murder hanging over Warren in Collin county, and that a reward of $800 is offered for his apprehension. If this be so, these boys richly merit it for their readiness and willingness to respond to the call of this single citizen of another county. . . ."

Perhaps recognizing that readers in Galveston might be interested in other news from Dallas County some distance to the north, G. obliged by abruptly changing the topic in the last paragraph to more mundane matters:

"The farmers are busy harvesting all around us now, with a promise of fine yield. One field near here, it is thought, will turn out forty bushels of wheat to the acre. The corn and cotton planted since the grasshoppers left is up and growing off finely. Weather is all right, with just enough rain to suit the crops. Local option working like a charm."

That small collection of letters, chosen only via a simple date-specific search of digitized newspaper archives, helps to illustrate that comments are not just extensions of their writers' personalities, but also artifacts that capture the vagaries of culture from specific times and places. While Delia's letter to *The Montour American* was focused on the annoyance of public smoking in her community, the other letters mentioned above are very much rooted in local issues of short-term interest in their own communities. The election of the "Secretary of the Board of State House Commissioners" was of little long-term significance, and of even less significance beyond the minutia of Indianapolis history. Without meaning any offense to possible descendants of M.N. Murray of Cincinnati, his letter is of no major significance, either, other than to remind us that "self-defense" shootings were somewhat controversial in the late 1800s (as they remain in the United States in the early 21st century). The Boston letter from "A Russian" reminds us that the performing arts always have been subject to harsh, biting reviews from unnamed critics, and the New York letter from "Coelebs (Not) in Search of a Wife" reminds us that grammar mavens have long tried to impose their rules upon all written communication. And from Texas, "G." reminds us that the American West could be wild in the 1870s, but such adventures did not preclude the importance of sharing the more important minutia of life, such as news about the recent weather and the vigor of local crops, and praise for the "local option," or the ability of counties and municipalities to ban or regulate controversial practices, such as gambling or the sale of alcoholic beverages, according to local customs.

Individually, the letters are amusing and interesting, and that alone may be justification enough for comments to figure more prominently in the historical research of journalists and journalism scholars. But read together, they construct a small narrative about the United States in 1877, early in the Reconstruction period (the Civil War, which ended in 1865, was still a raw issue). In the Northeast, we read of decidedly urbane issues—concerns about arts and letters and the rules of "common courtesy." In the Midwest, we see rhetoric that reflects lingering frontier attitudes, such as coarse political sniping and the use of firearms to resolve disputes. From Texas, we get a glimpse of true frontier life.

Of course, that narrative would only become richer and more meaningful if more letters from more newspapers published on that date were analyzed. The same could be true of letters published on any other date. What would we learn from a study of letters published December 6, 1941, the day before Pearl Harbor? Or on other "days before"—August 31, 1939? January 29, 1972? September 10, 2001? The typical approach to history would be to focus only on the feedback published after, and regarding, major events—Nazi Germany's invasion of Poland, the Bogside Massacre in Londonderry, Northern Ireland, on "Bloody Sunday," and the horrific terrorist attacks of 9/11. What the people were saying in their community news outlets leading up to such major events, or even independent of such events, is a far-too-often overlooked part of media research and criticism to this day.

CONTEXT BEFORE CHRONOLOGY

The following chapters will lay out a chronology of the evolution of news-media comment forums in the English-speaking world, starting with the London newsbooks of the 1600s—composed almost entirely from unsigned "letters"—and concluding with the chaotic cacophony found in the comment threads of modern media websites. Those chapters are most certainly focused on important milestones and significant moments, and the examples chosen may, of course, seem to favor the juiciest bits of the most tantalizing items. But before getting to that chronology, it might be helpful to consider the broader context of what comments have and have not been able to tell us over the centuries.

First, individual comments should be considered like individual snowflakes—each one different from the other, but only if you look closely enough. For going on five centuries, individual bits of audience feedback have been and remain decidedly idiosyncratic. An empirical content analysis may discern predictable patterns or consistent memes across relatively large and random samples, but that does not mean that each comment can be entirely defined by a pre-determined categorization or coding scheme. Audience feedback is far, far more complicated than that. Each original comment is a product of a unique person writing from a specific place within the cultural context of a particular time—even in the case of "astroturf" LTEs, in which individuals sign their names to memos that were pre-written by special-interest groups, the motivations to submit such feedback is often rooted in very individualized, personal beliefs and values. It is quite easy, for example, to spot similarities among comments written about America's war against North Vietnam circa 1974 and among comments about America's war against Iraq circa 2004, particularly in feedback discussions about "supporting our troops" and "protesting the war," but it would be folly to ignore the many things that made each wartime period unique, or to ignore that the former war originated many of the memes and tropes that were evoked in rhetoric concerning the latter. Similarly, Delia's letter against public smoking was not a harbinger of things to come, nor should it be used as "proof" of any widespread, popular anti-smoking campaigns in the late 1800s—all it means is that, in late May 1877, Delia had had enough of choking on the tobacco smoke of inconsiderate men in downtown Danville, Pennsylvania.

Second, and as experienced historians know quite well, comments should never be used to make assumptions about "public opinion at the time."

Several empirical studies throughout the 20th and early 21st centuries have provided overwhelming evidence that published comments are not accurate reflections of broader public opinion.[9] Comment forums may be promoted as being "open to the public," but not everybody in the public has participated in that process—nearly a century of research about letters to the editor has determined that, in the U.S. at least, letter-writing has been dominated by middle-aged, middle-class people with above-average educations.[10] Although research of online-comment forums is relatively nascent at this writing, early indications suggest that comment-writers also are not representative of the broader public, and tend to be younger and more educated than average.[11] Moreover, comment forums are highly susceptible to the construction of narratives that can create illusions of false majorities, misleading or exaggerated exemplifications, and the perpetuation of unfair stereotypes and common myths (that is, factual assumptions that are not reinforced by actual facts, such as the assumption that the Continental Congress voted to separate the American colonies from Great Britain on July 4, 1776—the vote actually occurred two days earlier).

Furthermore, relatively few comments submitted to managed forums get published, particularly with regard to letters to the editor in print media and audience comments broadcast on radio talk shows, which further erodes the utility of comments in predicting broader public opinion. Complicating the selection process further is that letter selection and editing is a highly subjective process that deals with many variables on a day-to-day basis—an editor may be willing to publish every letter on hand on a Wednesday, but may only choose to publish a small percentage of letters on hand that Friday. Some editors are happy to publish letters on any topic the writers choose, but others may automatically reject letters that are not directly responding to previous articles in the publication. Even the editor's mood on a particular day could influence whether a submission is published, the degree to which it is edited, etc. Simply put, comments can only be interpreted in the context of "what ended up being published," and never as a representative sample of what was submitted.

The third most important limitation in using comments for historical research is the human tendency to apply modern bias to interpretation of historical artifacts. For example, contemporary readers may interpret Delia's initial statement, "I am not a 'women's rights woman,'" as a right-wing, anti-feminist declaration. That might be a fair analysis if Delia had written the comment to one of the newspapers serving Danville in 2013, or even in 1973, but it would not be reasonable or intellectually rigorous considering that she wrote the letter in 1877. Although the U.S. Constitution would not be amended to enfranchise women voters nationwide until four decades later, in 1877 it was a controversial issue very much on the front burner of social dialogue. The territory of Wyoming had given women the right to vote in 1869 and the Utah territory followed in 1870 (and the latter repealed that policy in 1887). During the Reconstruction era in the U.S., many women protested their disenfranchisement by registering to vote and showing up to polling places in defiance of the law, clear acts of civil disobedience.[12] In 1877, the women's rights movement of that time was often viewed as a disruptive radical activity that was eschewed by many ideological and political moderates. At the time of Delia's letter, the liberal women's suffrage movement also was gradually being enjoined by another "radical" movement, the conservative Women's Christian Temperance Union, as both movements had at their core a belief that women could only exercise their moral authority in the home if they also had a voice in the voting booth.[13] Delia's letter suggests that she may not have been staunchly opposed to women's suffrage (she wrote only that she had "never asked . . . to vote" herself) and also that she was not an advocate of strict temperance (she did not call for smoking to be outlawed, only that smokers show some courtesy toward non-smokers in public spaces). Assuming the letter is an accurate reflection of Delia's socio-political leanings, it would be fair to surmise that she was essentially a moderate, and that declaring "I am not a 'women's rights woman'" was intended to distance herself, and her opinions, from radical, disruptive groups—and, by extension, proactively disarming potential criticisms from readers of *The Montour American* that her views about tobacco use may also be radicalized. Certainly, experts who have spent years studying both the Reconstruction period and the women's rights movement may have even more sophisticated, alternative interpretations. The point here is that without spending some time studying the historical context in which an individual comment was written, or a thread of such comments, the reader should not make assumptions about how that comment was interpreted at the time.

There are other limitations to studying comments to news media, but a fourth is to recognize that "the news media" is not a monolithic enterprise that has a tradition (or even a present) of standard universal practices. There are "common practices," certainly, but such norms are by no means universally accepted or consistently implemented, whether it involves the use or prohibition of anonymous sources, the publication or exclusion of "dead-body photos," whether and how to cover suicides, and so forth. The same has been and remains true for how various news outlets deal with audience feedback.

Many of the earliest English-language news publications, the "corantos" or "newsbooks" of the 1600s, were composed almost entirely of information gleaned from "letters." By the rise of newspapers in the 1700s "letters" were often prominently displayed alongside news items and advertisements, and many news reports and advertisements were also essentially "letters." Some newspapers and magazines began to separate "letters" into their own sections in the 1800s (such as *The New York Herald*'s "Our Complaint Book," which was mentioned earlier and is discussed in greater detail in Chapter 4). But not all did so. Some editors delighted in publishing harsh criticisms of their papers, while others were loath to print any such thing.[14]

Until the mid-20th century, anonymity in published feedback was the norm, not the exception, and the sometimes draconian "signature required" criteria many large news organizations apply to their "letters" section today simply did not exist for more than three centuries. The relative chaos of today's online forums are, in many ways, far more "traditional" than the sanitized, highly selective LTE sections of major publications, such as *The New York Times* or *The Times of London*, and the many thousands of smaller, community-focused newspapers and magazines currently in circulation. Even by the 20th century, when most newspapers and magazines started using the common label of "Letters to the Editor" and migrated those items to their opinion sections, each publication maintained its own way of handling submissions and constructing the forums, particularly among the multitude of community news outlets that greatly outnumber (in both quantity and total audience) the so-called "mainstream media."

Such differentiation continues to this day. The advent of online-commenting forums has only amplified that differentiation, with some publications implementing strict rules and pre-approval before allowing submissions to be posted, while others leave their forums more or less wide open to any and all comers. And although some might assume that the "newsbook" model of compiling whole publications from audience letters is lost to antiquity, the truth is there are still quite a few publications—both print and online—that are almost entirely composed of unsolicited, uncompensated submissions from readers.

Clearly, the news media's use and reliance upon feedback from their audiences has been not only a historical tradition that is maintained today as a vestigial, quaint practice, but is also a living reality of modern journalism practice, and is likely to remain so into the foreseeable future. The explosion of channels for public discourse enabled by the Internet and computer-mediated communication has created many new and interesting developments in the ways audience feedback can be solicited, gathered, sorted, used, and published. Those new practices also create new challenges and concerns for all involved, from the author-editors who manage such forums to the individual participants who turn to them as outlets for their expression.

Now more than ever, it is vitally important for those who manage, study, and use feedback forums to know more about the history of audience feedback, to tap into existing and emerging research about feedback, and to be more cognizant of the cultural importance of the phenomenon in modern society. As feedback forums become more sophisticated, so does the profession's thinking about those forums. The gut feelings, personal biases, and author-editor conceits that dominated feedback management through the late 20th century are just as important as Delia's complaint about public smoking, only in the context of what came before. They are far less useful, and appropriate, for what is happening now.

NOTES

1. Delia, "Editors of the AMERICAN" [letter to the editor], *The Montour American*, May 31, 1877, 3.
2. One of Them, "Gives it up. A candid candidate's phylosophy" [letter to the editor], *The Indianapolis Sentinel*, May 31, 1877, 3.
3. *The New York Herald*, "Our Complaint Book" [editor's note], *The New York Herald*, May 31, 1877, 9.
4. Coelebs (Not) in Search of a Wife, "Marriage Announcements" [letter to the editor], *The New York Herald*, May 31, 1877, 9.
5. Untitled note, *The Boston Daily Advertiser*, May 31, 1877, 2.
6. A Russian, "The Dani-Sheffs" [letter to the editor], *The Boston Daily Advertiser*, May 31, 1877, 2.
7. M. N. Murray, "A Card" [letter to the editor], *The Cincinnati Commercial*, May 31, 1877, 4.
8. G., "Horse Thief Arrested—Wheat and Corn" [letter to the editor], *The Galveston Daily News*, May 31, 1877, 3.
9. David L. Grey and Trevor R. Brown, "Letters to the Editor: Hazy Reflections of Public Opinion," *Journalism Quarterly* 47, 3 (1970), 450–56, 471; Sidney Forsythe, "An Exploratory Study of Letters to the Editor and Their Contributors," *Public Opinion Quarterly* 14, 1 (1950), 143–44; William D. Tarrant, "Who Writes Letters to the Editor?," *Journalism Quarterly* 34, 3 (1957), 501–2; Gary L. Vacin, "A Study of Letter Writers," *Journalism Quarterly* 42, 2 (1965), 464–65.
10. Bill Reader, Guido Stempel III, and Douglass K. Daniel, "Age, Wealth, Education Predict Letters to the Editor," *Newspaper Research Journal* 25, 4 (2004), 55–66.
11. Hans Meyer and Clay Carey (2013) "In Moderation: Examining How Journalists' Attitudes Toward Online Comments Affect the Creation of Community," *Journalism Practice* 8, 2 (2013), 213–228.
12. Angela G. Ray, "The Rhetorical Ritual of Citizenship: Women's Voting as Public Performance, 1868–1875," *Quarterly Journal of Speech* 93, 1 (2007), 1–26.
13. Amy R. Slagell, "The Rhetorical Structure of Frances E. Willard's Campaign for Woman Suffrage, 1876–1896," *Rhetoric & Public Affairs* 4, 1 (2001), 1–23.
14. This author once worked for a publisher who forbade the opinion-page editor of the newspaper to publish any letters that criticized the newspaper itself (criticisms of specific articles and editorials were fine). The daily newspaper was owned by a very large and well-known media company. That local prohibition was an awkward situation, to be sure, but illustrative of the dubious nature of claims regarding "professional standards" in journalism.

2 "Packets of Letters"
Audience Comments Before Freedom of the Press

Audience feedback obviously predates the printing press, because as long as there have been public statements there has been the potential for public response. For millennia, town criers and ad hoc stumpers were cheered and jeered by the crowds they addressed. Proclamations from on high were met with boisterous support or sullen complaint, and the brave few who made statements unfavorable to the public majority or the powers-that-be often experienced responses that were far more severe than heckling. After the start of the printing industry in Western Europe, printers also faced violent attacks (on property, person, or both) if the writings they published crossed the line in criticizing the aristocracy, the church, or any others with too much power and too little patience for dissent. Some editors printed dissent nonetheless, using loopholes, guile, and open defiance in various combinations. But even those who embraced authoritarian controls and published only "official" content were not immune from rebuttal. A pro-establishment pamphleteer in 17th-century London was quite likely to see his opinions denounced the next week in the pamphlet of an anti-establishment critic. Copies of a broadside hung around town could easily be torn down, defaced, or covered with copies of another broadside offering a different point of view.

With the development of the printing industry, the timely exchange of opinions en masse no longer required large groups of people to be in the same space at the same time. The ability to replicate ideas on multiple sheets of paper negated the temporal, geographic, and ephemeral limitations of oral discourse. The printing press was a game changer for human civilization, not just in facilitating communication from few to many, but also in empowering the many to directly participate in generating content that printer-editors would aggregate into their papers. What many 21st-century scholars call "participatory journalism," defined as "the act of a citizen, or group of citizens, playing an active role in the process of collecting, reporting, analyzing and disseminating news and information,"[1] is really nothing new. In fact, participatory journalism predates the Internet by more than four centuries, starting with the "newsbooks" of Europe of the 16th and 17th centuries.

ORIGINS: 'NEWSBOOKS' AS PARTICIPATORY JOURNALISM

The earliest evidence of letters to the editor in the West are found in the "corantos," or newsbooks,[2] of 17th-century Europe. The first European newspapers, in fact, were attempted in the early 1500s, perhaps in Venice where such publications cost one "gazetta," source of the Anglicized word "gazette."[3] They were not the first newspapers the world had seen—printed newspapers in China were evident from as early as the 9th century CE,[4] and hand-copied news sheets were commonly distributed in ancient Rome and Persia as well.[5] But early newsbooks were not just disseminators of official proclamations and public notices from authorities, as was the case of those earlier publications. Newsbooks were the progenitors of the practice that allowed readers to participate directly in the news-making process by submitting their own reports and opinions for possible publication—indeed, newsbooks and early newspapers were, arguably, the first attempts at what we now call "citizen journalism."

Although some historians consider them to be "newspapers," 17th-century newsbooks really were quite different from the broadsheets that would replace them the following century. Most were published in quarto from relatively small sheets of paper, with eight pages on each side of a sheet that was then folded, trimmed and bound—as such they were formatted like small books, most not much larger than a modern pocket-sized notebook. Quite a few were one-and-done publications, and as such could not have been conduits for continuing discourse among readers simply because there were no successive issues in which to publish any feedback that might have been delivered. A relative few newsbooks achieved periodical status, most of them published weekly over a span of several months or, in rarer cases, several years. Most newsbooks were focused on distinct political movements or specific topics, further making them more akin to niche magazines than general-interest newspapers.

But like the early newspapers that replaced them, many newsbooks relied heavily on submissions from readers to fill their pages—much of the content in newsbooks and early newspapers was attributed to "letters" from a variety of sources. One of the London newsbooks published during the late 1640s was even named *Packets of Letters*, each item beginning with the salutation "Sir" and written more as a personal note to the editor than as a general correspondence to the readers of the pamphlets. Relatively few of the letters found in newsbooks were attributed to the writers by name, as anonymity was both common and necessary in the era of strict control of the press.[6]

A distinction here should be made between those newsbook letters that were truly examples of audience submissions and those that were merely official statements or reprinted material from other sources. The letters found in archived editions of those newsbooks varied considerably in both purpose and form, and although clearly attributed as "letters," some clearly were not examples of audience feedback. Some of those letters were official proclamations signed by government officials or military officers that announced new laws, charges of misconduct, or victory in battle—although those, too, were letters sent to newsbook editors, they have been mostly excluded from this analysis because they were more akin to what we now call press releases than they were to letters to the editor. Newsbooks also paraphrased news from "letters" provided to them by regional officials and, during wartime, letters captured from "the enemy"—ostensibly, intercepted dispatches sent between military leaders. Those items also have been excluded from this analysis. A few newsbooks were composed of nothing more than the minutes of official meetings, such as a transcript of a hearing before Parliament or the summary of a synod among church leaders. Whether those types of communications could be deemed "letters *to* the editor" by today's standards is open to debate, surely, as all of those items attributed as "letters" were submitted to editors. Regardless, there are plenty of examples of letters that are much more in line with "audience feedback" as to not require much more discussion of those letters.

Overall, newsbook editors placed considerable emphasis upon letters containing unofficial news and analysis. Much of the "news" in the publications came from the personal observations of the letter writers, much of it content that blended opinions with factual claims, all of it presented with clear bias and flimsy sourcing, and quite often presented in less-than-remarkable prose. Newsbook editors relied on receiving such letters, and in aggregating the content supplied by their readers (that is, supporters of their various positions or interests), editors mentioned those "letters" regularly and prominently. In doing so, whether by design or simply by custom, those editors created a modicum of transparency about their work, and also constructed a narrative of community involvement in the dissemination of news. An early example of that attribution is from November 1623,[7] when *The Proceedings of Bethelem Gabor in Hungary* attributed its news about the Thirty Years' War to various letters to the editor: "From Cullen againe, other Letters have it thus: Wee understand by the Letters from Prague, and Vienna, which are sent dayly hither, that Bethelem Gabor's Armie advanceth it selfe mightily, having blocked up many Fortresses and Holds in Hungary, and passed so farre into Moravia. . . ."[8] Even when summarizing and paraphrasing the content of such letters, newsbook editors felt it important enough to mention that the information came from letters they received regularly.

Such thin attribution was almost certainly a cautionary reaction to the censorship and regulation of the press of that era. In 1632, the Star Chamber under King Charles I abolished the publication of newsbooks in Britain altogether. But after the Star Chamber was abolished by the Habeas Corpus Act of 1640,[9] publication resumed with renewed vigor, and the newsbook industry bloomed in the English-speaking world. The disbanding of the Star Chamber was not the only cultural impetus; the concepts of free speech and freedom of the press were gaining popular support at that time throughout

Europe—that was the same time John Milton produced his *Areopagitica*, an influential treatise against censorship and advocating for freedom of speech, itself published without license.[10] Further, the cultural milieu preceding and during the English Civil War was reflected in (and enabled by) fierce partisanship on the part of newsbook editors and their partisan contributors.

Letters remained a dominant source of news and opinion for the newsbooks of the 1640s. For example, the June 11, 1645, edition of the *Exchange Intelligencer* had the following introductions to various news items: "There came a letter this day from a person who is dayly with Sir Thomas Fairfax, as having great relation to him. . . .";[11] "From Rome: By letters sent very lately from thence, by an English Gentleman gone to one that was lately chiefe justice of England. . . .";[12] "By letters from Amsterdam bearing the date of June 6, 1645, we are certified that there arrived thither June 5 [ten] ships out of Bresill. . . ."[13] Another example is from the *Flying Eagle* newsbook published December 11, 1652: "This day we understand by severall Letters from Rumney Marsh in Kent, and severall parts in Sussex, that the Dutch Fleet (who now lye neer Rys) have come a shore and plundered the people, and driven away much sheep and cattel of a considerable value. . . ."[14] Similar language can be found in most of the remaining newsbooks from that era.

For editors of those newsbooks, letters of suitable quality surely were scarce and valuable, their production dependent on a relatively small pool of correspondents who were both willing and able to gather information and write it down. It was surely "citizen journalism," but as we know, not everybody enjoyed the rights of citizenship in 17th-century England, and that made education and literacy far from a common thing. In the 1600s, even "crude literacy" rates were low—and "crude literacy" was measured only by the ability to sign one's name. In much of Europe and its far-flung colonies, crude literacy was estimated to be in the neighborhood of 35 percent to 40 percent overall.[15] Crude literacy is not, of course, an indication of the ability to write prose; as such, the potential pool of newsbook correspondents was quite limited to begin with. The ability to both read and write was mostly a benefit of wealth or status, and tended to be enjoyed mostly by urban elite males, as "upper status and male occupations demanded literacy more than the jobs allowed to the poor and to women. Cities provided concentrations of population to support schools and printing presses, and they provided jobs requiring literacy."[16] Amid such segregation of class and gender, letters to the editor of the 17th century could in no way have been broadly representative of "the people," and that limitation would continue as public education and literacy expanded over the centuries, and endures in some ways even into the 21st century.[17] The mere mention of a "letter" in a 17th-century newsbook signified that the information was from a learned person of status—that is, a "citizen" in the classical sense, not the modern sense.

For women, there were even more barriers through much of that century, as "social prohibitions . . . generally prevented women from reading in public, let alone writing their own material for publication."[18] Because so few of the letters published in newsbooks bore the writers' names, many literate women were able to circumvent those "social prohibitions" and contribute directly to publications in the mid-1600s,[19] and many more of various social standings did so openly by the end of that century.[20] In fact, anonymous writing, the norm in newsbook publishing, allowed far broader participation in public discourse than the "social prohibitions" of the era would have normally tolerated.

ANONYMITY IN THE AGE OF CENSORSHIP

With the exception of official declarations, the letters mentioned or reprinted in newsbooks rarely included the names of the writers, a detail that is of considerable historical significance to media professionals of the 21st century, who may have concerns about the anonymous nature of today's online discussion forums.

The culture of the 17th century helps explain why so few of the (wo)men of letters who contributed to newsbooks were identified by name. Repressive authorities throughout many of Europe's realms and colonies clearly attempted to circumvent criticism of their reigns through strict licensing and censorship initiatives. Many of the newsbooks circulating in England through that century were, in fact, printed in the more libertarian cities of the Netherlands specifically to circumvent such controls across the North Sea, and especially to get around the ban on newsbook printing imposed by Charles I in 1629.[21] Likewise, printers of German-language newsbooks operated from the Netherlands because in the central European kingdoms and principalities "power-conscious rulers preferred to allow Dutch papers into their domains rather than permit a native free press."[22] It was only between the end of the Star Chamber in 1641 and the British Parliament's resumption of prior restraint via the Licensing of the Press Act of 1662 that English newsbooks enjoyed their 20-year period of relative freedom and popularity. The use of anonymous writing and editing was dominant in English newsbooks of that era.

Complicating the issue is the fact that most newsbook editors were deeply partisan, and as such their newsbooks served distinct subgroups with shared ideologies, the printing equivalent of singing to the choir. It wasn't response from their own readers that newsbook editors feared, but rather retaliation and harassment from their opposition. The most obvious source of retaliation came from the "other" dominant authority (at that time in England, either Parliamentarians seeking to reduce the power of the monarchy or Royalists who were trying to protect the crown's absolute power). It also came informally via harassment, vandalism, or socio-political ostracism within more nuanced communities. Complaints were seldom published within the newsbooks being criticized, but rather in oppositional titles, such that the English Civil War also was fought by partisans in the press. The

Kingdomes Weekly Intelligencer in 1643, for example, argued in regard to another newsbook that was critical of the king, ". . . it is hoped that the Protestant party about him will acquaint his Majesty therewith, and get the Author and Printer thereof punished. . . ."[23] Pro-Parliament newsbooks similarly attacked editors and printers of Royalist publications.

Moreover, the work of compiling, printing, and distributing news-books was not an enterprise of "authorship" so much as an enterprise of "sharing"—that is, the intent often was not necessarily to buy and sell intel-lectual property for profit, but rather to nurture and serve the information needs of ideological communities (and, perhaps, earn enough money to sus-tain the enterprise). Each newsbook may have been edited and printed by just one or two people, but it took a virtual community of like-minded writers and readers to keep it going. British scholar Marcus Nevitt explained the realities of such "collective activity" this way: "This overlap between authorship, publishing, and printing had certain advantages, both economic and strate-gic, for contemporary workers in the news trade, so that, whilst costs could be cut, it also made the job of the censor or licensor more difficult. How was a seditious intention to be traced amid such a complex network of creative activity, when even hawkers selling the newsbooks at street level could be found politicizing the texts they sold in radical and seditious ways?"[24]

Anonymity in newsbooks not only confounded officials seeking to sup-press dissent, but also, if unwittingly, exemplified and gave authority to the collective nature of news work, something that continues to this day in the modern press. A 21st-century news enterprise may have a few well-known contributors, usually high-profile anchors and columnists, but the vast majority of journalists work behind the scenes in relative anonymity—in the public dialogue, the discussion is not so much about "today's analysis piece by Adam Liptak" as it is "today's analysis of a Supreme Court case in *The New York Times*." As is often the case today, in the age of newsbooks it was the title that had the authority among readers, not the individual editors and writers. In fact, each newsbook itself became a personality, the nexus of its own community of anonymous reader/contributors, and itself the target of praise from anonymous supporters or denouncement from anonymous critics.

'PAMPHLETS SCARRILOUS, AND VILE'

The communities that supported the English newsbooks naturally were just as partisan as the papers themselves, and the rhetorical warfare could at times be vicious, though certainly never as vicious as the physical battles between Royalist and Parliamentarian armies. Even many of their titles and subtitles set a decidedly hostile tone toward their ideological opponents. Examples include the pro-monarchy *Mercurius Bellicus or an Alarum to All Rebels* (c. 1648) or its contemporary nemesis, *Mercurius Anti-Mercurius*, which made the claim of "Impartially Communicating Truth, correcting falshood, reproving the wilfull, pittying the Ignorant, and opposing All false and scandalous aspersions unjustly cast upon the two Honourable Houses of PARLIAMENT."[25] The level of disdain and disrespect individual news-books held toward their ideological opponents was even more evident in the pages of such journals. By the time of the Restoration in 1661, the language in newsbooks had become far removed from the lofty prose found in the government-licensed books produced by artists, scholars, and respected statesmen, and also was not on par with the elegant prose in more sophisticated journals elsewhere, such as the *Journal des Sçavans* of mid-17th-century France.[26] In London, newsbooks had embraced the more rancorous and emotionally charged rhetoric of "common" citizens, and the effect was to enable a predominantly rough-and-tumble form of dialogue. It is not surprising, then, that letters sent to the editors also embraced that tendency of "free" expression—expression that was not only free from authoritarian control, but also free from many social inhibitions. Newsbook editors thus constructed and endorsed the mythos of "the people's forum," a meme that has been applied with varying degrees of accuracy to audience comment forums ever since.

Because many of the newsbooks explicitly rejected the authoritarian conventions of authorship (a necessity of licensing) and deference to the elitist social pressures that defined "polite" society (a by-product of censorship), they also were the targets of scorn from cultural elites of the period. A somewhat famous example of elitist disdain toward the "scurrilous press" was a pamphlet titled *The Great Assises Holden in Parnassus*, published in 1645 and attributed to "Edward Husbands" (believed by some to be a pseudonym used for that purpose by Spenserian poet and satirist George Wither).[27] The pamphlet presented an allegorical poem in which several newsbooks of the day were put on trial, with the Greek god Apollo serving as judge and the jury comprising a number of respected writers and poets, including the playwright William Davenant, the playwriting team of Francis Beaumont and John Fletcher, and "The Lord Verulam, Chancellor of Parnassus," a reference to Sir Francis Bacon. The reference to Francis Bacon is not to be taken lightly: Bacon had died about 20 years earlier, and his *Novum Organum* was, in part, a treatise against "common" discourse that Bacon and other elites considered to be addled by "the mist of tradition, or the whirl and eddy of argument. . . ."[28] Among the "malefactours" listed for trial were the newsbooks *Mercurius Britanicus, Mercurius Aulicus, The Scout*, "the writer of Diurnals," "the writer of Passages," and "The Scottish Dove, &c."[29] Evoking the intellectual elitism of Bacon and others, *The Great Assises* was particularly harsh toward the newsbook editors of the day:

> "For it is now imploy'd by Paper-wasters,
> By mercenary soules, and Poetasters,
> Who weekly utter, slanders, libells, lies,
> Under the name of specious novelties . . ."[30]

The outcome of the allegorical trial was a judgment that agents of the "court" of important authors should imprison or kill those newsbook editors:

> ". . . bring in alive, or dead, each one
> That had discovered been, or to defile
> The Presse with Pamphlets scarrilous, and vile."[31]

The Great Assises initiated a string of responses in the various newsbooks, many defending the accuracy of their claims, but also debating whether newsbook publication should be curbed or protected. Several issues of the "malefactour" *Mercurius Britanicus* were dominated by point-by-point rebuttals of complaints in other journals, one such example being the multi-page rebuttal to the newsbook *Academicus* in the issue published February 2, 1646:

> "Come, come on Academicus, down with your Pack, and let's see what Pedling stuffe you have brought to town: How, a comment upon Britanicus! That work had befitted someone more Reverend, and the Novice might have had the manners to give his elders leave first. But I see the Oxford Pamphleteer means to forestall Design and spoile the Mercat at London, though I can tell you I value no such Farthing-projects, for they are easily pufft away in half a Page, my Ink immediately destroyes all Paper-worms. . . ."[32]

Such response was an early case of news media being used not just to discuss politics and social issues, but also as conduits to debate the role of the press itself. The practice of giving readers the ability to essentially "talk back" to the media within those media was launched, and the role of news media as forums for truly "common" debate—and not necessarily polite or lofty debate among intelligentsia—also started to evolve.

The tendency (or, perhaps, necessity) of anonymity in newsbooks also may have been a factor in those bitter and prolonged rivalries among partisan editors themselves. One newsbook that was targeted by several competitors during the English Civil War was *Mercurius Aulicus*, a Royalist publication that ridiculed one of its challengers in 1643 with another nasty, point-by-point rebuttal, even referencing page numbers of particular passages (in parentheses):

> "Then a very new Author ('twill be a week old on Monday) calls himselfe A WEEKLY ANSWER TO MERCURIUS AULICUS; and he sayes (25) that 'he only writes to Undisceive those who love the truth' (let His Majesties words alone, you see you cannot spell them.) . . . [and] 30, That 'the Lord Capells Officers doe take away mens Horses'; They onely tooke one Mare which your Brother Rebell was buggering. . . ."[33]

"Aulicus" attracted the ideological scorn of many other newsbooks. The mid-September, 1643, issue of *Mercurius Britanicus* rejoiced in reporting that "The grand newes is, *Mercurius Aulicus* was surprized on Wednesday last by the Militia of the City of London; a few only escaped, and no fewer than five hundred lies were taken prisoners. . . ."[34] A writer to *The Spie* rejoiced earlier that year: "Aulicus, both the Author and the Pamphlet are departed the World together, and for ought I know, neither of them are likely ever to rise againe. . . . I am perswaded we shall ere long have another villaine in Print under the name Aulicus, who will endeavor perhaps as mischievously against the State as the former."[35] The following spring, the *Mercurius Britanicus* again commented: "The olde Aulicus, the single sheeted Author, hath his liberty this weeke, and writes not . . . that he may recover his braine, and thinke, and contrive, and invent, . . . that he may be able the next week to tell the stronger and more considerable lies. . . ."[36]

More often, though, such feedback came in the form of rebuttals to other letter writers, either to correct perceived errors of fact or to challenge opinions. Consider this anonymous "correction" letter, published in 1643:

> "And here it is to be observed, that in a London Pamphlet which came out since Christmasse, report was made of a great battell fought in this very place (when none such was fought) and that this Collonel Cavandish who was now victorious had beene slaine therein, with divers other Gentlemen of name and note, when neither he nor they had then took up Armes for the defence and service of His sacred Majesty. The author of which pamphlet is he pretended (as some of them doe) to the spirit of Prophesie, mistooke the time; though he guessed rightly at the place, and failed in pointing out the Victors, though he found a battell: but if he intended to write an history, his is now better furnished then before."[37]

Today's observers of comments, particularly in anonymous online forums, might note that the intermixing of disagreement with personal insults is not a new phenomenon by any stretch, and probably has a lot more to do with human nature and social psychology than with Internet-based communication. Rancor, vitriol, name-calling, and general disrespect all are centuries-old realities of discourse in the popular press. It is no wonder, then, that once news-media publishers began the practice of publishing direct feedback from their audiences, many of those participants emulated the rhetoric that they saw used by the newsbook author-editors.

DISCERNING FEEDBACK FROM OTHER LETTERS

As mentioned earlier, newsbooks used the term "letter" to refer to nearly all communication arriving to their editors, and indeed many writers referred to items they had read in newsbooks as "letters" (versus "articles"). But there clearly were some items published then that were prototypes of what we today would consider audience feedback, and gradually some newsbooks began to treat those items differently from other letters they would utilize.

One of the earliest newsbooks circulated in London included, in its back pages, just such an item. It was published in October 1623, and challenged an earlier report that had claimed the "Antichrist" had been born:

> "Master B.: Give me once leave to beare a part in your weekly newes: A late Booke of yours reported to us the strange birth of Antichrist, to the stairing of the haire of the simple, the insultation of the super-stitious, the derision of the wife. . . . Now let it be my newes to the world by you, that the Elder Brother of this very same Antichrist was borne in Babylon, in the yeare of our Lord God, 1532. That credulous foules may not be guiled with these sycophancies, let any Reader but call at your shop for Sir Richard Barkleyes Booke of the Felicitie of Man, printed in London, for William Ponsonby, in the yeare 1603. . . . See now, honest Reader, what flyes the blind man swallowes, and judge whether this Babylonian Antichrist be any other than an old tale new furbusht; and smile at the shifts of the guiltie imposters, who whiles they tell us of a new Antichrist raising up the dead, have themselves revived an old Antichrist, of some fourescore and ten yeres agoe. Laugh at the teeth, and feare the tongue of Antichrist, another Antichrist in another Babylon. . . . M.D.H."[38]

That early LTE bears a number of characteristics that have come to define the form even into the 21st century. It begins with a salutation to the editor, a practice that continues to this day in many publications, including some that add the salutation "To the Editor" whether the original writer included it or not. The above example also includes a request for publication, signifying that the writer did not presume that his submission would be published—that is, an acknowledgement of the editor's gatekeeping role. The writer makes reference to an earlier news item that inspired the response, thus maintaining the structure of dialectic and also evoking the classical concepts of both the Socratic method and of "audi alteram partem"—the right to reply. The essay also makes reference to the "Reader," signifying the letter was not intended only for the editor's eyes, but rather was submitted for the newsbook's audience. Finally, the letter was "signed," simply with the initials "M.D.H.," thus maintaining the convention of closing such letters with some sort of signature to indicate "authorship" by someone other than the editor.

An early attempt to give such common expressions designated spaces within publications was seen in the London newsbook titled *Some Speciall and Considerable Passages from London* (c. 1643). The editor of that newsbook compiled a number of letters in sequence, each demarked with a salutation such as "Dear Friend" or simply "Sir."[39] Unlike letters from correspondents relaying news, which were usually summarized and paraphrased by the editors, opinion-based letters often were published verbatim and with (it seems) minimal editing, such as this one from the *Flying Eagle*, published in early December 1652 in London (this excerpt only includes the introduction and closing statements):

> "Sir,
> "I Have received both your Letters; I give you many thanks for the communication of your printed Paper, and the two Orders of Parliament. It is a grievous, and a lamentable thing that the Parliament should need Remembrances, much more importunate Sollicitorys in the behalf of those whose flesh and blood they eat; and drink; to say nothing of the Honour given them. . . .
> And now I suppose you are as weary with reading as I with writing; But if I might heare a word or two from you sometimes, and might thereby understand that the pulse of the publique Affairs beats healthfully, you should thereby refresh very much the often wearied spirits of,
> Your very faithful friend
> R.B."[40]

In between those two paragraphs were many long, bloated passages that are not remarkable in either historical or literary considerations—the letter complained of the ages-old practice of government officials misusing their positions for personal gain to the detriment of the public. In addition, the prose is not necessarily engaging, nor are the opinions all that insightful or compelling. The writer aspired to be artful and poignant, it seems, but the end product indicate the writer's aspirations were limited by his or her talents. It is unclear just who "R.B." is—no mention of his or her occupation, place of residence, or any credentials to suggest the person was offering an insider's critique of the inner workings of government. In many ways, the letter evokes the previously discussed notion of "relative anonymity"—even a modern revelation of the writer's name is unlikely to make the letter worthy of any serious historical note. Like the vast majority of LTEs published over the centuries, the letter by "R.B." is, essentially, a common opinion submitted by a common citizen.

'HAVING ENCOURAGEMENT BY A GREAT MANY LETTERS TO CONTINUE OUR GAZETTE'

The 1662 Press Act effectively shut down the printing of partisan news sheets in England for about three decades thereafter (essentially creating a monopoly for the official newspaper of Parliament, *The London Gazette*). But the public's desire for less official publications did not wane. British media historian Helen Berry noted that, "The Press Act curbed the reporting of foreign and domestic news before 1695 through censorship, which encouraged the development of new and experimental forms of print, dealing with less politically sensitive subjects."[41] One of the most notable examples of that was *The Athenian Gazette or Casuistical Mercury* (later renamed *The Athenian Mercury*), the brainchild of London printer John Dunton.

The Athenian is believed to be the first publication to adopt the "question-and-answer" format, an enduring practice in which a news publication solicits questions from the public to be answered in the medium—today, the most common forms are advice columns and call-in advice shows on radio. *The Athenian* printed summaries of selected questions along with responses from Dunton and his social club, The Athenian Society, who reportedly discussed the questions when they met in their favorite coffeehouse.[42] It was a twice-weekly publication, first published under the pseudonym "P. Smart," but later under Dunton's real name.[43] The mission of the publication was expressed in the introduction of the first issue, dated March 17, 1690: "The Design is briefly, to satisfy all ingenious and curious Enquirers into Speculations, Divine, Moral and Natural, etc. and to remove those Difficulties and Dissatisfactions, that shame or fear of appearing ridiculous by asking Questions, may cause several Persons to labour under, who now have opportunities of being resolv'd in any Question without knowing their Informer."[44] By the second issue, *The Athenian* claimed to be receiving considerable volumes of both questions and positive audience feedback, stating, "Having encouragement by a great many letters to continue our Gazette, as an undertaking that will be very useful to many, (for we never expected of accomplishing that impossible task of pleasing every body,) we shall endeavour as general a satisfaction as we can, by answering whatsoever questions or objections as are sent us, that are consistent with modesty and pertinent for information."[45] After more than a year of publication, and with a total readership estimated to be thousands of men and women, *The Athenian* made frequent reference to being inundated with submissions, once asking its readers to "hold their Hands and Pens, and let us take Breath awhile, and get rid of those CART—LOADS of Questions which are yet upon the File."[46]

Some early critics of *The Athenian*, as well as some present-day scholars who have studied the texts, suggested that Dunton and his peers simply made up the questions, ostensibly to create the appearance of public involvement. Berry disputes that claim:

> "[A]t least some of letters were authentic, although it is usually difficult to say precisely which ones. There is unfortunately no thrilling cache of

Figure 2.1 The emblem of The Athenian Society, engraving by Frederik Hendrik van Hove for *The History of the Athenian Society*, by Charles Gildon.

original letters to the Athenian Society against which to compare the printed text. . . . It matters, however, that the *Athenian Mercury* was not just a prototype epistolary novel, written in solitude by an unidentified Grub Street hack in a garret, but a randomly mutating social document . . . composed by many authors, and developed week-on-week, shaped by the exercise of editorial control and actual inquiries from readers. . . . [I]t was a deeply woven text that interacted with, and was influenced by, the social circumstances of its own particular community of readers."[47]

The popularity of *The Athenian* was the result of a complex formula of editorial tactics, not the least of which was constructing a narrative of "community" through the careful selection and editing of audience feedback. The emblem of the Athenian Society illustrates that imagined community[48] quite well. At the top of the woodcut is depicted a long table, behind which the bewigged, anonymous gentlemen of the Society sit, reading and discussing the letters handed to them from men and women, scientists and artists, menial laborers and the privileged wives of noblemen, all crowding at the front of the table. The accompanying text states, "Behind the scenes sit mighty we, nor are we known nor will we be, the world and we exchanging thus."[49] In the tier below, a cluster of "noisy fools" is depicted as lining up to submit their questions to the Society members. Behind the queue of "noisy fools" are drawn the "lost wretches," including a man at the gallows, and another man being threatened with a woman bearing a knife and a stick (the man saying "Help, help, noble Athenians"). The illustration offers an obvious metaphor for the evolving class of author-editors and their classifications of their audience: the preferred elite at the table, the "noisy fools" participating from afar, and the "lost wretches" who are not part of the audience. In the case of *The Athenian*, the illustration puts the "editorial board" apart from letter writers, not just physically (via the table) but also in terms of social status. The woodcut and description suggesting that the forum provided by the Athenian Society (and dominated with the author-editors' lengthy responses to obviously truncated and edited questions) was believed by its publishers to be a service provided by an elite group of intellectuals to the common people.

The popularity of *The Athenian* continued into the 1700s, and that popularity surely inspired other printers to be much more willing to accept, and publish, submissions from the general public. And in so doing, those early news sheets set the stage for the 18th-century evolution of news sheets from mere conduits of "fact" to rich, vibrant forums for public discourse. The concept of "audience feedback" was exported to the European colonies in the Americas, and in those wild frontiers, legal authorities were less able to impose and maintain controls on the press. The champions of freedom of the press in the Old World had their dreams realized not just at home, but also in the New World, where the role of the press as a forum for truly "public" discourse blossomed and thrived through the 18th century.

NOTES

1. Shayne Bowman and Chris Willis, *We Media: How Audiences Are Shaping the Future of News and Information* (Reston, Va.: The Media Center at The American Press Institute, 2003). Accessed November 23, 2012, from www.hypergene.net/wemedia/download/we_media.pdf.
2. For more about 17th-century newsbooks, see Joad Raymonds, *The Invention of the Newspaper: English Newsbooks 1641–1649* (New York: Oxford University Press, 1996).
3. "From *gaza*, wealth, is formed the Italian word *gazetta*, which denotes a small coin, given for a newspaper when they were first published. The first newspaper or *Gazette* that appeared was published in 1536 in Venice, and appeared every six months. In the library at Venice there are 30 volumes of this *Gazette*. Lord Chancellor Burleigh published from time to time a Gazette, called 'The English Mercury' [c. 1585–1605]. . . . In 1612 appeared the first Gazette in Germany, and in 1630 the first in Paris." From Richard Harrison Black, *The Student's Manual, Complete: Being an Etymological and Explanatory Vocabulary Derived from the Greek and Latin Languages* (London: Longman, Green & Co., 1874), 186.
4. Warren Chappell and Robert Bringhurst, *A Short History of the Printed Word* (Port Roberts, Wash.: Hartley & Marks Publishers, 1999), 141–44.
5. Isaiah Thomas, *The History of Printing in America*, ed. Marcus A. McCorison (New York: Weathervane Books, 1970), 8–9.
6. *Packets of Letters* was a London newsbook published in 1648, "concerning the Transactions of the Parliament of Scotland." That and other newsbooks mentioned in this chapter were accessed via the British Library's 17th–18th Century Burney Collection Newspapers, www.bl.uk/reshelp/findhelprestype/news/newspdigproj/burney/index.html.
7. All dates in this book are those used in the cited publications, and not adjusted to modern convention. Prior to 1751 in Britain, the Julian or "Old Style" calendar was official, not the modern Gregorian calendar, now about 13 days out of sync. Until 1752, England marked the new year on March 25 (meaning February 1648 came after December 1648, for example). Readers who wish to convert the dates given from Julian to Gregorian standards can use any number of online conversion applications, such as the one at www.csgnetwork.com/juliangregcalconv.html.
8. Unknown author, "November 12, 1623," *The Proceedings of Bethelem Gabor in Hungary*, November 26, 1623, 3.
9. Unknown author, "Charles I, 1640: An Act for [the Regulating the Privie Councell and for taking away the Court commonly called the Star Chamber," *Statutes of the Realm: volume 5: 1628–80* (1819), 110–12. Accessed March 26, 2013, from www.british-history.ac.uk/report.aspx?compid=47221.
10. John Milton, *Areopagitica: A Speech for the Liberty of Unlicensed Printing to the Parliament of England.* Accessed August 21, 2014, from www.gutenberg.org/files/608/608-h/608-h.htm.
11. Untitled article, *The Exchange Intelligencer*, June 11, 1645, 29.
12. Untitled article, *The Exchange Intelligencer*, June 11, 1645, 31.
13. Untitled article, *The Exchange Intelligencer*, June 11, 1645, 32.
14. Untitled article, *The Flying Eagle*, December 11, 1652, 2.
15. Eugene R. Kintgen, Barry M. Kroll, and Mike Rose, *Perspectives on Literacy* (Carbondale, Ill.: SIU Press, 1988), 103–4.
16. Kintgen et al., *Perspectives on Literacy*, 104.

17. Bill Reader, Guido Stempel III, and Douglass Daniel, "Age, Wealth, Education Predict Letters to the Editor," *Newspaper Research Journal* 25, 4 (2004), 55–66.

18. Helen M. Berry, *Gender, Society, and Print Culture in Late Stuart England: The Cultural World of the Athenian Mercury* (Burlington, Vt.: Ashgate Publishers, 2003), 36.

19. Marcus Nevitt, "Women in the Business of Revolutionary News: Elizabeth Alkin, 'Parliament Joan,' and the Commonwealth Newsbook," in Joad Raymond, ed., *News, Newspapers and Society in Early Modern Britain* (London: Frank Cass Publishers, 1999), 84–108.

20. When printer John Dunton launched *The Athenian Gazette and Casuistic Mercury* in the 1690s, its target audience was explicitly both men and women, and it accepted letters of inquiry from both men and women. Its 1693 spin-off, *The Ladies Mercury*, was certainly intended for a female audience. See Berry, *Gender, Society, and Print Culture in Late Stuart England*.

21. Chappell and Bringhurst, *A Short History of the Printed Word*, 143.

22. Chappell and Bringhurst, *A Short History of the Printed Word*, 143.

23. Untitled article, *Kindomes Weekly Intelligencer*, May 16, 1643, 149.

24. Nevitt, "Women in the Business of Revolutionary News," 86.

25. Unknown author, *Mercurius Anti-Mercurius*, Oct. 2, 1648, 1.

26. Harcourt Brown, "History and the Learned Journal," *Journal of the History of Ideas*, 33, 3 (1972), 365–78.

27. Edward Husbands, *The Great Assises holden in Parnassus*, London, 1645. Reprinted with annotation in David Hill Radcliffe, ed., *Spencer and the Tradition: English Poetry 1579–1830* [website]. Accessed September 28, 2012, from http://spenserians.cath.vt.edu/TextRecord.php?action=GET&textsid=33437.

28. Francis Bacon, *Novum Organum*, section LXXXII (1620). Accessed January 21, 2013, from www.constitution.org/bacon/nov_org.htm.

29. Husbands, *The Great Assises holden in Parnassus*.

30. Husbands, *The Great Assises holden in Parnassus*.

31. Husbands, *The Great Assises holden in Parnassus*.

32. Untitled article, *Mercurius Britanicus*, February 2, 1646, 1.

33. Untitled article, *Mercurius Aulicus*, December 17, 1643, 734.

34. Untitled article, *Mercurius Britanicus*, September 19, 1643, 1.

35. Untitled article, *The Spie*, June 6, 1644, 145.

36. Untitled article, *Mercurius Britanicus*, March 6, 1644, 191.

37. Untitled article, *Mercurius Aulicus*, April 16, 1643, 195.

38. M.D.H., "The true and undoubted Newes, of the birth of Antichrist, by M.D.H.," *October 2, Number 50 Our Last Newes Containing a Relation of the Last Proceedings*, October 2, 1623, 20–22.

39. Untitled article, *Some Speciall and Considerable Passages from London*, January 11, 1643, 181–82.

40. Unknown author, "A Letter Sent to a Friend Concerning the Publique Faith," *The Flying Eagle*, December 11, 1652, 11–13.

41. Berry, *Gender, Society, and Print Culture in Late Stuart England*, 28

42. Bertha-Monica Stearns, "The First English Periodical for Women," *Modern Philology* 28, 1 (1930), 45–59.

43. Berry, *Gender, Society, and Print Culture in Late Stuart England*, 21.

44. Untitled article, *The Athenian Gazette and Casuistic Mercury*, March 17, 1690, 1. From *The Athenian Oracle: Being an Entire Collection of all the Valuable Questions and Answers in the Old Athenian Mercuries, by a Member of the Athenian Society* (London: The Athenian Society [1703–1704]), 2.

45. *The Athenian Gazette and Casuistic Mercury*, March 24, 1690, 1.

46. *The Athenian Gazette and Casuistic Mercury*, September 1691, cited in Berry, *Gender, Society, and Print Culture in Late Stuart England*, 36.
47. Berry, *Gender, Society, and Print Culture in Late Stuart England*, 35.
48. The term "imagined community" stems from Benedict Anderson, *Imagined Communities* (New York: Verso, 1991).
49. Unknown author, "An Emblem of ye Athenian Society, 1692," The British Museum. Accessed November 1, 2014, from www.britishmuseum.org/research/collection_online/collection_object_details.aspx?objectId=3069867&partId=1&searchText=The+Athenian+Society&page=1

3 "A Sure Sign of Liberty, and a Cause of It"
Audience Feedback and the Emergence of the Free Press

It is not a stretch to argue that the very concept of "freedom of the press" was exemplified and hard-won through the publication of myriad letters in newspapers during the 17th and 18th centuries. Expanding the right to publish ideas to the "capite censi" was, and remains, a complicated and difficult cultural endeavor. In the present day, professional journalists often express disdain toward anonymity in general and toward coarse online commentary in particular, mostly directed at anonymous online forums. That is not much different from the disdain of the 17th century literati toward anonymous newsbooks, "Who weekly utter, slanders, libells, lies, Under the name of specious novelties. . . ."[1] Unlike today, editors of the popular press in the 18th century were far less obstructionist toward providing forums for the often vitriolic and offensive rhetoric of "A Farmer," "A Soldier," and "A Citizen." That may have been due in large part to the partisan nature of such publications, but certainly reflected the anti-establishment, free-expression zeitgeist of the late Enlightenment Era.

That is not to say that 18th-century newspaper editors were uniformly libertarian and egalitarian—or that they were "uniform" in any sense of the term. As is still the case today, editors of the 1700s were mostly eccentric and idiosyncratic people, often more interested in doing things their own ways than in establishing or adhering to any broad professional standards. One such enigmatic editor was James Franklin, editor and printer of the hell-raising *New England Courant* of the 1720s. Projecting the classical ideal to "Hear both sides," Franklin's *Courant* printed criticisms not only of his own writings, but also rebuttals to letters printed in previous editions. That was a departure from the more common approach of the previous century, in which editors would use their publications to criticize opponents and defend against complaints published in opponents' newsbooks. The *Courant* brought multiple sides together in one forum, and thus provided a single forum for true dialogue. One front-page letter in the *Courant* condemned the disruptiveness of letter-printing newspapers (such as the *Courant*), as opposed to carefully written and edited books by solo authors. It was signed "Dic. Buckrum," which could have been a real name, but given the context might well have been a pseudonym ("buckrum" is a variant spelling of "buckram," the rugged cloth used to cover books):

> "To the Author of the New-England Courant:
>   SIR,
>   The wise man tells us that where there are no Tale-bearers, there Strife ceaseth. When a Club, or Knot of Men set themselves up to scan and CANVASS every thing that is acted (both in Publick and Private) among a People, what else can be expected but Contention and every evil work. . . ."[2]

Above all, though, Franklin regularly published letters of all kinds, whether partisan essays from his "Couranteers," or regular writers, or odd missives from people unknown to him. That was the case of the most famous letters published in the *Courant*, the fourteen penned in 1722 by "Silence Dogood." Today it is well known that "Silence Dogood" was the pseudonym used by 16-year-old Benjamin Franklin, but a less-considered fact is that young Benjamin had adopted not just a pseudonym, but in fact a complete alternative persona to evade the gatekeeping of his older brother. James Franklin had refused to publish the works handed to him in person by Benjamin, so Benjamin created the character of an aged widow from the countryside and surreptitiously left "her" letters at the print shop for James to find, read, and publish.

The essays of Silence Dogood are often discussed as curious artifacts from the early life of a great historical figure, but considered on their own merits, the Dogood essays were trendsetting archetypes of letters to the editor despite the dubious nature of their authorship. The first Silence Dogood letter was published in the April 2, 1722, issue of the *Courant*, and began:

> "Sir,
>   It may not be improper in the first Place to inform your Readers, that I intend once a Fortnight to present them, by the Help of this Paper, with a short Epistle, which I presume will add somewhat to their Entertainment. . . ."[3]

That salutation reveals the dual audiences of letters and comments—they are most often written to the individual editor, but within the context of being published for all to read. An important subtext is that "verifiable authorship," a dogmatic norm of the late 20th century, has always been of dubious merit. Had the elder Franklin known the true identify of the writer, he might not have even bothered reading the submissions, let alone publishing them; thanks to Benjamin Franklin's dissembling, the Silence Dogood essays saw print and entered posterity. For a few weeks in 1722, when James Franklin was imprisoned for printing a passage that offended local government officials, Benjamin took over printing duties, but continued to publish the Silence Dogood letters under that pseudonym. Although James Franklin was infuriated upon learning that he had been deceived, he also was not averse to being deceptive himself. The following year, when he was again punished for "offending the magistrates" and refusing to reveal the identity of the "Couranteer" who wrote the letter in question, James Franklin was banned from printing anything without official sanction; to evade the authorities, he continued to produce the *Courant* but listed his younger brother as the printer.[4]

An ocean away and at about the same time, the *London Journal*, and later the *British Journal*, had been publishing a series of letters from "Cato." "Cato" was the pen name of two prominent Whigs, John Trenchard and Thomas Gordon. The duo chose that pseudonym in honor of Cato the Younger, the incorruptible senator of classical Rome who defiantly committed suicide in Utica in 46 BC rather than flee from or surrender to Julius Caesar's tyranny.[5] Their true identities were not publicly verified until 1724, shortly after Trenchard's death and a few months after the last letter was published. Gordon wrote in 1724, in the preface to one of several bound volumes of *Cato's Letters*, "Who were the authors of these letters, is now, I believe, pretty well known. It is with the utmost sorrow I say, that one of them is lately dead, and his death is a loss to mankind."[6]

Trenchard's and Gordon's pseudonymous letters began as excoriations against the merchants, bankers, and politicians responsible for the 1720 collapse of the South Sea Company. The South Sea Company had fallen to an investment scandal rife with insider trading and unlawful profiteering; its collapse triggered an economic crisis throughout Britain.[7] Cato's letters initially called for criminal prosecutions of those responsible as well as for economic policy reforms, but soon broadened to cover a variety of social topics that condemned political corruption in general and the tyrannical tendencies of those in power. In so doing, the routine evoked the democratic philosophies of John Milton, John Locke, and Algernon Sidney (two of the letters, No. 26 and No. 37, are essentially long excerpts of Sidney's *Discourses Concerning Government*, for which Sidney was tried and executed in 1683).[8] *Cato's Letters* were soon compiled and reprinted in other newspapers, and they enjoyed broad popularity in both Britain and in the British colonies. In America, *Cato's Letters* were frequently cited or even serialized in several pro-liberty newspapers, and their opinions had a marked effect on restless colonials—20th-century historian Clinton Rossiter famously wrote, "No one can spend any time in the newspapers, library inventories, and pamphlets of colonial America without realizing that *Cato's Letters* rather than Locke's *Civil Government* was the most popular, quotable, esteemed source of political ideas in the colonial period."[9]

Of all of the 138 original Cato letters, those concerning "libels" were largely responsible for promoting the post-licensing concept of "freedom of the press." The word "libel" at the time meant any unflattering statement, and unlike today, "truth" was not a legal defense against a charge of "seditious libel." The printing of an unflattering truth could incur harsh judgment and heavy penalties, hence the aphorism, "the greater the truth, the greater the libel"—the explanation being that "a man would be more likely to commit a breach of the peace when the matters alleged against him were true than if they were false, in which latter case he might, perhaps, afford to treat them with contempt."[10] *Cato's Letters* suggested a different approach. Cato argued that a free society must tolerate harsh opinions, even though they could be "a sort of writing that hurts particular persons, without doing good to the publick" and that "no Man in England thinks worse of libels than I do."[11] One of the most quoted statements from letter No. 32, "Reflections upon Libelling," is "I would rather many Libels should escape, than the Liberty of the Press should be infringed."[12] Trenchard and Gordon insisted, moreover, that publication of "base and mean" writings, including antisocial and incivil missives by "monsters," is an unavoidable consequence of freedom of the press:

> "As long as there are such things as printing and writing, there will be libels: It is an evil arising out of a much greater good. And as to those who are for locking up the press, because it produces monsters, they ought to consider that so do the Sun and the Nile; and that it is something better for the world to bear some particular inconveniences arising from general blessings, than to be wholly deprived of fire and water. . . . [H]onest men, with clear reputations, which they know foul mouths cannot hurt, will always be for preserving it open, as a sure sign of liberty, and a cause of it."[13]

Routine publication of such libertarian arguments about freedom of the press was relatively new in English culture of that era, and also quite controversial. Censorship and licensing itself had only ceased a couple of decades earlier in 1695, when the British House of Commons allowed the Licensing Act to expire. The laws against "seditious libel" were retained, however, and continued to exert a chilling effect on anti-establishment publishing. Although one reform said that juries, and not judges, were to determine the verdict in sedition trials, crown-appointed judges were to determine the facts that could be presented and to interpret the application of the law, essentially controlling the jury's process—"these restraints were practically as despotic as the edicts of the Star Chamber . . . the result was a practical denial of the right of trial."[14] Although Cato did not face serious government action, many others did, and succumbed to trials rigged by partisan judges.

Those legal restraints on freedom of the press, specifically the freedom to publish opinions from the people, were put the test about a decade after *Cato's Letters* entered syndication. The trial of the era took place not in England, but in an important English colony across the Atlantic.

'THE FALSEHOOD MAKES THE SCANDAL, AND BOTH MAKE THE LIBEL'

Among the newspapers in America that reprinted some of *Cato's Letters* was *The New York Weekly Journal*, launched in 1733 by political opponents of the recently appointed governor of New York, William Cosby, and produced by a young, struggling German-born printer, John Peter Zenger.

Like James Franklin's *New England Courant* a decade earlier, *The New York Weekly Journal* was primarily a vehicle for anonymous letters espousing strong opinions against the colonial government in general, and specifically against the authoritarian administration of Governor Cosby. The *Journal* was among the first (some scholars suggest it was *the* first) partisan newspapers in the New World. It was started by Lewis Morris[15] and other New York politicians who disagreed with Cosby's policies and practices; they used the *Journal* to publish their pseudonymous arguments against Cosby and his regime.[16] Zenger was the printer, but not really the editor—many scholars believe the editor was one of Morris' group, most likely colonial lawyer James Alexander.[17] Morris, Alexander, and a small group of their supporters "wrote practically everything but the news notices" in the newspaper.[18] By the tenth issue, "the articles begin to take the form of letters apparently written by the subscribers."[19]

Cosby was outraged and wanted the shadows running the *Journal* to be outed and punished. The governor's hand-selected chief justice, James DeLancey, in January 1734 convened a grand jury to investigate "some Men with the utmost Virulency" who had "endeavored to asperse his Excellency and vilify his Administration . . . The Authors are not certainly known, and yet it is an easy Matter to guess who they are."[20] Most likely owing to Cosby's increasing unpopularity, no indictments were returned by the grand jury. DeLancey tried again and again to charge grand juries and issue court orders seeking "the Discovery of the Authors or Writers of these Seditious Libels,"[21] but he was consistently foiled by properly assembled juries of citizens.

In 1734, Cosby assembled a "special" council, and through his hand-picked committee had a warrant of dubious legitimacy issued in November for the arrest of Zenger.[22] Zenger was denied bail, and remained in jail for refusing to identify the authors of the anonymous letters he had printed in the *Journal*. Within a few months, Zenger's case was brought to trial.

Likely *Journal* writer James Alexander attempted to represent Zenger, but was disbarred by DeLancey for doing so. Andrew Hamilton, a renowned and respected lawyer from Philadelphia, agreed to take up Zenger's defense; Hamilton's renown prevented DeLancey from intervening. The trial was filled with high rhetoric and clever debate from both sides. Yet in defending Zenger, Hamilton successfully argued that "it is not our bare Printing and Publishing a Paper, that will make it a Libel. You will have something more to do, before you make my Client a Libeller; for the Words themselves must be libellous, that is, *false, scandalous*, and *seditious*, or else we are not guilty."[23]

Hamilton prevailed on two important arguments: First, citizens have the right to speak and write critically of public officials if they "suffer under a bad Administration."[24] Second, "the Falsehood makes the Scandal, and both make the Libel."[25] The jury's acquittal of Zenger set a precedent for both standards. The third most notable precedent established by the Zenger acquittal was that juries, and not judges, had the authority to determine the facts and make judgments in libel cases. The ability of authoritarian officials to silence their critics suffered a huge and long-remembered defeat that day. What is often forgotten (or simply not considered) is that the Zenger case was focused on whether a newspaper publisher had the right to publish anonymous letters to the editor and to keep the identity of the writers confidential. In many ways, the Zenger case was a victory for the libertarian ideal that the press's primary role was to provide forums for anonymous public discourse.

'A DESPOTIC SCHEME OF GOVERNMENT'

The Zenger verdict only somewhat weakened authoritarian tendencies of those in power. In the decades (and centuries) that followed, the freedoms won in that landmark legal case were and continue to be tested and challenged repeatedly by government officials.

A noteworthy example occurred in 1779 in the United States, when the Continental Congress tried to uncover the identity of "Leonidas," who had written a letter to a Philadelphia newspaper alleging that corrupt members of Congress had harmed the economy of the emerging nation.[26] A Massachusetts delegate moved to bring the printer of *The Pennsylvania Packet* before Congress, ostensibly to out "Leonidas." That effort was rebuffed primarily by delegate Merriweather Smith of Virginia, who read a passage from the letter by "Leonidas" and declared: "When the liberty of the Press shall be restrained . . . the liberties of the People will be at an end."[27] John Penn, a delegate from North Carolina, also defended "Leonidas," saying the anonymous writer "no doubt had good designs" and that "the liberty of the Press ought not to be restrained."[28] The action against the *Packet* was stopped. Years later, it was revealed that "Leonidas" had been Benjamin Rush of Pennsylvania, a signatory of the Declaration of Independence.[29]

Across the Atlantic, another landmark trial reinforced freedom of the press about 50 years after Zenger's acquittal and a few years before the American colonies declared their independence. The famous "Letters of Junius," a series of caustic letters to the editor published in the London newspaper *The Public Advertiser* from 1769 through 1772, resulted in a trial of the newspaper's editor to compel identification of "Junius." The jury found the printer "[g]uilty of printing and publishing only,"[30] which was essentially an acquittal of the charge of printing seditious libel. Junius's identity has not been definitively established, although many scholars support the theory that it was the Parliamentarian reformer Philip Francis.[31]

A few years later, in 1779, the New Jersey legislature debated a similar case when printer Isaac Collins, editor of the *New Jersey Gazette*, was ordered by a state legislative council to disclose the identity of "Cincinnatus," who had written a satirical attack on Governor William Livingston for the newspaper. Collins refused, saying "Were I to comply . . . I conceive I should betray the trust reposed in me, and be far from acting as a faithful guardian of the Liberty of the Press."[32] The matter was dropped.

There also was some discussion among newspaper editors and their readers about the issue of accountability in letters to the editor. A notable debate began in the October 4, 1787, edition of the *Boston Independent Chronicle*, when a self-identified Federalist[33] (writing anonymously) raised concerns that anonymity would allow "foreign enemies" to undermine the emerging Constitution by "filling the press with objections." The writer urged printers not to publish anonymous commentary without first obtaining the true identities of the writers.[34] Benjamin Russell, editor of the Federalist *Massachusetts Centinel*, responded by adopting a policy of not publishing Anti-Federalist[35] comments unless the writers provided their names—not to be published with the letter, but "to be handed to the publick, if required."[36] The *Massachusetts Gazette* followed, and published a letter from "A Citizen" who agreed that anonymous writers should be compelled to leave their names with the publisher. Similar arguments were made by anonymous letters to the *Philadelphia Independent Gazetter*.[37] Criticisms of Russell's policy were soon published in various newspapers, mostly from writers with obvious Anti-Federalist leanings. In their demand for a Bill of Rights to the U.S. Constitution, specifically what was to become the First Amendment, those letter-writers argued vociferously that freedom of the press must include the right to anonymity. Wrote a "Federal Farmer" (the pseudonym of a prolific, but unknown, Anti-Federalist writer): "What can be the views of those gentleman in Boston, who countenance the Printers in shutting up the press against fair and free investigation of this important system in the usual way?"[38] "Philadelphiensis" also lashed out, calling the Federalists-backed idea a "despotic scheme of government," and arguing: "Here we see pretty plainly through (the Federalists') excellent regulation of the press, how things are to be carried on after the adoption of the new constitution."[39] In *The New York Journal*, "Detector" wrote that the Federalist effort would "reverse the important doctrine of the freedom of the press" and was "the introduction of this first trait of slavery into your country."[40] In Rhode Island, the *Providence United States Chronicle* ran a letter from "Argus," who viewed the effort as an attempt by "our aristocratical Gentry, to have every Person's Name published who should write against the proposed Federal Constitution, [which] has given many of us a just Alarm."[41] In light of such criticism, Russell reprinted several anonymous essays from all sides of the debate, and wrote that he did so to demonstrate that allegations that he opposed free speech "had not any foundation in truth"; the *Massachusetts Gazette* further refused to release the names of Anti-Federalist writers whose letters had been published in the newspaper.[42]

Anonymous letters and essays were common in the 18th-century press, and it is important to note that even those who signed their names to such documents as the Declaration of Independence and the U.S. Constitution wrote pseudonymous letters to newspapers of their time, such as:

- "Letters from a Farmer in Pennsylvania," a dozen essays from the 1760s signed "A Farmer" that were later revealed to have been written by prominent revolutionary John Dickinson;[43]
- The Federalist Papers by "Publius," the pseudonymous newspaper letters penned by James Madison, Alexander Hamilton, and John Jay to promote passage of the U.S. Constitution in the late 1780s—the true identities of "Publius" were not revealed until after Hamilton's death in 1804.[44]
- The various authors of the "Anti-Federalist" responses to "Publius," including another "Cato" (believed by scholars to have been New York governor and later vice-president of the United States, George Clinton); "Centinel," who was probably either Samuel Bryan or his father, Pennsylvania judge and legislator George Bryan; and "Brutus," who may have been Richard Henry Lee, a signer of the Declaration of Independence.[45]

Despite the undeniable role of anonymous letters in arguing for and defending freedom of speech and of the press in those formative years of Western democracy, anonymity continued, and continues, to be attacked by offended officials. In 2010, an Ontario court ruled in *Warman v. Wilkins-Fournier* that the right for an online letter-writer to remain anonymous is not absolute,[46] an extension of British Common Law that many criticize as stifling free expression.[47] A more explicit example is from New York state in 2012, in which a group of state lawmakers introduced bills that would basically have made Governor William Cosby's arguments against John Peter Zenger into law, thus undoing nearly three centuries of legal protections for anonymous comments. The proposed law (Senate Bill S06779, House Bill A08688), sought to require that "[a] web site administrator upon request shall remove any comments posted on his or her web site by an anonymous poster unless such anonymous poster agrees to attach his or her name to the post and confirms that his or her IP address, legal name, and home address are accurate."[48] A similar bill was introduced in Illinois in 2013, and similar efforts had been attempted at about the same time in Arizona and Tennessee.[49] Couched in terms of curbing "harmful" expressions, those proposed laws violate the very principles of "freedom of the press" championed by

Cato, employed by Zenger and "Junius," and enshrined in the First Amendment to the U.S. Constitution, enacted December 15, 1791.

'FOUL EBULLITIONS OF PREJUDICE AND MALICE'

Legal challenges to free expression are often motivated by public sentiments against certain types of speech. Even in the relatively "free" parts of the English-speaking world, there remained through the 18th century much disdain toward the publication of opinions from the common people—that is, "men of small talents."[50] The concern was not so much that common people were reading those publications—that was celebrated, particularly among those who wanted to use the papers to instruct the lesser classes in matters of morality and acceptable conduct. It was the ability of "the rabble" to have their thoughts and observations published that became a point of contention.

In *A Brief Retrospect of the Eighteenth Century*, first published in 1803, renowned theologian Samuel Miller lamented what he saw as a century-long decline of the "virtuous" press in 18th-century America:

"Too many of the conductors of our public prints have neither the discernment, the firmness, nor the virtue to reject from their pages the foul ebullitions of prejudice and malice. Had they more diligence, or greater talents, they might render their Gazettes interesting by filling them with materials of a more instructive and dignified kind."[51]

Noted printer Isaiah Thomas agreed somewhat, but suggested that the problem was not that editors of the day were unqualified, but rather their journals were reflective of the political divisiveness in the new United States: "There are among the men who conduct the public journals of America, many, whose literary acquirements are not inferior to those of their predecessors. The great difficulty proceeds from the rage of party spirit, which is kept alive by the frequent of elections, in which the conductors of newspapers engage as partizans."[52]

Political speech was not the only speech contained in letters to the editor of the 18th century, however; nor were pseudonyms used only to obscure the identities of big thinkers espousing revolutionary rhetoric. For example, in the October 1, 1776, issue of *The General Evening Post* of London, a letter signed by "VIATOR" suggested that imprisoned felons be put to work to clean up the English "waste lands" to "give the most pleasing, plentiful, and flourishing appearance to the face of the country."[53] Likewise, the November 9, 1778, issue of the New York–based *Royal Gazette* included a letter from "Pacificus" disputing the alleged size and might of the French navy.[54] In late 1771, a number of colonial newspapers reprinted a letter signed "A DRAGOON" that had originally been published in *The General Evening Post* in London. The letter attacked the integrity and honor of a previous letter-writer who had used the pseudonym "Johnny Britain." "Dragoon's" letter to the *Post* was reprinted within a few weeks in *The Pennsylvania Journal*, *The Pennsylvania Chronicle*, and *The Connecticut Gazette*, and possibly others.[55]

Pseudonyms may have protected writers from direct retaliation, but it did not protect either them or their opinions from harsh criticism. A good example is from a frontier newspaper, *The Kentucky Gazette*, in 1791, in which "Rob the Thrasher" challenged the integrity of several previous writers, a "Mr. A.B.C.," a "Will Wisp" and a "Felte Firebrand":

> "Then Will Wisp appeared, he did well to stile himself so . . . he could not venture to reason, vapour like, without heat or information, only comes forward to deceive, and he could not even do that, for the wind was against him, his origin given by naturalists is out of stinking marshes and graveyards, and his existence they say is short. . . .
>
> Next comes Felte Firebrand on the stage, we expected from his name to hear something lively, ingenious, and suitable to the name, as fire brands are destructive instruments. He attempted satyr without possessing a genius suitable to the undertaking, and mounting a horse he was not capable to command, he came slap into the nastiest rut between Limestone and Lexington, and was all covered over with bombast and nonsense. . . ."[56]

Such insulting rhetoric could be found in 18th-century newspapers throughout the English-speaking world. The very first item in the January 25, 1786, issue of *The Madras Courier* in India, was a letter signed by "Job," asking the editor,

> "When, my good Sir, will you do us the favour to finish the controversy which has so long subsisted between a noisy Subaltern Officer and a troublesome declamatory Gentoo? . . . Cannot you find out, instead of a page in your paper, some corner of your office where these gentry may be disposed of? Apropos, as they are men of Letters, do be so good to let one of your Devils shew them the way to your literary Hell, there they may settle these disputes in an eligible manner, and without the danger of driving your Readers stark staring mad."[57]

Criticisms of such harshness are inevitable when the press attempts to accommodate the public broadly, and each person writing comments brings to the enterprise his or her own interests, perspectives, and emotions. Moreover, 18th-century newspapers were not nearly as compartmentalized (or even as organized) as the more professionalized media of the late 20th and early 21st centuries. A typical newspaper of the 1700s was a catchall for a variety of letters from the public, covering the gamut—items political, cultural, commercial, and personal.

The newspapers serving the various British colonies (or former colonies) reflected that diversity. Quite common were letters regarding the sale, purchase, and recognition of land and property. A 1793 edition of *The Oracle of Dauphin and Harrisburgh Advertiser*, for example, carried a letter from the heirs of William Penn announcing that they were selling in Northumberland County, Pennsylvania, "the whole manor of Pomfret, consisting of sixteen good farms, containing near 300 acres each. . . . The improvements on these farms are valuable—Good comfortable log houses, and convenient barns and stables, on all of them. . . ."[58] Another example is from the February 14, 1789, edition of the *Kentucke Gazette* (later changed to *Kentucky Gazette*): a letter from noted frontiersman John May[59] stating, "I Hereby give notice that the law establishing a Town at the Mouth of Limestone [Limestone Creek] will probably be altered, And I do hereby forbid the Trustees from acting under the former law, and further forewarn all persons from purchasing John May's land, under the description of John May's and Simon Kenton's. . . ."[60] A few weeks earlier, another letter to the editor was published in the *Kentucke Gazette*, "Fifteen Guineas Reward," announcing the theft from the writer's home of "a green silk knit purse . . . in which were sixty Guineas (English and French) and five half Joannes's: I will give the above reward to any person who will detect the thief and bring him to Justice, or ten Guineas for the money and no questions asked."[61]

That and similar "reward" letters were common in American newspapers of the era; many featured numerous such letters per issue. Most often rewards were offered for the return of livestock, and in time letter-writers were offering rewards for escaped slaves and indentured servants. The *South Carolina Gazette* had four such letters in its September 10, 1736, edition, as well as five letters announcing horses that were "Stray'd or Stolen," and a letter offering a reward for information about the location of five deserters from the garrison at St. Simons, Georgia.[62] The *Pennsylvania Packet* of May 30, 1774, had six letters offering rewards for escaped slaves and indentured servants, compared to just two letters arguing for Americans to declare their own freedom from England ("Brothers! Shall we despair amidst the rattling chains which are formed to bind us hand and feet, God forbid? Let every breast swell with disdain at the impious thought."[63]).

A 1793 letter from rural central Pennsylvania, submitted by "M.S." to *The Sunbury and Northumberland Gazette*, demanded freedom of another kind: "Fish are a species of animals which ought to be exempt from our tyranny. They inhabit an element of their own; they encroach not on our rights; nor do they destroy our property. . . . [T]o see the harmless trout driven from one end of its habitation to the other, in the most agonizing distress, till spent and breathless he yields to his destiny, and the savage arts of man."[64] That was two centuries before People for the Ethical Treatment of Animals, or PETA, would encourage its supporters to argue the same thing (usually for more charismatic and "popular" animals than the humble trout). The 18th century saw the advance of truly "public" forums that would convey opinions of all manner from members of the public. They became, in their own limited way, the best reflections that society had of itself.

'. . . AND THEREFORE DESIRES YOU WOULD ALLOW IT ROOM IN YOUR PAPER'

Letters to the editor in the 18th century were free from many of the restrictions encountered by writers today. Since the late 20th century, most newspapers have automatically rejected letters about personal disputes, for example, or letters making claims of wrongdoing against others, statements of "fact" that are not independently verifiable, even letters that are longer than a couple hundred words.[65] Whether those modernizations are a benefit or a detriment to contemporary comment forums is a matter of considerable debate that will be discussed in later chapters. The tradition of handling audience feedback, however, began in the early days of the Free Press era, and the approach then was unmistakably libertarian and accommodating of diverse opinions and heated prose.

Letters frequently were used to make personal attacks, as well as to defend against those attacks. One genre of comment from that era is the "honor letter," or a letter written with the intent to stifle rumors and address mischaracterizations among private citizens. One such letter to the *India Gazette* of Kolkata, India, in 1790, was written by Paul Jodrell (son of playwright Richard Paul Jodrell) to respond to

> ". . . the calumny and detraction promulgated through the channel of the Madras Courier; and although we have ever considered it a disgrace to have our names appear by our own authority in a publication where malevolence has assumed the lead, and trampled upon every principle of honour and of truth . . . we have at last resolved, however painful the measure, to make use of it in order to destroy reports . . . which have been industriously propagated by two or three individuals. . . . We do solemnly and unequivocally declare that Miss Paulina Elizabeth Margaret Jodrell is the daughter of Sir Paul and Lady Jodrell."[66]

Honor letters were published in other parts of the world, such as this example from Ireland's *Dublin Mercury* in 1770, in which the writer announced that:

> "[S]ome evil minded person or persons did of late at two several times forge letters in the name and signature of me Charles Mayne of Cootehill, Esq., joint agent to the right hon. the Earl of Bellamont . . . And whereas the said forged letters did, in every article, contain insidious, malicious, and notorious falsehoods, Now I the said Charles Mayne do hereby promise to pay the sum of Fifty Pounds sterling as a reward to any person (the immediate author of the same excepted) who shall in

six calendar months from the date hereof, discover one or more person of persons concerned in committing said forgeries."[67]

Another genre of letter common of that era, and that would have a hard time today finding an accommodating editor, were "miracle cure" letters. Those letters made specific medical claims, often offering cures for all manner of common ailments, usually for a small remittance. Not all such letters asked for payment, however. An example is from Scotland, in a 1730 issue of the *Eccho or Edinburgh Weekly Journal* that included an unsigned letter from "A Physician who for many Years has experienced a pleasant, safe and never but effectual Medicine, if applied in Time, for those convulsive, strangulating Coughs in Children vulgarly called the Chin or Whooping Cough . . . and therefore desires you would allow it Room in your Paper."[68] (The suggested remedy was broth made from boiled coltsfoot leaves, a once common homeopathic treatment now widely suspected to cause liver disease.)

Many letters of the 18th century were quite obviously unpaid advertisements, another genre that modern editors typically reject or refer to their advertising salespeople. Frequently, letters were used to announce performances, public sales and auctions, temporary exhibits, and the like. A rather lengthy example is from the *Maryland Gazette*, published in Annapolis in 1749—a letter from "The Operator" promoting an exhibit of about two dozen "Experiments on the newly discovered Electrical Fire; not only those that have been made and published in Europe, but a Number of new ones lately made in Philadelphia; by which several of the principal Properties of this wonderful Fire are demonstrated. . . ."[69]

Considered as a whole, letters to the editor in the 18th-century press of the American colonies provided an eclectic mixture of factual claims and counterclaims, criticisms (often harsh, sometimes outlandish), political treatises, commercial announcements, and personal statements of belief and conscience. The forums were used to convey interpersonal squabbles, to send messages to far-flung friends and family, and to announce births, marriages, and deaths. A letter asking a long-lost brother to write home was just as likely to appear as a letter challenging a new law or policy of local officials, and a clumsy, awkward complaint about a barking dog was just as likely to appear in the same issue as a letter from an aristocrat or renowned public figure. Media historians Michael and Edwin Emery made this note of the American frontier press during the late 18th and early 19th centuries:

"On the whole, they were small, hand-set, scrubby publications. It is apparent that there was no place on them for large staffs, regular correspondents, or columnists furnishing opinions for readers too busy to form their own. There was plenty of opinion, of course, but most of it was contributed by readers. Usually there was a column or two of local news, sometimes printed as scattered items without benefit of headlines.

There might be half a column of exchanges or news gleaned from other newspapers arrived by the last post. The remaining material, exclusive of the notices, or advertisements, was very likely submitted by readers. Every subscriber who could wield a pen sooner or later appeared in the columns."[70]

Largely unencumbered by the selection criteria that evolved through the 19th and 20th centuries, editors of those early forums seemed far more likely to publish whatever crossed their desks, and in so doing provided truly free forums for personal expression and collaborative journalism. As Emery and Emery observed, that resulted in some content that was "strident and in bad taste," and was prone to "distortion, flamboyance, and vindictiveness."[71] Yet that was the press that both shocked and mesmerized Alexis de Toqueville early in the 19th century, and very much what he had in mind when he wrote that the American press "constitutes a singular power, so strangely composed of mingled good and evil that it is at the same time indispensable to the existence of freedom, and nearly incompatible with the maintenance of public order."[72] The cultural chaos necessary for a truly free society was reflected in those early newspapers, warts and all.

NOTES

1. Edward Husbands, *The Great Assises holden in Parnassus*, London, 1645. Reprinted with annotation in *Spencer and the Tradition: English Poetry 1579–1830* [website], ed. David Hill Radcliffe. Accessed September 28, 2012, from http://spenserians.cath.vt.edu/TextRecord.php?action=GET&textsid=33437.
2. Dic. Bukrum, "To the Author of the New-England Courant," *New-England Courant*, January 7, 1723, 1.
3. Silence Dogood, "To the Author of the New-England Courant," *New England Courant*, April 2, 1722, 1.
4. Massachusetts Historical Society, "Benjamin Franklin—Newspaper Publisher and Runaway," *Silence Dogood: Benjamin Franklin in the New England Courant* (Boston: Massachusetts Historical Society, 2013). Accessed March 13, 2013, from www.masshist.org/online/silence_dogood/essay.php?entry_id=204.
5. Ronald Hamowy, "Introduction," in Ronald Hamowy, ed., *Cato's Letters, or, Essays on Liberty, Civil and Religious, and other Important Subjects, Volume One* (Indianapolis, Ind.: Liberty Fund, 1995), xx.
6. Thomas Gordon, "The Preface," in Ronald Hamowy, ed., *Cato's Letters, or, Essays on Liberty, Civil and Religious, and other Important Subjects, Volume One* (Indianapolis, Ind.: Liberty Fund, 1995), 17.
7. Hamowy, "Introduction," xxii.
8. Hamowy, "Introduction," xxii.
9. Clinton Rossiter, *Seedtime of the Republic* (New York: Harcourt Brace and Co., 1953), 141.
10. Thomas McIntyre Cooley, *A Treatise on the Constitutional Limitations Which Rest Upon The Legislative Power of the States of the American Union* (Boston: Little, Brown and Co., 1868), 464.

11. John Trenchard and Thomas Gordon, "Reflections upon Libelling," in Ronald Hamowy, ed., *Cato's Letters, or, Essays on Liberty, Civil and Religious, and other Important Subjects, Volume One* (Indianapolis, Ind.: Liberty Fund, 1995), 228.
12. Trenchard and Gordon, "Reflections upon Libelling," 233.
13. Trenchard and Gordon, "Reflections upon Libelling," 232–33.
14. Livingston Rutherfurd, *John Peter Zenger: His Press, His Trial, and a Bibliography of Zenger Imprints* (New York: Dodd, Mead and Co., 1904), 130.
15. Lewis Morris later was appointed the crown's governor of New Jersey; his great-grandson, Gouverneur Morris, attended the Constitutional Convention of 1787 and is widely credited as being "the penman of the Constitution." See "Creating a Constitution," Library of Congress website, http://memory.loc.gov/ammem/collections/continental/constit.html.
16. David Paul Nord, "The Authority of Truth: Religion and the John Peter Zenger Case," *Journalism Quarterly* 62, 2 (1985), 227–35.
17. Nord, "The Authority of Truth."
18. Rutherfurd, *John Peter Zenger*, 29.
19. Rutherfurd, *John Peter Zenger*, 32.
20. Rutherfurd, *John Peter Zenger*, 33.
21. Rutherfurd, *John Peter Zenger*, 41.
22. Rutherfurd, *John Peter Zenger*, 45.
23. Rutherfurd, *John Peter Zenger*, 70–71.
24. Rutherfurd, *John Peter Zenger*, 74.
25. Rutherfurd, *John Peter Zenger*, 80.
26. Gerard W. Gawalt and Ronald M. Gephart, *Letters of Delegates to Congress, 1774–1789, v. 13* (Washington, D.C.: Library of Congress, 1986), 141
27. Gawalt and Gephart, *Letters of Delegates to Congress*, 139
28. Gawalt and Gephart, *Letters of Delegates to Congress*, 139
29. Dwight Teeter, "Press Freedom and the Public Printing: Pennsylvania, 1775–83," *Journalism Quarterly* 45 (1968), 445–51.
30. Francis Jennings, *The Creation of America: Through Revolution to Empire* (Cambridge: Cambridge University Press, 2000), 107.
31. T. H. Bower, "Junius, Philip Francis, and Parliamentary Reform," *Albion: A Quarterly Journal Concerned with British Studies* 27, 3 (1995), 397–418.
32. Richard F. Hixson, *Isaac Collins: A Quaker Printer in 18th Century America* (New Brunswick, N.J.: Rutgers University Press, 1968), 95–96.
33. At the time, a "Federalist" supported a strong centralized government for the new United States, whereas an "Anti-Federalist" favored a weaker union that reserved more independence for the individual states. Both factions supported U.S. independence from Britain, and each comprised groups of well-known "patriots." For example, James Madison and Alexander Hamilton were staunch Federalists; Thomas Jefferson and James Monroe were among the most vocal Anti-Federalists.
34. John P. Kaminski and Gaspare J. Saladino, *Documentary History of the Constitution, Vol. 13* (Madison, Wis.: State Historical Society of Wisconsin, 1981), 315.
35. See footnote 33.
36. Kaminski and Saladino, *Documentary History of the Constitution*, 312, 315–16.
37. Kaminski and Saladino, *Documentary History of the Constitution*, 317–20.
38. Herbert J. Storing, *The Complete Anti-Federalist* (Chicago: University of Chicago Press, 1981), 254.
39. Storing, *The Complete Anti-Federalist*, 102–3.
40. Kaminski and Saladino, *Documentary History of the Constitution*, 318.
41. Kaminski and Saladino, *Documentary History of the Constitution*, 320–21.

42. Kaminski and Saladino, *Documentary History of the Constitution*, 313–14.
43. National Humanities Center, "To Divide, and Thus to Destroy: Letters from a Farmer in Pennsylvania" (Research Triangle Park, N.C.: National Humanities Center, 2013). Accessed December 25, 2012, from http://nationalhumanities center.org/pds/makingrev/crisis/text4/dickinsonletters1767.pdf.
44. John Kincaid, "Who was Publius—the Real Guy?" (Easton, Pa.: Robert B. and Helen S. Meyner Center, Lafayette College, 2012). Accessed December 25, 2012, from http://meynercenter.lafayette.edu/publius/.
45. Storing, *The Complete Anti-Federalist*.
46. George B. Delta and Jeffrey H. Matsuura, *Law of the Internet, Volume 2* (Austin, Tex.: Wolters Kluwer, 2011), 123–24.
47. The Libel Reform Campaign "Free Speech is Not For Sale" (London: The Libel Reform Campaign, 2012). Accessed March 27, 2013, from www.libel reform.org.
48. State of New York Senate Bill S06779, introduced March 21, 2012. Accessed March 20, 2013, from http://assembly.state.ny.us/leg/?default_fld=&bn=S067 79&term=2011&Summary=Y&Text=Y.
49. Josh Peterson, "Illinois State Senator Pushes Anti-Anonymity Bill," *The Daily Caller*, Washington, D.C., February 21, 2013. Accessed March 21, 2013, from http://dailycaller.com/2013/02/21/illinois-state-senator-pushes-anti-ano nymity-bill/.
50. Samuel Miller, *A Brief Retrospect of the Eighteenth Century* (New York: T. & J. Swords, 1803), 254.
51. Miller, *A Brief Retrospect of the Eighteenth Century*, 254–55.
52. Isaiah Thomas, *A History of Printing in America*, ed. Marcus A. McCorison (New York: Weathervane Books, 1970), 20.
53. Viator, untitled [letter to the editor], *The General Evening Post*, London, October 1, 1776, 2.
54. Pacificus, untitled [letter to the editor], *Royal Gazette*, New York, November 11, 1778, p. 2.
55. The letter from "A Dragoon" was printed December 12, 1771, in *The Pennsylvania Journal*; December 16, 1771, in *The Pennsylvania Chronicle*; and January 3, 1772, in the *New London Gazette*. The reprints were found via the "America's Historical Newspapers" database of NewsBank.
56. Rob the Thrasher, untitled [letter to the editor], *The Kentucky Gazette*, Lexington, Ky., December 24, 1791, 2.
57. Job, "To the Editor of the Madras Courier" [letter to the editor], *The Madras Courier* Madras, India, January 25, 1786, 1.
58. Gerard Stropnicky, Tom Byrn, James Goode, and Jerry Matheny, *Letters to the Editor: Two Hundred Years in the Life of an American Town* (New York: Touchstone, 1998), 23.
59. John May was a contemporary of North American frontiersmen Daniel Boone and Simon Kenton, and along with them founded Maysville, Kentucky, an important port on the Ohio River at that time. See Allan W. Eckert, *The Frontiersmen* (Ashland, Ky.: Jesse Stuart Foundation, 2001).
60. John May, untitled [letter to the editor] *Kentucke Gazette*, Lexington, Ky., February 14, 1789. Accessed January 3, 2013, from The Kentucky Digital Library, http://kdl.kyvl.org/catalog/xt7sbc3svk87_2?.
61. R. M'Gillice, "Fifteen Guineas Reward" [letter to the editor], *Kentucke Gazette*, Lexington, Ky., January 3, 1789. Accessed January 3, 2013, from The Kentucky Digital Library, http://kdl.kyvl.org/catalog/xt79w08wb19m_2.
62. Unknown author, untitled [letter to the editor], *South Carolina Gazette*, Charleston, S.C., September 10, 1736, 1–4.

63. An American, "Americans!" [letter to the editor], *The Pennsylvania Packet* or the General Advertiser, Philadelphia, Pa., May 30, 1774, 2–3.

64. M.S., "The rights of fish," in Stropnicky et al., *Letters to the Editor: Two Hundred Years in the Life of an American Town*, 27.

65. Suraj Kapoor, "Most Papers Receive More Letters," *The Masthead* 17, 2 (1995), 18–21.

66. Paul Jodrell and Jane Jodrell, "Affidavit" [letter to the editor], *The India Gazette*, Calcutta, India, February 22, 1790, 2.

67. Charles Mayne, untitled [letter to the editor], *The Dublin Mercury*, Dublin, Ireland, January 18, 1770, 3.

68. Unknown author, untitled [letter to the editor], *Eccho or Edinburgh Weekly Journal*, Edinburgh, Scotland, August 19, 1730, 3.

69. The Operator, "Notice is Hereby Given to the Curious" [letter to the editor], *The Maryland Gazette*, Annapolis, Md., May 10, 1749, 2.

70. Michael Emery and Edwin Emery, *The Press and America: An Interpretive History of the Mass Media* (Boston: Allyn and Bacon, 1996), 82.

71. Emery and Emery, *The Press and America*, 82.

72. Alexis de Tocqueville, *Democracy in America, Volumes 1 and 2, Unabridged*, trans. Henry Reeve (Stilwell, Kans.: Digireads, 2007), 137.

4   Commodification of Comments
Professional Bias and Gatekeeping of Letters to the Editor

In 1803, the first machine that could make paper into continuous rolls went online in Hertfordshire, north of London.[1] Not very long thereafter, inventors began figuring out ways to apply the printed word to those rolls of "endless paper."[2] By the end of that century, reel-fed presses were widely adopted by newspaper publishers, and the rapid growth of the news industry through the 1800s drove innovations in printing technology.[3] Of course, the dramatic rise of newspapering as an industry, rather than as a craft, depended heavily on the expansion of the newspaper audience, and that meant attracting readers beyond those in the socio-political elite—"readers" being a euphemistic term for what those audience members truly became: customers. And over time, they also became unpaid contributors of content to help editors fill and sell those endless pages.

There are some who celebrate industrialism's influence on the news media, and there are many others who lament the commercialization of "freedom of the press." The early 19th-century shift from the partisan press to a more populist, general-interest approach had the benefit of expanding public access to the press, but it also began a long, slow process of diminishing the "open forum" approaches of the past—by the mid-1800s, audience feedback became less common than in previous eras, with a slow uptick later in that century and into the 1900s. By the mid-20th century, however, audience feedback exploded, and most serious newspapers and magazines created special "letters to the editor" sections. Along with that dramatic increase in submissions from the public came a decreasing liberalism among the editors receiving those submissions, and the forums became much more restricted and commodified than in the past. Through the gatekeeping process, feedback features became more reflective of editors' ideals about public discourse than of broader society.

The pioneers of the popular press—the "penny press"—made great claims about serving the informational needs of the public, yet there is little evidence to suggest that the first generation of press barons were committed to providing broad forums for public discourse compared to previous newspapers. The penny papers frequently did print items that were deemed "letters," but those were most often from correspondents, such as the

"Washington letter-writers" who reported about political activities in the U.S. capital, or similar correspondents from the major cities of the world (many of them writing anonymously or under pseudonyms).[4] Audience feedback items usually were not labeled as "letters" but were set off from other items by some kind of lead-in text, such as "Dear Editor:" or "To the Editor of The Times." And unlike the correspondent letters, which were both plentiful and quite lengthy, feedback letters tended to be both short and scarce. Media historian Brian Thornton conducted a content analysis of four New York newspapers published in 1835,[5] and remarked that "[a] modern reader . . . might be surprised by the scarcity of published letters to the editor in 1835," noting further that the two conservative, elite newspapers he studied published "far more" letters than their penny-press competitors, the *Herald* and the *Sun* (the two elite papers published 181 letters over a five-month period, compared to 37 total by the two "penny papers").[6] Thornton's findings are sustained when looking through archives of newspapers from later in that century as well—compared to other forms of content, letters appear infrequently and sporadically, perhaps as few as just one or two per week published in daily newspapers of the era. It is hard to tell whether that observed scarcity was due to a lack of submissions or a lack of accommodation by the newspapers of the mid-19th century.

One thing that can be observed from the mid-1800s to the mid-1900s is that the handling of audience feedback became more deliberate and commercialized. The evolution was slow and fickle, as some obvious efforts to showcase audience feedback came and went. By the 1870s, for instance, *The New York Herald* had organized its letters into a feature called "Our Complaint Book." The section, located in the back pages of the newspaper, contained a rudimentary submission policy, stating, "Letters intended for this column must be accompanied by writer's full name and address to insure attention. Complainants who are unwilling to comply with this rule simply waste time in writing."[7] LTE selection in the Industrial Age also seemed to shift away from the "anything goes" approach of the Enlightenment press to a much more deliberate, constructed-narrative approach that benefited the newspaper's commercial success. The construction of audience feedback as a form of "fan mail" was the most obvious example of the early commodification of audience feedback.

FEEDBACK AS 'FAN MAIL': THE CASE OF JAMES GORDON BENNETT'S *NEW YORK HERALD*

To a certain extent, audience feedback had always included occasional expressions of flattery and support toward news publications. But the practice of printing fan mail—generic praise for the newspaper and/or its famous editor, with little or no reference to any other content in the publication—became more common practice after the advent of the penny press.

One of the most noteworthy characteristics of the penny press was its penchant for sensationalism, and that went hand in hand with brash and bold celebrity editors who put their egos on full display and seemed to adopt the age-old showbiz mentality that "there is no such thing as bad publicity." Literary critic and historian David S. Reynolds mused, "Penny newspapers, aimed at the wallets and the tastes of America's increasingly rowdy working class, supplanted the respectable sixpennies of the past with a new brand of journalism that was brash, zestful, and above all sensational."[8] In regard to *The New York Herald's* James Gordon Bennett Sr., Reynolds noted that the editor would "print shocking stories with little or no moral comment, and he even courted insults to gain publicity."[9] There are many examples of such baiting by Bennett, but one that very clearly dovetails with his practice of printing "fan mail" is from September 1839, in which Bennett responded to a lament from "Emily" who claimed that her husband had prevented her from reading *The Herald* ("Oh! do, dear Bennett, tell me how to get a chance to read it. I have stated my case to you, and now, like a good doctor, tell me how to get your paper—but stop, I hear him on the stairs."[10]). Bennett's response began "Humbug!—It is too late in the day to talk about the morals of the *Herald*. The clamor was originally got up by the Wall Street editors and politicians, who are, individually and collectively, a gang of the most lazy, ignorant, demoralized rogues, not yet adjudged to eternal punishment. . . ."[11]

Of particular note were items published as letters that extolled the talents and "genius" of Bennett himself and the celebrity of the *Herald*. One such letter, from the spring of 1837, discussed the writer's winter travel "on the road between Baltimore and Washington, when we were almost perishing with cold," at which point "a lady of our party drew from her bag a number of the HERALD, and commenced reading a few extracts. The original wit and sprightliness of your editorial remarks soon began to enliven us, and by awakening our spirits gave warmth to our bodies."[12] A somewhat critical letter of the same era rather politely complained about inaccurate reporting of monetary exchange rates, concluding, "It gives me pleasure to observe your independent course, but allow me to say that you are at times rather radical for my taste, and think and write too much about your own self."[13] And a critical letter to the *Herald* the following year challenged the veracity of claims that the newspaper had received locks of hair from seven women: "You ought not attempt to deceive your readers, by saying you received seven locks of hair, and such like stuff. What young ladies would send them—tell me that?"[14] The response to that letter offered, "Very well, Quiz, we will tell you partly. We cannot give their names in full—but here are their Christian names, and a full description of their persons, sent with the hair. . . . Lydia; Tall, fine person, with black brilliant eyes . . . Eliza; Middle size, with blue eyes . . . Caroline; Rather above the middle size, black eyes. . . ."[15]

In that manner, the *Herald* used both laudatory and critical LTEs as opportunities to turn the conversation to benefit the newspaper. Such letters gave Bennett and his editors occasion to restate their opinions about various issues and concerns. An interesting submission from October of 1837 includes a letter requesting a subscription to "your valuable Herald," to be mailed to Columbus, Ohio, and to be paid with a note from a Wall Street exchange company run by "men of eminence," to which Bennett added a rejoinder to castigate the writer's faith in that particular Wall Street company, calling the company officers "shinplasters" and "impudent humbugs," and essentially refusing the subscription request because of the writer's affiliation with those men.[16]

Whether any or all such letters were really from the public, or constructed by the *Herald*'s staff to read like letters from the public, may never be truly known. The practice of newspapers writing their own letters was not widely discussed, but may have been somewhat common, based on suggestions by some media critics and scholars.[17] Suspicions that the *Herald* sometimes wrote its own LTEs may be forgiven when considering letters published on the front page (top-left column) of the March 2, 1837, issue. All three letters heaped praise upon the paper—the first, datelined Detroit, commending Bennett for an editorial encouraging tenants to revolt against increased rent from landlords:

> "Now, friend Bennett, (I call you friend because I believe you are a friend to mankind in general), allow me to finish the picture, but inviting all such as will resist, to partake of the advice set forth in your article . . . Your philanthropic bearing is noticed even out here; we know of no man better calculated to reform society than yourself. . . . P.S. You know not what a hue and cry there is here after your little 'Herald' whenever the mail arrives. We have lots of New Yorkers here. . . ."[18]

Another such letter was from "Paul Pry" in September 1836: "Sir—The avidity with which all classes read your paper, proves the estimation you are held in as an editor, for talent, and possessing in an eminent degree that kind of tact for conducting a public journal, which must make your paper more sought after than any other daily paper in this city. . . ."[19]

Bennett's *Herald* was by no means a typical newspaper of the era (if there really was any "typical" newspaper then), and so this brief case study should not be considered indicative of the norms of the era. Most newspapers published most letters without rejoinders, and, arguably, those that were less sensationalistic did not receive the number of reputation-defense letters received by the *Herald* (which, again, did not publish very many letters at all in the mid-1800s). But the case does illustrate, perhaps to an extreme, the level to which audience feedback can be packaged and manipulated by news outlets that are less interested in providing truly public forums for dialogue about the issues at hand than they are in developing discussions about the publications themselves.

DEFINING THE FORUMS: PACKAGING
OF AUDIENCE FEEDBACK

At the turn of the 19th century, it was not uncommon for newspapers to reprint letters to the editor from other newspapers, either those published nearby or those from afar, even overseas. For example, *The Scioto Gazette and Chillicothe Advertiser* of south-central Ohio published a letter in 1800 originally published in Rhode Island regarding congressional elections,[20] and the *National Intelligencer and Washington Advertiser* in 1801 reprinted a letter from Paris complaining about the distances between Parisian institutes and gardens.[21] Over time, that practice ceased, and publications only published letters submitted to them directly, almost always initiated with a label such as "To the Editor of The Gazette" or some such. Front-page LTEs became increasingly rare, although some exceptions could be found (*The New Mississippian* of Jackson, Mississippi, published front-page letters as late as 1883, for example[22]). Adolph Ochs became publisher of *The New York Times* in 1896, and wrote that the newspaper's goal was to provide "a forum for the consideration of all questions of public importance, and to that end to invite intelligent discussion from all shades of opinion."[23] Over the following decades, the newspaper began publishing letters in a regular, fixed location on its inside pages.

By the early 20th century, it was common practice for newspapers to gather letters together, two or more in succession, sometimes (but rarely, until the mid-1900s) under very clear section headers—"Letter to the Editor" by far the most common, but sometimes with other titles, such as "Our Complaint Book" (other than Bennett's *Herald*, the title was also used for the letters segment of the *Galveston Daily News* of coastal Texas[24]), "Communications," used by *The Liberator* of Boston, Massachusetts,[25] and "The Kick Kontest" of *The Citizen* of Honesdale, Pennsylvania, which gave prizes to the best "kicks" (complaints) submitted from readers and which were printed on the front page.[26] *The Chicago Tribune* used the header "Voice of the People" starting in 1908; by the 1920s, *The New York Times* had aggregated its feedback into the right-hand column of its editorial page and added the section header "Letters to the Editor" in 1931.[27] By the middle of the century, nearly all newspapers and magazines that published audience feedback had standalone and clearly marked "letters to the editor" forums, and that came with many very distinct practices for editing LTEs.

Rejoinders were somewhat common in the newspapers of the era. A letter in the *Herald* in 1844 complaining that a previously published LTE had "dragged up from the grave, the bones of my mother, who has now been dead some fifteen years, and paraded her name before the readers of your paper, with abusive remarks. . . . I skulk behind no anonymous signature, but satisfied that James Gordon Bennett, who has felt the malignity of this same Philadelphia clique, is above their malice and their lies." To which the newspaper responded, "If any clique hate us, [they] do so solitary and alone—we cannot return the sentiment—and care nothing about their love or hatred."[28]

As Bennett and his editors often did in the *Herald*, many editors would also take advantage of letters to offer replies and rejoinders, often with a bit of snarky attitude. *The Inter Ocean* newspaper of Chicago was especially prolific and adroit in that regard. Through the 1870s, it was common for the daily *Inter Ocean* to publish one or two LTEs each week from its upscale audience, and many of those letters were accompanied by a rejoinder (usually titled "REPLY") that were as long or longer than the original letters. Sometimes the replies were to questions (such as explaining the extent and duties of the U.S. ambassadors around the world when requested to do so in a letter,[29] or responding to questions about specific government policies, such as Wyoming's early efforts to end prohibitions against women voting[30]). But the replies sometimes would be more than informational and would reveal the editor's political stance on issues (the *Inter Ocean* was well known for being staunchly Republican throughout its succession of owners and editors[31]). Sometimes, the replies would be a bit caustic, as in this example:

"Oskaloosa, Iowa:
To the Editor of The Inter Ocean:
1. Is it right that the people of this country should be made a police force to enable moneyed corporations to oppress labor?
2. What avails the ballot in the hands of the poor when money is so potent to bribe our legislators, judges and officers, as at the present time?
3. Have we reached that point in our history where the soldier and bayonet are the only efficient means of keeping the peace between capital and labor?

M.D'Lyle
REPLY

1. No.
2. Do you know of any case where legislators or judges have been bribed without exposure or punishment? If so it is your duty to squeal on such persons at once. If you do not, it is hardly fair to make your assertion so sweeping.
3. We reached a point a few days ago in Chicago, where sharp clubbing by the police was required to keep a lot of pretended workmen from burning and plundering the city. We don't know how it was in Oskaloosa."[32]

The second letter published that day, an offer to provide information about recent fires in various U.S. cities and wars in Europe as reported by a Thomas Stackpole, was met with a terse reply: "So far as his offer is concerned to give us a 'full account,' it is declined. We have published a good many full accounts of the fires named, and, so far as the war is concerned, we can beat Stackpole two to one with our cable dispatches. His spiritual lines are down somewhere."[33]

Some editors were less caustic and more playful with their rejoinders. A fascinating example was the aforementioned "Kick Kontest" of *The Citizen* newspaper of Honesdale, Pennsylvania, in the Pocono Mountains. Launched in the spring of 1911, the feedback forum was set up as a front-page feature through which residents of Wayne County could complain and grumble. A house advertisement for the feature encouraged readers to "Kick to the Editor!!!," and enticed them by asking "Have you a kick coming? Is there anything that displeases you? Are you unhappy and need cheering up? Has any little thing gone wrong? Tell us your troubles. . . . There must be something you don't like. Kick about it. What good is an editor anyway except to fix up the kicks of his readers?"[34] The newspaper gave a cash prize—"a brand new crisp one dollar bill"—to the writers of "the three best kicks each week,"[35] and was declared to be "[o]pen to everyone alike, men, women and children, subscribers and non-subscribers. Old and young, rich and poor."[36] The newspaper suggested a few topics: "The weather, of course. Tight fitting shoes. The high cost of living. The hobble skirt and the Harem trousers. High hats on week days. Suffragism, etc., etc., etc. The funnier the better. . . . The more original the subject the better chance for a prize."[37] The "kicks" could be prose or poetry, but were limited to 50 words in length, and shorter ones were encouraged: "A clever fifteen-word kick may win a prize over a full-length fifty-word one. . . . For the best kick of ten words or less The Citizen will pay an additional prize of one dollar."[38] The printed "kicks" all began with the same salutation, "Editor The Citizen," and most were followed by a humorous "answer," such as these few examples from the April 12, 1911, edition:

> "Editor The Citizen:
>   I kick because Congress has been so long standing pat that I must go without a new Easter hat.
>   D.M. PENNELL, Hawley, Pa.
>   Answer: Presuming that you are married and recalling the stories we've heard about the price of Easter bonnets we're willing to modestly assert that your husband is rightly grateful to Congress.
>   Editor The Citizen:
>   I kick because we widows,
>   A big tax have to pay;
>   Must be as meek as Moses,
>   And not have a word to say.

MRS. A. A. GEARY
Answer: Well, madame, our gallantry is only exceeded by our good (?) looks so allow us to inform you that you wouldn't be a widow long if we—but, oh, pshaw, we blush at our boldness. Our P.O. Box Number, however, is 825. . . ."[39]

The editor's rejoinder, as a professional practice, is an interesting artifact of the evolution of editorial control. The most obvious act of editorial control with regard to feedback is the decision over whether to publish—basic gatekeeping—as well as the degree to which that feedback is edited, packaged, and presented. Corralling letters into distinct, segregated, and relatively small spaces was another journalistic routine that imposed editorial control over the forums. Those were all practical considerations, however, as newspapers and magazines adapted to the growing number of submissions and the reduced reliance on unsolicited feedback to fill pages. The use of LTE rejoinders extended the control from the merely practical to the philosophical, as it gave editors the means to co-opt the moment of an individual having her say in public to an opportunity for the editor to engage in self-promotion, to put forth an editorial opinion, and to otherwise turn the conversation among the audience members back toward the publication's overall agenda. An editor's note seems like an obvious courtesy when responding to a direct question, and indeed the impetus for the editor's response may be simply to engage in a conversation. Yet the end result it that (with apologies to Walter Gieber[40]) feedback forums are what editors make them. They no longer were the reflections of broad, diverse opinion that LTEs were in previous eras; from the Industrial Age through the 20th century, the forums became narratives constructed by editors from the raw materials of audience feedback.

RISING ELITISM AND THE AURA OF AUTHORSHIP

As the emphasis on editing shifted from merely providing forums to the more deliberate structuring of those forums, editors naturally spent some time thinking about their practices and sometimes sharing their thoughts with other editors and publishers. The increasingly professionalized approach to feedback management came with a cost, however—an obvious elitism through which editors began to favor the more "literate" submissions from educated audience members over the often coarser, less-articulate (and often anonymous) submissions from more common folk. In time, that institutional bias was transmuted into an assumed "professional standard" that further eroded the diversity of opinion in the forums.

That elitism was on full display in a 1921 column in *Editor and Publisher* by Philip R. Dillon, who noted, "I freely express my pleasure at the steadily rising quality of the letters to the editor, printed each day in most of the daily newspapers. I am led to believe that these voluntary contributions have come to be one of the most desirable features of the large city dailies, as well as the country weeklies which have carried this custom of printing letters from correspondents form the earliest days of journalism."[41] Dillon clearly valued letters in *The Times* of London, which often featured the comments that were "signed by a doctor, lawyer, educator, clergyman, army officer, engineer, or business man in almost any line of trade, written with force, clearness and elegance; written as well, in fact, as a professional writer could do it, and often better than the average professional writer."[42]

He continued:

> "The talent for language expression is widespread among all cultural classes outside of the strictly literary class, in Britain and her colonies. The average British professional man unlike the American business man does not drop his habit of good writing and speaking after he leaves the university or secondary school. We are evidently growing conscious of what I call out national shiftlessness in language expression. The finer quality of the daily letters to the editor is another strong piece of evidence going to prove the growth of culture in America."[43]

Dillon also lamented that many American editors "seem to frown upon letters from members of their staffs. . . . Unquestionably, letters to the editor by trained journalists tend to raise the standard of all letters to the editor, and help to establish in the public mind the right of the publication to insist on a certain standard for all letters that aim to attain publication."[44] That statement suggests that editors of the era were not necessarily applying an elite bias intentionally, and that many had a genuine desire to make feedback forums spaces for the readers and the broader public, not just another space for professionals to dominate. Rather, editors succumbed to a more subconscious accretion of professionalism and elitism that slowly eradicated the vibrant pluralism of the forums.

"Raising standards" was very much a theme of forum management throughout the 20th century. A trade publication devoted to newspaper opinion editors, *The Masthead*, often included articles and essays focused on feedback-forum management, including a few collections of different views that were labeled as "symposia." One such "symposium," published in 1951, noted a shifting practice away from publishing LTEs that were anonymous with the intent of "improving quality." Jack Kilpatrick of *The Richmond News Leader* in Virginia wrote about his newspaper's recent decision to no longer publish anonymous letters to the editor, writing, "It was our feeling then, and it remains our feeling as this is written six months later, that in general one signed letter is worth two from DISGUSTED. . . . Signed letters seem to have a little more thought in them than the average run of unsigned letters."[45] Additional essays published in *The Masthead* through the 1950s and 1960s evoked similar themes: "[T]he average reader detests letters from 'Observant Citizen' or 'A Reader' who apparently lacks guts to put his name to his opinion"[46]; "A letter has no value if printed under a pen-name"[47]; "[Prevent] haters and hollerers from cluttering up the column and scaring off other writers . . . we stopped printing any letters that did not carry the author's name and address. The new rule worked."[48] Exactly what that editor meant by "the new rule worked" is not evidenced, but a reasonable assumption would be that it meant the newspaper received more submissions that pleased the editor, and fewer that challenged his preferences.

Much of the anti-anonymity rhetoric of the time constructed a mythical ideal around the concept of "signing one's name," a mythos that can perhaps be called the "aura of authorship." Here I borrow liberally from Walter Benjamin's concept of "the aura of authenticity,"[49] put forth in his 1936 essay "The Work of Art in the Age of Mechanical Reproduction." Benjamin was considering why an original work of art is considered more culturally valuable than a reproduction, and why mechanical reproduction lacks the "aura" of the original, but he briefly extended the argument to include a consideration of audience feedback in newspapers:

> "With the increasing extension of the press, which kept placing new political, religious, scientific, professional, and local organs before the readers, an increasing number of readers became writers—at first, occasional ones. It began with the daily press opening to its readers space for 'letters to the editor.' And today there is hardly a gainfully employed European who could not, in principle, find an opportunity to publish somewhere or other comments on his work, grievances, documentary reports, or that sort of thing. Thus, the distinction between author and public is about to lose its basic character. . . . At any moment the reader is ready to turn into a writer. As expert, which he had to become willy-nilly in an extremely specialized work process, even if only in some minor respect, the reader gains access to authorship."[50]

The "aura of authorship" was (and remains) an assumption that the act of authorship is more culturally valuable than the mere act of writing. The anti-anonymity arguments made by editors from the mid-1900s forward have been imbued with that assumption, with considerable discussion about how much "better" signed LTEs tend to be compared to unsigned letters—"better" of course being measured against the professional norms and standards of the editors themselves. The privileging of "readers turned authors" can be traced through the gradual extinction of letters from "A Farmer," "A Soldier," and "A Citizen" in the mainstream press. At first, pseudonyms disappeared entirely, replaced by the quasi-anonymous use of the writers' initials; eventually, even the accommodation of initials waned. *The Los Angeles Times* would publish "name withheld" letters with initials only into the 1960s,[51] but switched to a "must sign" approach, which required names to be published with letters, in June 1969.[52] *The Columbus Dispatch* in Ohio's capital published letters signed only with initials at least as late as 1970, but soon thereafter ceased the practice.[53] The very first LTE to *The New York Times*, published in 1851, was signed only "Visitor"[54]; by the 1940s, the *Times* no longer published letters without names except in very rare instances,[55] and in 1973, the newspaper made the rule firm with this printed policy: "Letters must be signed."[56] By the mid-1990s, an estimated 84 percent of U.S. newspapers required published letters to include the writers' names, and 94 percent rejected purely anonymous letters.[57] Although a few publications continued to provide space for anonymous and/or pseudonymous comments from the audience, the overall trend through the 1990s was not only to reject the centuries-old tradition of liberally accommodating all submissions, but also to construct a revisionist mythology that somehow "signing one's name" is essential to the democratic principle of freedom of speech—and that banning anonymous comments was somehow an act of professional ethics. That assumption was, and remains, utter nonsense given the historical record, and yet it is perhaps the most enduring myth professional journalists have about the evolution of modern-day practices and standards.

LETTERS AS 'HAZY REFLECTIONS OF PUBLIC OPINION'

Concurrent with increasing professional discussion about how to manage audience feedback was the scholarly study of feedback forums, especially a number of early studies that tried to discern the demographics of successful LTE writers. One of the first such studies was conducted by Sidney Forsythe of Alabama College, whose 1950 article in *Public Opinion Quarterly* set the stage for future research.[58] Forsythe studied published letters in the Louisville, Kentucky, *Courier Journal*'s "Point of View" column over a one-year period, starting June 1, 1946. He sent questionnaires to the writers of signed LTEs, and found that the writers were "overwhelmingly in the middle and old age-groups . . . male in sex, predominantly . . . conservative in their viewpoints . . . above average in formal education . . . 'native white American' . . . lived in the localities in which they now reside for an average of 18 years . . . [and] members of the white collar, business and professional occupational groups, overwhelmingly. . . ."[59] He concluded, "It seems quite clear that these writers, on a number of the counts, are far from being representative either of their communities or of the nation."[60] Forsythe also found that 44 individuals accounted for 385 letters published in the newspaper over that 12-month period, with a median of eight letters each—at least one writer had 23 letters published that year. That one study, focused on a specific place in a very short time period, provided some evidence that feedback forums under the management of professionalized journalists was dominated by submissions from people much like those professional journalists—educated, middle-aged professionals, overwhelmingly men of heightened social status.

A number of similar "who writes?" studies were conducted thereafter, all producing similar results. A master's student at the University of Oregon, William D. Tarrant, sent questionnaires to people whose LTEs had been published in the Eugene, Oregon, *Register Guard* newspaper during a month in 1956, and found that "[c]onsidering all letter-writers, in comparison to the general public, it was found that letter-writers were better educated, less mobile, more religious . . ., more mature, more self-expressive, better read, more individualistic and much older than the average citizen."[61] A few years later, another graduate student, Gary Vacin at Kansas State University, focused on three dailies in that state in 1964, including two of the largest in Kansas at the time, the *Topeka Daily Capital* and the *Wichita Eagle*.[62] Vacin also sent questionnaires to successful letter writers, and found that most respondents were 55 or older, "predominantly well-educated," "male, by a three-to-one ratio," longtime residents of their communities (averaging 20 years in the same community), and predominantly white-collar workers.[63] Decades later, a nationwide telephone survey in the U.S. found similar patterns—most successful letter writers were older, wealthier, and better-educated than the average population.[64] Studies of editors' views about their forums found a surprising large number, sometimes 60 percent or more, believed their LTE forums represented public opinion, even though very few did any independent surveys of letter-writers to verify such assumptions.[65] Quite contrary to editors' beliefs in the mythos of the "virtual village square," empirical research found that published letters infrequently matched public opinion, findings that started in 1937[66] and remained essentially unchallenged throughout the 20th century. Scholars David Grey and Trevor Brown surmised in 1970 that the forums of the mid-20th century were so heavily edited that they offered only "hazy reflections of public opinion.[67] They argued: "Editors . . . seem to be asking 'What do we want to hear?' and not so much 'What do the writers want to say?' By implication, those with minority or less popular viewpoints tend to be kept out of the mainstream of discussion."[68] They further argued:

> "More letters are apparently being written to newspapers, but are they published? And is the demographic profile of the typical letter-writer changing? Since most of the 30 years of research on letters-to-the-editor has been based on only those published, if may be that the profile which has emerged reflects less the writers themselves than the selection of editors. A broader but largely invisible cross-section of Americans may have been writing for some time; theirs may be the inarticulate, sometimes abusive letters screened from print. Until more systematic knowledge of editorial selection decisions is available, we may be losing valuable indicators of political attitudes, frustrations and change."[69]

There is no way to discern whether the elitism found in 20th-century LTE forums was caused by increased selectivity by editors or a self-selection among the general public, but the research of the era made it quite clear that, first, those who got letters published were cultural elites, and editors who assumed their forums to be more egalitarian were, essentially, clueless about that fact. Editors banned anonymity, curbed length limits, and largely rejected submissions that they considered sub-standard according to their increasingly high standards of journalism, and in so doing made their letters-to-the-editor forums less like true public squares and more like gated communities for the educated middle class. And that educated middle class began to participate in unprecedented numbers. A 1977 report estimated that there were some 10 million active LTE writers in the U.S. alone[70]—but that was only about 4 percent of the nation's population at that time,[71] further debunking the myth that LTE forums of the era could be representative of broader public opinion.

FEEDBACK AND THE ALTERNATIVE PRESS

While the feedback forums of mainstream media became less accessible to all but the educated middle class, advances in printing technology in the mid-20th century allowed for a dramatic expansion of alternative newspapers and niche magazines, many of which were far more accommodating of submissions from their communities. From the raucous DIY newspapers of urban punk-rock fans to the more sedate back-to-the-land magazines of rural homesteaders, the alternative press maintained and expanded upon the traditional role of news media as forums for community discourse. Expanded efficiencies in printing—most notably high-speed, offset lithography—allowed newspapers to expand their printing businesses to include "job printing" for third parties. The relatively inexpensive costs of having a small-circulation DIY newspaper or magazine printed created many opportunities for various communities to develop their own news media.

Alternative media are not simply smaller, more focused versions of larger media outlets. More akin to 18th-century newspapers, the alternative press of the 20th century relied heavily on audience participation, to the point that the content of some publications consisted almost entirely of unpaid, unsolicited letters, essays, and articles from readers. Media scholar David Abrahamson explains that interconnection between alternative publications play "a special role in their readers' lives, constructing a community or affinity group in which the readers feel they are members."[72] Abrahamson further argued:

> "When contemplating the typical relationship between the magazine journalist and his or her readers, and then contrasting it with a similar consideration in the newspaper world, it is quickly evident that something special is apparent. In most cases, the editors and writers of magazines share a direct community of interest with their readers. They are often, indeed literally, the same people. There is no journalistic distance."[73]

One of the oldest and most obvious examples of that is *The Budget*, a weekly newspaper produced out of rural Sugarcreek, Ohio, that circulates internationally to various settlements of Amish and Mennonite communities. Started in 1890 as a typical local newspaper, *The Budget* quickly gained popularity among Amish who had moved from the Sugarcreek community to other parts of Ohio, or even other U.S. states, and within two years it was sent to more than 450 post offices in 18 states.[74] The content of the newspaper was almost entirely made up of letters from various Amish and Mennonite settlements, produced regularly by community representatives the newspaper calls "scribes." The letters read more like "letters from home," often filled with trivia about community events, weather, births, weddings, and the like.[75] The most recent information about *The Budget* at this writing puts its weekly circulation at about 18,000, with an typical page count of 44, and content is made up of between 450 and 500 letters each week from a roster of about 840 scribes.[76] The newspaper is very accommodating of the scribes, only limiting certain types of commentary, such as overt religious proselytizing or potentially libelous statements; publisher Keith Rathbun told a researcher in 2012 that "[p]art of our unwritten agreement is if they write it, we'll get it into the paper."[77] The editor of the national paper, Fannie Erb-Miller, told the same researcher that intimacy between scribes and the newspaper means there are very few problems with submissions: "They know what we do or do not leave in. So actually a lot of [the letters] are pretty much processed and left the way they come in as far as their style of writing and the way they write it, and it's not edited except for certain things we don't put in."[78]

That lack of "journalistic distance" is also clear in the monthly fanzine *Maximum Rocknroll*, which was launched in 1982 and inspired by a radio show of the same name in the San Francisco Bay region.[79] The all-volunteer publication has a core staff of volunteer editors who handle monthly production, but the vast bulk of content comes from readers: "Every month, MMR publishes tons of submissions-based band interviews, from the latest buzz bands to the most obscure punx from the far reaches of the universe. In addition, scene reports from across the globe keep the worldwide scene connected."[80]

Tapping into reader submissions was also crucial to the Reiman Magazines company, started by Roy Reiman in the mid-1960s with a small magazine focused on agricultural structures, but expanded in the 1970s to include rural lifestyle magazines aimed primarily at women in farming communities.[81] By 1991, the company had an estimated 5 million subscribers and was valued at $67 million,[82] and the small publishing empire eventually expanded to include nearly a dozen titles, including *Country Woman*, *Farm & Ranch Living*, and its most successful title, *Taste of Home*.[83] An estimated 80 percent of all content in the magazines has come from reader submissions, from short items and photographs to full-length feature articles.

Another niche publication that relies almost entirely on reader submissions is the *Small Farmer's Journal*, launched in 1977 by sustainable-agriculture advocate Lynn R. Miller; at this writing, the publication has a worldwide circulation of more than 30,000 in 72 countries.[84] As the publication approached its 40th anniversary, Miller described the quarterly magazine this way:

> "More like a community odyssey than a periodical, *Small Farmer's Journal*'s large, beautiful format is packed to over-full with more information than you might find in three or four conventional magazines. Supported 100% by its readership, this folksy and feisty publication, a true clarion of free speech in the best old sense of the phrase, is a vibrant and exciting platform for engaging far-flung ideas about anything pertinent to the small family farm experience."

Such publications serve very important roles in the personal and communal lives of all readers, but especially of those who contribute content, particularly letters to the editor. Very clearly, they commodify audience feedback as a primary source of content that they can in turn sell to subscribers and advertisers, but for the most part the business model of the alternative press seems to be less about converting feedback into finances, and rather about creating genuine, inviting forums where like-minded people can engage in virtual community (even offline via print periodicals). A systematic analysis of letters published in such magazines can reveal the shared values and beliefs of those virtual communities. They also can give individual members of those virtual communities a sense of agency and involvement, through which they can not only share their views and experiences but also ask for assistance and advice, console or encourage other writers, or even organize in-person meetings and gatherings.[85]

The forums provided by such alternative publications were, and remain, far more vibrant and conversational than the heavily packaged forums developed by the mainstream press. Few alternative publications include strict rules about submissions, such as limiting length or the frequency of submissions, or prohibiting the use of pseudonyms. The mainstream press, on the other hand, seemed to spend much of the latter half of the 20th century developing more and more complicated reasons to reject and control audience feedback.

FEEDBACK SUBMISSION POLICIES

The slow, steady movement of mainstream newspapers toward making audience feedback forums more favorable toward cultural elites corresponds with editors' efforts to justify their increasingly obstructionist approach to providing public forums in their pages. The mid-20th century also saw the rise of the "letters policy," or formal statements published in newspapers that provided guidelines for submissions. On their face, such policies were usually simple (even terse) enumerations of the criteria editors used to sort through submissions, and in that regard they represented editorial transparency, which itself was increasingly viewed as a professional imperative through the 20th century.

Whereas editors of earlier eras would often publish LTEs that were poorly written, long, vitriolic, or coarse, by the mid-1990s the criteria for rejection had grown considerably among professional forum editors. Grey and Brown's 1970 review of previous research and input from journalists they met "yield the following lists of reasons or rationalizations for rejecting or selecting letters:"

"For rejection: libelous, unfair personal attack, groups using paper as a billboard, promoting private business, unsigned, writer wishes to monopolize column, lives out of circulation area, letters to a third person, some types of harsh controversy, exhausted subjects, bad taste, thank you's, say nothings, poorly written, too long, repetitive of points made by others or earlier writers, correspondence closed, letter has appeared in another journal or newspaper, crank or nut, bogus letter with faked signature, editor tries to balance opinions so rejects one in favor of another with a different point of view not yet represented.

"For selection: short and articulate, authority of writer, relevance of content, suitability of content to the paper's readership, right of reply to other letters writers and to editors or reporters, correction or clarification of reports, light relief or humor, reflects a shade of opinion not yet represented."[86]

From a classic liberalism perspective, such policies were a bit anathema to the ideals of freedom of expression and the mythos of feedback forums as virtual "village squares." Whereas newspapers and magazines began to devote considerable space to long, rambling treatises and bloated prose from their own writers, they somehow expected their audience members to respond in terse, focused comments of just a couple of hundred words, sometimes no more than a paragraph or two. As the news media became more professionalized, they also became, via their feedback policies, less accommodating of non-journalistic submissions from their audiences. One editor summed up the professional attitude of the 1970s press in an interview with media critic David Shaw, saying "We would prefer to print those (letters) that are more in accord with our editorial policy."[87]

One of the most common restrictions imposed in newspaper letters policies was a limit on length. As with the gradual implementation of "must sign" policies, the imposition of length limits was gradual, and by no means universal. By the 1990s, about 75 percent of U.S. daily newspapers limited letter writers to no more than 500 words (many set the cap at 250 words or fewer).[88] Smaller newspapers (those with circulations below 50,000) and weeklies generally were less restrictive in that regard, but large and mid-sized dailies tended to be more strict about imposing length limits and automatically rejecting overly long letters. An obvious reason for imposing length limits, especially among the large urban newspapers, was that they received proportionately larger numbers of submissions than smaller publications. *The Chicago Tribune*'s "Voice of the People" section included the following notice in the mid-1960s, for example: "Writers should confine themselves to 200 or 300 words . . . Space for letters is obviously limited. Incoming mail far exceeds it. The right to condense letters is reserved."[89] Interestingly, there is nothing in that editor's note that encourages letter-writing—it was an instruction, not an invitation, and a sideways suggestion that to a large, celebrated publication such as the *Tribune*, a feedback forum was not so much an accommodation of broad public discourse as it was a lottery open only to the lucky few, with the newspaper editors picking the winning numbers.

BEYOND COMMODIFICATION: REACTING TO FEEDBACK

Concurrent with their imposition of professional standards on the selection and packing of audience feedback, journalists also developed a complex array of uses for audience feedback, such that the designated forums became ubiquitous and treated as significant and distinct roles in the newsroom. Mid-sized and large daily newspapers started creating separate "opinion" departments to produce editorial and op-ed pages; the larger publications received so many submissions that they would sometimes have an editor assigned just to letters-to-the-editor, sometimes with an assistant or even a small staff. In 1977, *Los Angeles Times* media critic David Shaw offered this estimation of the size of the phenomenon at that time in the United States:

> "Today, more letters to the editor are being written than ever before. It is estimated that there are more than 10 million letter-writers in the country, and even though few papers publish more than one of every 10 or 15 letters they receive, more letters are being published than at any time in American history. Most newspapers devote at least 20%–25% of their daily editorial pages to letters. Many papers devote 35%–40% of their page."[90]

The public therefore only saw a relatively small selection of all the letters submitted to news media, despite many good-faith efforts among editors to publish a variety of opinions. The problem with those highly professionalized forums was not necessarily a lack of willingness by editors to accommodate all comers, but a lack of space in which to publish those submissions. Time, also, was a limiting factor, as the process of sorting, reading, selecting, editing, and typesetting LTEs, many of them hand-written, was often laborious. Selectivity was, quite simply, a necessity for editors of the day. What made the forums decidedly less egalitarian was not the mere act of selection, but rather the professional biases of the selection process. Still, unpublished LTEs were useful to the news media in ways that were harder to discern by the public. Many editors would use LTEs and other forms of feedback to get some ideas about issues that mattered to their communities and/or their audiences,[91] but some would certainly get ideas for news stories or columns from letters that were rejected (most often due to anonymity).

For the reading public, however, the forums were promoted as an idealized public square open to all, yet in reality the forums became controlled and manipulated features of the increasingly elite news media. The phenomenon now commonly referred to as "gatekeeping" was very much on display in the forums. In the early 1960s, two scholars studied how more than 20 newspapers covered how colleges there reacted to on-campus speeches by Communist organizer Gus Hall. The research found that newspapers that published staff-written editorials on the topic were also more likely to publish LTEs about the topic, leading the authors to surmise that either editors who didn't write about the issue didn't publish letters about it, either, or that "the letters served as stimuli to editorial writers or . . . the editorials served as stimuli to letter writers."[92] A later, more robust study of 10 metropolitan newspapers over three decades found evidence that newspapers that ran a lot of front-page news about crime also tended to run a lot of letters about crime.[93] Although such studies can only show correlations, the fact that editors get to pick and choose which issues they will editorialize upon, as well as choose which LTEs will be published (and to what extent), makes it reasonable to believe that the narratives of feedback forums is whatever editors want them to be. Some editors may want forums to be more open-ended, some may prefer to be more limiting and controlling. The former approach tended to be more common in the community press, where small newspapers serving small rural communities or distinct urban neighborhoods could come closer to publishing every LTE they received, while the more restrictive approach was adopted by large-circulation newspapers and magazines.[94]

Larger media may have been more restrictive, but that does not mean they were necessarily less responsive to audience feedback. As mentioned earlier, research found correlations between the priorities in published letters and editorial positions of newspapers,[95] and in some cases overwhelming audience feedback could even reverse earlier decisions. Most often, "overwhelming" was measured in terms of volume. For example, *Time* publisher Henry Luce in 1932 ended a popular series in the magazine called "The March of Time." Later in the year, after receiving more than 22,000 letters, he relented and restored the series, and also published some of the protest letters to demonstrate the reason for his change of mind.[96] Many larger publications began to focus more on selecting letters that were about the publications, such as comments on previously published articles or editorials—one assessment of letters in *The Philadelphia Inquirer* in the mid-1970s found that three-fourths of all letters published in one month "were commenting on something previously published in the Inquirer—a far higher percentage than in any other paper examined for this survey."[97]

Over many decades, it was argued that a strong letters section was seen as an indicator of the publication's popularity and credibility.[98] A good LTE section became a good marketing tool for the publications as well, as indicators that the readers were involved in the news-making process.

By the autumn years of the 20th century, journalism had segregated itself into a *de facto* league system, and much of the discussion of such things as "best practices" and "professional standards" were focused only on the elite, large-audience news outlets, not on the far-more numerous mid-sized and small news outlets. Journalism scholar John C. Merrill referred to the major league entities as "the elite press," which he defined as media that exhibited "high standards, serious purpose, and international significance,"[99] and which stood out (in his opinion) from the "common" media of the time—"a heterogeneous hodgepodge of triviality, too busy entertaining and flashing atypical and distorted images before its readers to pay much attention to presenting a sane, dignified, and balanced world view."[100] Merrill, and indeed many similar acolytes of the "big leaguers" of the news business, articulated a general disdain toward the workaday journalism that did not reflect that kind of elitist attitude against "the popular and middle-level press"[101]: "It is vulgar in the truest sense of the word—speaking to the masses of semiliterates who feel they need to read something called a 'newspaper' but who have no desire to understand the vital issues of the day, and even less desire to concern themselves with these issues."[102] Merrill gave credit to the ways some of the "elites" gave space to letters—he noted that "letters to the editor are quite common in most quality papers of the world,"[103] mentioning specifically such elite publications as *The Times* of London and Italy's *La Stampa*. Merrill also noted that the Soviet newspaper *Izvestia* had a robust letters section that received an estimated 350,000 submissions per year in the 1960s:

> "All of the letters are not published, of course, but they are read and those which are not printed are answered. A staff of about fifty, mostly women, handle the increasing flow of letters. All complaints (and there are many) are investigated. Through letters to *Izvestia*, and to other Soviet newspapers, the people can feel a part of the country's journalism."[104]

"Feel a part of the country's journalism." But only "feel." The 20th century saw many advancements in the quality of journalism practice, including the evolution of a sense of professional ethics and social responsibility among the elite news media of the world. Part of that sense of obligation resulted in a sophisticated approach to handling audience feedback. But in so doing, the press had become detached from the public, and also largely detached from the public-forum traditions of the free press. Policies and practices developed by editors to make the public forums more in line with the professional standards applied to news and commentary had the (perhaps unintentional) consequence of making those forums less reflective of the public they ostensibly served. So while the professional press may have been publishing more feedback than it ever had in the past, it also was publishing feedback that was far less egalitarian. By the late 20th century, that left an opening for electronic media to step in and expand, dramatically, the ways media could make money from the raw materials of audience feedback.

NOTES

1. British Association of Paper Historians, "History of Papermaking in the United Kingdom." British Association of Paper Historians [website]. Accessed December 6, 2013, from www.baph.org.uk/ukpaperhistory.html.
2. James Moran, *Printing Presses: History and Development from the Fifteenth Century to Modern Times* (Berkeley, Calif.: University of California Press, 1973), 173–77.
3. Moran, *Printing Presses*, 211–14.
4. Mark Stegmaier, "Window on Washington in 1850," *American Journalism* 15, 1 (1998), 69–82.
5. Brian Thornton, "The Moon Hoax: Debates About Ethics in 1835 New York Newspapers," *Journal of Mass Media Ethics* 15, 2 (2000), 89–100.
6. Thornton, "The Moon Hoax," 94.
7. "Our Complaint Book," *The New York Herald*, May 31, 1877, 9.
8. David S. Reynolds, *Beneath the American Renaissance: The Subversive Imagination in the Age of Emerson and Melville* (New York: Oxford University Press, 2011), 174.
9. Reynolds, *Beneath the American Renaissance*, 174.
10. Emily, "Waverly Place, August 28th, 1839: Very Dear Sir" [letter to the editor], *The Morning Herald*, New York, September 6, 1839, 2.
11. Bennett, James Gordon Sr., "Remarks," *The Morning Herald*, New York, September 6, 1839, 2.
12. Gertrude de M._____, "New York, April 21, 1837" [letter to the editor], *The Morning Herald*, New York, May 1, 1837, 2.
13. Sound Currency, "Boston, May 16, 1837: James G. Bennett" [letter to the editor], *The Morning Herald*, New York, May 24, 1837, 2.
14. Quiz, "To the Editor of the Herald" [letter to the editor], *Morning Herald*, New York, May 10, 1838, 1.
15. Quiz, "To the Editor of the Herald," 1.
16. John R. Davis, "James Gordon Bennett Esq., Editor of the Herald" [letter to the editor], *The Morning Herald*, New York, October 27, 1937, 2.
17. Philip R. Dillon, "Easy Talk," *Editor & Publisher* 53, 32 (1921), 30.
18. Unknown author, "Detroit, Feb. 15, 1837. Dear Bennett" [letter to the editor], *The Morning Herald*, New York, March 2, 1837, 1.
19. Paul Pry, "Mr. Gordon Bennett" [letter to the editor], *The Morning Herald*, New York, September 9, 1836, 1.
20. Unknown author, "From Rhode Island: Extract of a Letter to the Editor," *The Scioto Gazette and Chillicothe Advertiser*, Chillicothe, Ohio, November 27, 1800, 2.
21. Unknown author, "Extract of a Letter to the Editor from Paris," *The National Intelligencer and Washington Advertiser*, Washington, D.C., March 25, 1801, 2.
22. *The New Mississippian* ran two letters in the far-right column of its front page on October 16, 1883.

23. Kalman Seigel, *Talking Back to* The New York Times: *Letters to the Editor, 1951–1971* (New York: Quadrangle Books, 1972), 3–4

24. *The Galveston Daily News* used "Our Complaint Book" regularly in 1877 as a segment title for its letters to the editor.

25. The Liberator, "Communications" [letters to the editor], *The Liberator, Boston*, March 1, 1834, 34.

26. The Citizen, "Krafty Kicks Kome Skampering In: No Let Up To Interest and Enthusiasm Aroused by Citizen's Weekly Kick Kontest," *The Citizen*, Honesdale, Pa., April 12, 1911, 1.

27. Bill Reader, "Anonymity in Newspapers' Readers' Forums: Policies and Practices Applied to Letters to the Editor and Anonymous Call-In Forums," master's thesis, The Pennsylvania State University (2000).

28. George Lippard, "James Gordon Bennett, Esq., Editor of the New York Herald" [letter to the editor], *The New York Herald*, November 15, 1844, 1.

29. E.J.D., "To the Editor of the Inter Ocean" [letter to the editor], *The Inter Ocean*, Chicago, June 3, 1874, 4.

30. A.M. Walker, "To the Editor of the Inter Ocean" [letter to the editor], *The Inter Ocean*, Chicago, June 3, 1874, 4.

31. Rufus Blanchard, *Discovery and Conquests of the North-West, with a History of Chicago, Volume 2* (Chicago: R. Blanchard and Co., 1900), 237–40.

32. M. D'Lyle, "To the Editor of the Inter Ocean" [letter to the editor], *The Inter Ocean*, Chicago, August 7, 1877, 4.

33. Edwin Drood, "To the Editor of the Inter Ocean" [letter to the editor], *The Inter Ocean*, Chicago, August 7, 1877, 4.

34. The Citizen, "Kick to the Editor" [advertisement], *The Citizen*, Honesdale, Pa., May 5, 1911, 1.

35. The Citizen, "Kick to the Editor," 1.

36. The Citizen, "Kick to the Editor," 1.

37. The Citizen, "Kick to the Editor," 1.

38. The Citizen, "Kick to the Editor," 1.

39. The Citizen, "Krafty Kicks Kome Skampering In," *The Citizen*, Honesdale, Pa., April 12, 1911, 1.

40. Walter Gieber, "News is what Newspapermen Make It," in Lewis A. Dexter and David Manning White, eds., *People, Society and Mass Communication* (New York: Free Press, 1964), 172–80.

41. Dillon, "Easy Talk," 30.

42. Dillon, "Easy Talk," 30.

43. Dillon, "Easy Talk," 30.

44. Dillon, "Easy Talk," 30.

45. Jack Kilpatrick, "Dear Sir, Your Cur!" *The Masthead* 3, 3 (1951), 39.

46. M.Carl Andrews, "Pity the Editor without Letters," *The Masthead* 20, 3 (1968), 12.

47. C. Carpenter, "The Letter Litter," *The Masthead* 19, 2 (1967), 78–81: 80.

48. John G. Craig, "Priming a Balky Pump," *The Masthead* 20, 3 (1968), 27.

49. Walter Benjamin, "The Work of Art in the Age of Mechanical Reproduction," trans. Harry Zohn, University of California Los Angeles School of Theater, Film and Television [website]. Accessed July 21, 2014, from www.marxists.org/reference/subject/philosophy/works/ge/benjamin.htm.

50. Benjamin, "Art in the Age of Mechanical Reproduction."

51. Reader, "Anonymity in Newspapers' Readers' Forums."

52. Reader, "Anonymity in Newspapers' Readers' Forums."

53. Michael J. Saks and Thomas M. Ostrom, "Anonymity in Letters to the Editor," *Public Opinion Quarterly* 37, 3 (1973), 417–22.

54. Seigel, *Talking Back to* The New York Times.

55. Reader, "Anonymity in Newspapers' Readers' Forums."
56. Reader, "Anonymity in Newspapers' Readers' Forums," 19.
57. Suraj Kapoor, "Most Papers Receive More Letters," *The Masthead* 17, 2 (1995), 18–21.
58. Sidney A. Forsythe, "An Exploratory Study of Letters to the Editor and Their Contributors," *Public Opinion Quarterly* 14, 1 (1950), 143–44.
59. Forsythe, "An Exploratory Study of Letters to the Editor and Their Contributors," 143.
60. Forsythe, "An Exploratory Study of Letters to the Editor and Their Contributors," 143.
61. William D. Tarrant, "Who Writes Letters to the Editor?" *Journalism Quarterly* 34, 4 (1957), 501–2.
62. Gary L. Vacin, "A Study of Letter-Writers," *Journalism Quarterly* 42, 3 (1965), 464–65.
63. Vacin, "A Study of Letter-Writers."
64. Bill Reader, Guido Stempel III, and Douglass K. Daniel, "Age, Wealth, Education Predict Letters to the Editor," *Newspaper Research Journal* 25, 4 (2004), 55–66.
65. Grey and Brown, "Letters to the Editor: Hazy Reflection of Public Opinion"; Steve Pasternack, "Editors and the Risk of Libel in Letters," *Journalism Quarterly* 60, 2 (1983), 311–15, 328; Ernest Hynds, "Editorial Page Editors Discuss Use of Letters," *Newspaper Research Journal* 13, 1&2 (1992), 124–36.
66. H. Schuyler Foster Jr. and Carl J. Friedrich, "Letters to the Editor as a Means of Measuring the Effectiveness of Propaganda," *American Political Science Review* 31, 1 (1937), 71–79.
67. David L. Grey and Trevor R. Brown, "Letters to the Editor: Hazy Reflection of Public Opinion," *Journalism Quarterly* 47, 3 (1970), 450–56, 471.
68. Grey and Brown, "Letters to the Editor: Hazy Reflection of Public Opinion," 450.
69. Grey and Brown, "Letters to the Editor: Hazy Reflection of Public Opinion," 471.
70. David Shaw, "Pathos, Rage: Readers Let Fly in Letters to the Editor," *The Los Angeles Times*, Los Angeles, Calif., November 5, 1977, 1, 30–32.
71. According to the U.S. Census Bureau's online "Population Clock," the U.S. population on July 1, 1980, was 227,224,681. Accessed July 24, 2014, from www.census.gov/popclock/.
72. David Abrahamson, "Magazine Exceptionalism: The Concept, The Criteria, The Challenge," *Journalism Studies* 8, 4 (2007), 667–70: 669.
73. Abrahamson, "Magazine Exceptionalism," 669.
74. George R. Smith, "History of the Budget," *The Budget*, Sugarcreek, Ohio, May 16, 1990, 2.
75. M. Clay Carey, "A Plain Circle: Imagining Amish and Mennonite Community Through the National Edition of The Budget," master's thesis, Ohio University (2012). Accessed June 24, 2014, from https://etd.ohiolink.edu/!etd.send_file?accession=ohiou1337286843&disposition=inline.
76. Carey, "A Plain Circle: Imagining Amish and Mennonite Community Through the National Edition of The Budget," 61.
77. Carey, "A Plain Circle: Imagining Amish and Mennonite Community Through the National Edition of The Budget," 65.
78. Carey, "A Plain Circle: Imagining Amish and Mennonite Community Through the National Edition of The Budget," 65–66.
79. Maximum Rocknroll staff, "About," maximumrocknroll.com. Accessed July 24, 2014, from http://maximumrocknroll.com/about/.
80. Maximum Rocknroll staff, "About."
81. Sheila M. Webb, "The Narrative of Core Traditional Values in Reiman Magazines," *Journalism & Mass Communication Quarterly* 83, 1 (2006), 865–82.

82. Lisa Gubernick, "Blooming in the Recession," *Forbes*, November 11, 1991, 114–15.
83. Webb, "The Narrative of Core Traditional Values in Reiman Magazines."
84. Lynn R. Miller, "About Us," smallfarmersjournal.com. Accessed July 24, 2014, from http://smallfarmersjournal.com/contact-us/about/.
85. Bill Reader and Kevin Moist, "Letters as Indicators of Community Values: Two Case Studies of Alternative Magazines," *Journalism & Mass Communication Quarterly*, 85, 4 (2008), 823–40.
86. Grey and Brown, "Letters to the Editor: Hazy Reflection of Public Opinion," 451.
87. Shaw, "Pathos, Rage: Readers Let Fly in Letters to the Editor."
88. Kapoor, "Most Papers Receive More Letters."
89. The Tribune, "Voice of the People" [editor's note], *The Chicago Tribune*, August 27, 1965, 16.
90. Shaw, "Pathos, Rage: Readers Let Fly in Letters to the Editor," 1.
91. Susan Herbst, "Assessing Public Opinion in the 1930s–1940s: Retrospective Views of Journalists," *Journalism & Mass Communication Quarterly* 87, 4 (1990), 943–49.
92. Hal Davis and Galen Rarick, "Functions of Editorials and Letters to the Editor," *Journalism Quarterly* 41, 1 (1964), 108–9.
93. David Pritchard and Dan Berkowitz, "How Readers' Letters May Influence Editors and News Emphasis: A Content Analysis of 10 Newspapers, 1948–1978," *Journalism & Mass Communication Quarterly* 68, 3 (1991), 388–95.
94. Jock Lauterer, *Community Journalism: Relentlessly Local* (Chapel Hill, N.C.: University of North Carolina Press, 1995), 150–151.
95. Davis and Rarick, "Functions of Editorials and Letters to the Editor"; Pritchard and Berkowitz, "How Readers' Letters May Influence Editors and News Emphasis."
96. James L. Baughman, *Henry R. Luce and The Rise of the American News Media.* (Baltimore, Md.: Johns Hopkins University Press, 1987), 77.
97. Shaw, "Pathos, Rage: Readers Let Fly in Letters to the Editor," 32.
98. Forsythe, "An Exploratory Study of Letters to the Editor and Their Contributors"; Grey and Brown, "Letters to the Editor: Hazy Reflection of Public Opinion"; Hynds, "Editorial Page Editors Discuss Use of Letters"; Jock Lauterer, *Community Journalism: Relentlessly Local*; Shaw, "Pathos, Rage: Readers Let Fly in Letters to the Editor."
99. John C. Merrill, *The Elite Press: Great Newspapers of the World* (New York: Pitman Publishing, 1968), 4.
100. Merrill, *The Elite Press*, 5.
101. Merrill, *The Elite Press*, 7.
102. Merrill, *The Elite Press*, 6.
103. Merrill, *The Elite Press*, 77.
104. Merrill, *The Elite Press*, 96.

5   Professional Journalism's Transformation of "a Quaint Tradition"

By the early 20th century, the mainstream news media had transcended from being instruments of revolution and reform for "the common people" to being a major hegemonic institution, owned by fabulously wealthy individuals and families and operated by author-editors at or near the top of the socio-economic class structure. Many of the press barons of the late 1800s had stunning rags-to-riches stories, but by the early 1900s many had become the heads of powerful and influential families: the Hearsts, the Pulitzers, the Harmsworths, the Newhouses, the Murdochs, and so on. The generations who followed were often raised in luxury and had little real-world knowledge of the struggles and conditions faced by the working-class people who read their newspapers or tuned in to their radio stations. They were socio-economic elites referred to as "press barons" by their critics, especially during the severe socio-economic divisions of the Great Depression.

Journalism scholar Fred Blevens remarked that in the United States the press barons were largely opposed to many of the governmental policies aimed at helping the working class (a series of reforms popularly called "The New Deal"):

> "By 1933, the American newspaper industry was under considerable pressure to control profits and improve working conditions, a signal that First Amendment protection on the business side was eroding. Publishers joined forces with influential business associations to fight for what they considered 'free press' issues threatened by new federal laws and proposed legislation designed to promote social welfare, regulate commerce, and reform child labor practices. . . . At the same time, some press critics, decrying the development of journalism as 'big business,' harshly criticized newspapers for exhibiting class bias and becoming less and less representative."[1]

The paradigmatic shift of the common or "low press" led to a perceived disconnect between the press and the best interests of society, and that detachment was very much the impetus for the Commission on Freedom of the Press. Chaired by University of Chicago president Robert Hutchins in the mid-1940s, the commission was composed of about a dozen high-profile academics and a few former government officials, most of them from the United States and focused on U.S. media. The commission formed in 1943 and was the brainchild of *Time* and *Life* publisher Henry Luce, whose company contributed $200,000 to the effort. After four years of studying the content of news media and talking with media professionals and civic leaders, the "Hutchins Commission" issued a highly critical report of the state of the media in the United States: "A Free and Responsible Press," which was subtitled "A General Report on Mass Communication: Newspapers, Radio, Motion Pictures, Magazines, and Books." That report began by suggesting that the concentration of ownership and control of the media "has greatly decreased the proportion of the people who can express their opinions and ideas through the press."[2] The commission clearly believed that there was not enough voice from the people in the news media.

Harkening back to the idealized forum function of the press during the 18th and 19th centuries, the commission lamented that the news media had transformed from a localized practice "which provided variety and interchange of opinion and easy individual access to the market place of ideas" into "an enormous and complicated piece of machinery. As a necessary accompaniment, it has become big business."[3] As a result, the commission argued,

> "The right of free public expression has therefore lost its earlier reality. Protection against government is now not enough to guarantee that a [person] who has something to say shall have a chance to say it. The owners and managers of the press determine which persons, which facts, which versions of the facts, and which ideas shall reach the public.... [The press] must be accountable to society for meeting the public need and for maintaining the rights of citizens and the almost forgotten rights of speakers who have no press."[4]

The Hutchins Commission was so concerned about the apparent erosion of audience participation in news content, as well as the role of news media to provide truly public forums for discourse, that it made the forum function its second-ranked priority (after calling for accuracy and clarity in reporting the news of the day). The commission urged that "the great agencies of mass communication should regard themselves as common carriers of public discussion,"[5] not necessarily to print everything submitted, but to accommodate a variety of views via a variety of channels: "The individual whose views are not represented on an editorial page may reach an audience through a public statement reported as news, through a letter to the editor, through a statement printed in advertising space, or through a magazine article."[6] What emerged from the commission's work was formalization of "social responsibility theory of the press,"[7] a major theoretical shift from the libertarian theory hatched in the era of Milton, solidified in the era of

Franklin, commercialized in the era of Bennett, and institutionalized in the era of Hearst and Pulitzer.

For the most part, the targets of the commission's criticism—mainstream news media—were skeptical, and at first the Hutchins Report was met with either tepid curiosity or outright hostility from working journalists. Renowned columnist Walter Lippmann supported the commission's recommendation that the press be critiqued regularly, but suggested that criticism would be better from external observers rather than internally, as the commission recommended: "The good critic should be an outsider," Lippmann argued, "for personal detachment is necessary to good criticism."[8] Not all reactions to the report were so positive. *The Louisville Courier-Journal's* Barry Bingham questioned the practicality of the report's recommendations, suggesting that those intellectual elites' "lack of familiarity with the mores of newspaper offices resulted in a certain naiveté and awkwardness in exploring unfamiliar ground."[9] *The Chicago Tribune* editorialized strongly against the commission, calling it "a group of totalitarian thinkers . . . who want to discredit the free press of America or put it under a measure of government control."[10] Conservative syndicated columnist George Sokolsky openly ridiculed the commission as "dumb professors" because they listed radio as part of "the press": "Radio is not a newspaper any more than vaudeville. Radio is a show. A newscaster . . . is hired for his voice. He reads stuff dished up by one of the newspaper wire services."[11]

The reforms proposed by the Hutchins Commission did not effect immediate change in the news media, but over the latter half of the 20th century many media outlets slowly moved away from the fierce libertarianism of previous eras toward the social-responsibility model of ethical practice.[12] With regard to audience feedback, that resulted in a far more sophisticated approach toward gathering and packaging submissions from the public, although that sophistication also, ironically, tended to make the forums far less reflective of broad public opinion. The rough-and-tumble realities of true public discourse did not disappear entirely from the news media just because mid-20th century newspapers had begun gentrifying their forums. But true, unfettered public discourse was largely purged from the "socially responsible" mainstream media, and instead found more inviting forums in the less-elitist realms of the underground press, community media, talk radio, and, by the 1990s, the Internet.

RADIO AND TELEVISION AS FORUMS
FOR PUBLIC DISCOURSE

Unlike print media before them, many of which started out as conduits for unsolicited commentary from the public, broadcast media were very much one-way conduits of communication for much of their formative years—at least in terms of on-air content. It should be noted here that, unlike the printing presses of previous eras, radio transmitters in the 1920s were relatively easy to come by, and many basement tinkerers were able to solder together transmitters that could reach thousands, then millions, of household receivers. Do-it-yourself radio, often dubbed "squatter radio" or "pirate radio," provided a direct means for individuals to circumvent larger, organized media in order to express views and ideas.[13] Because many of those innovative DIY broadcasters eventually ended up working for larger, commercial stations and networks, they naturally took with them much of that grassroots attitude of informality, such that it was not uncommon for presenters to effect a "folksy" persona and to honor personal requests from listeners as to which records to play, whose birthdays to announce, and the like.[14] Radio historian Elena Razlogova found that "[s]mall stations welcomed such requests," whereas "[l]arge metropolitan stations soon developed decorous radio formats that posited a more formal relationship between broadcasters and the excitable lay audiences."[15] That schism mirrored what was happening in the newspaper industry of the time as well, with smaller-scale media retaining their more informal, "good-neighbor" approach to accommodating audience feedback, and larger media outlets becoming more detached and formal, even elitist.[16] The dominance of the latter in many countries also led to the genesis of "community radio," which provided typically low-powered, volunteer-run radio stations that the public could access to create its own programming. Commercial and public broadcasting typically overpowered such small community stations, however, in terms of audience share, financial resources, talented staff, and cultural significance—in order to really have their voices heard beyond their own cultural bubbles, audience members had to strive for access to the mainstream media.

It was rare for radio and, later, television news segments to share audience feedback with their audiences, yet there is no doubt that feedback played a significant role in how broadcasting pioneers made programming and content decisions. But much of that was behind the scenes, as broadcasters would not use airtime to read letters and telegrams or to talk via telephone with listeners.[17] Using radio (and then TV) as a bona fide forum for audience discourse would not come until many decades later.

An early proponent of creating a broadcasting equivalent of letters to the editor was Dick Salant, who headed CBS News in the 1960s and 1970s.[18] Estimating that CBS News received some 150,000 letters each year, Salant recalled in his memoirs that he would respond to many letters personally because the network had no conduit for sharing those complaints and opinions with the general audience: "Because broadcasting is such an extraordinarily one-way street with not even a regular letters-to-the-editor opportunity, it was important, as a safety valve, to try to respond to mail."[19] Salant did get his wish eventually, albeit in a very small way, when the popular news magazine *60 Minutes* created a periodic "letters from viewers" segment, which broadcasting historian Richard Campbell noted "is perhaps the only program in the history of prime-time American television that, within its limited and carefully edited forum, explicitly encourages diverse and alternative readings of its own narrative interpretations."[20] Another U.S. network, National Public Radio (later changing its name to just "NPR"), also incorporated "letters from listeners" into many of its programs, which was a way for the expansive network to construct a narrative of community among and accountability to its millions of listeners.[21] Similar efforts were used by a variety of broadcasters, including BBC News Hour's "World Have Your Say" segments and the "Listener's Letters" segments on Australian Broadcasting Corporation's "By Design" radio show. Such segments were, and remain, much like the segregated "letters to the editor" sections of major newspapers—highly selective and truncated snippets from only a mere fraction of the total submissions received. Such segments usually encouraged the submission of feedback and would use second-person pronouns to suggest informality, such as, "And now, we read from your letters" or "Here is what some of you have to say about. . . ." Rarely have such short, selective segments been able to provide accurate reflections of the breadth and depth of the feedback received by specific programs and stations, but they do provide a hint of audience engagement and, more importantly, exhibit that such broadcasters are interested in hearing from their audience members.

One possible explanation for the historical lack of on-air audience feedback was the chilling effect of broadcasting regulations, specifically widespread "right of reply" regulations and policies. In many free-press states, the right of reply is mostly focused on people who are specifically mentioned in news reports, such as the BBC's editorial guideline, which states, "When our output makes allegations of wrongdoing, iniquity or incompetence or lays out a strong and damaging critique of an individual or institution the presumption is that those criticised should be given a 'right of reply,' that is, given a fair opportunity to respond to the allegations."[22] In the United States, the right of reply was manifest in the "Fairness Doctrine" of the Federal Communications Commission, which began in 1949 and lasted until 1987. After both formal and informal censorship during the World Wars, primarily aimed at deterring extreme views on U.S. airwaves that could be considered unpatriotic,[23] the Fairness Doctrine paralleled the social-responsibility model put forth by the Hutchins Commission. Although meant to require broadcasting companies to provide opportunities for the public to respond to the opinions of presenters and on-air guests, the result was a widespread avoidance of such content beyond straight news reports, as airing commentaries might have triggered demand for on-air replies via the Fairness Doctrine.[24] With the repeal of the Fairness Doctrine in 1987, many previously low-profit AM stations in the U.S. switched to the "talk radio" format through which very strong opinions (predominantly right-wing) could be aired, including opinions from listeners who called in and voiced their own opinions.[25] That relatively new freedom for U.S. broadcasters led to an uptick of call-in segments (also known as "talkback" segments) on radio and television, and corresponded with similar efforts around the globe, such as local talkback shows on Australian Broadcasting Corporation affiliates (such as Radio 612 Brisbane's "Mornings with Madonna King"[26]) and the like.

Talkback radio, also known as "call-in radio," is arguably professional broadcasting's most robust attempt to provide forums for public discourse. Some talk shows have significant "call-in" segments, such as those provided by NPR's "The Diane Rehm Show" and, until its cancellation in 2013, "Talk of the Nation." Other programs are entirely driven by audience participation, such as the popular programs on Honduras's Radio América network, "El Médico y Su Salud," in which a medical expert answers health questions, and "Orientación Legal," hosted by a lawyer who takes calls from the audience.[27] Honduras radio stations also feature a lot of what is called locally "social service programming," a broadcasting equivalent of newspaper classified ads through which people can call in and make all manner of announcements, such as job openings, cars for sale, or personal news such as birthdays and death notices.[28] Talkback radio is almost entirely anonymous in terms of audience participants—most shows will only ask callers to give their first names and cities of residence, thus giving a bit of privacy and anonymity to the broader listening audience.

The call-in advice show is a popular format for daytime radio. Such shows are usually focused on specific topics such as personal health and fitness, relationship advice, and financial advice. One of the most celebrated advice shows in the U.S. was NPR's "Car Talk," in which two brothers who ran an automotive repair shop in Boston would try to diagnose problems the callers had with their cars and trucks—the show ran from 1977 until 2012, after which the weekly program continued via edited reruns.[29] Another well-known advice show in the U.S., "The Dr. Laura Program," ran from 1994 to 2010 over the airwaves, and started out as a personal advice show before the host, Laura Schlessinger, began using the show for long lectures espousing her conservative views on morality and politics.[30] Such shows rely almost entirely on audience participation to drive the conversation and to give the hosts something to talk about. Those shows also tend to be pre-recorded and heavily edited prior to syndication, and therefore they are often missing the same spontaneity and real-time interaction as other forms of call-in broadcasting. A more authentic approach to giving the public its say over the airwaves is via live talkback shows.

Talkback radio in Australia has been the topic of considerable study, and as such may be better understood at this time than talkback radio in many other cultures. The format in Australia predates 1967, when regulations were modified to allow the format for commercial radio.[31] After decades of study, that growing body of scholarly research finds stark differences between the content of talkback programs compared to more common, traditional scripted shows: The language is more informal and the responses more spontaneous and "real,"[32] the format is especially good at building social cohesion and a sense of community during natural disasters,[33] and talkback radio has decidedly different influences on political activity and views compared to traditional scripted radio.[34] However, the format also is often criticized for emphasizing controversy and stirring strong emotions, some argue in a manner that is of dubious ethics and to the detriment of more measured, professional radio programming.[35]

Many media elites and academics are highly critical, even condemning, of the "outrage" rhetoric common in such audience-participation programming.[36] Some elite journalists, such as NBC's John Chancellor, complained about the rising popularity of call-in radio as diminishing the influence of professional journalists in such important areas as campaign coverage.[37] Yet a dispassionate consideration of the content of such shows suggests that they fill a much more traditional role in society as a true "social safety valve"—a means through which the anonymous citizenry can express its frustrations about politics and social problems in a manner that may seem hostile, angry, and at times anti-social, but that in the end is not violent or overly disruptive (such as organized protests). In that way, call-in radio shows partially filled the void in civic engagement that was created when newspaper letters-to-the-editor forums became less accepting of truly public opinion, particularly by rejecting anonymous comments or comments that those editors deemed "outrageous."

Despite concerns about the tone of the commentary in such shows, research has found a number of social benefits provided by talkback radio. For example, call-in radio especially may be more effective in conveying information than more controlled formats. A 1985 study had research subjects perform tasks with radio playing in the background; those who listened to the call-in format reportedly learned more about the issue than did those who listened to a more scripted interview format.[38] Another study from the mid-1980s found that among Jamaicans of lower socio-economic status, call-in radio tended to be more influential in political choices than more authoritative formats.[39] Anecdotally, observers suggest that politicians in the 1990s may have fared better in elections when they participated in call-in radio shows,[40] offering a potential foil for more orchestrated campaign events and advertisements. Whether such findings could be replicated in the 21st century is open for debate, but it would be intellectually dishonest to wholly condemn talkback radio as a format simply because the comments can, at times, be outrageous.

THE RADIO HOST: REFEREE OF THE DIALOGUE

Talkback radio is formatted so that the hosts choose the topics and guests for each segment; other than that, the participating audience tends to drive the conversation. Long-time talkback radio host Thomas Kelly of Cleveland, Ohio, described his role as more of a referee. "We're pretty wide-open.

We have a call screener, a board operator, and a producer, and they hardly screen anybody," Kelly explained in a telephone interview in early 2014.[41] "We get a lot of calls . . . over three hours, we'll take maybe 20 or, if it's really hot, up to 40 or 50 calls." The screener asks what the caller wants to comment on, only rejecting calls that could go off-topic or present serious problems. Kelly, as the host, does a lot of real-time editing by trying to guide callers and managing their airtime. "I tend to go a little long with callers. I like to be polite, so unless [the phone line is] really jammed up, the caller becomes part of the show. The caller becomes a performer, and if they're really hot, I'll let them go a while. If the caller is fumbling and bumbling, though, we get rid of them." Kelly said he tries not to just cut off the speaker like, say, Fox News's Bill O'Reilly is wont to do. Rather, Kelly said, "I try not to make the caller feel bad. If a caller's just nervous, which happens quite often, I say 'It's OK to be nervous, don't worry,' then cut to break or something. There are usually easy ways to ease the caller off." Kelly also said that he prefers callers who see things differently than he does. "We have a pretty intelligent audience. We try to be very open to callers who go against the tide. If everything is going one way, you welcome the caller who offers a counterpoint. . . . As long as they are not profane or out of line in some way, I let them go. The controversy is good. Controversy and disagreement, that's all good for the show." In the end, though, Kelly said the host is still running the show. "Never let a caller take control. The host is in control and you have to keep control. And that doesn't mean restricting the caller or anything. If the caller is so forceful that they're almost impossible to slow down or interrupt, you have to hurry them up and move on to the next caller." The overall theme of my interview with Kelly was framed around respect for the callers as the most important part of the show. "I really have a problem with hosts who forget that they're just a host, and the callers are the guests and they should be treated as guests," Kelly said. "If you're talking about topic that has a wide range of opinions, you don't want to be nasty with a caller who disagrees with you. . . . Be gracious with the callers. Let them talk. Don't interrupt them, don't argue with them."[42]

Kelly's approach to talk radio is not uncommon at the local level in many localized markets. Doug Fabrizio, host of the "RadioWest" talkback program on KUER public radio in Salt Lake City, Utah, is known for his calm, respectful, and encouraging treatment of both callers and guests, for example. Likewise, Sharon Elliott of the "Viewpoints" call-in show on WAIS in Nelsonville, Ohio, deals with a more raucous group of listener-callers with both patience and wry humor. But not all local call-in shows are so genteel, for certain, and there are any number of "shock jocks" who host shows in which crude humor and rude insults are the norm. That is no different than other media forms—some newspapers are sophisticated, some have a "good-neighbor" type of informality, and some relish in their roles as sensationalistic scandal sheets; magazines range from the literary sophistication of Harper's to the sophomoric potty humor of MAD (on down to the dregs of crass pornography). The range of approaches to talkback radio is reflective of the range of tastes in society.

ANONYMOUS CALL-IN FORUMS: A GHETTO FOR 'LINGUISTIC INFIDELS'

The growth of talkback radio through the 1980s led some newspapers to reconsider their "must sign" policies toward letters to the editor. Taking a cue from the popularity of talkback radio and its "anonymous callers," some newspapers created their own versions—anonymous call-in forums—which met with much of the same elitist criticism that has been heaped on talkback radio.

Anonymous call-in forums relied upon advanced telephony, specifically automated call-management technology (voice mail). To submit comments, people would call a telephone number (often toll-free) and record their messages. Daily, someone at the newspaper (often a clerk) would transcribe the messages, and an editor would decide which ones to publish. The forums often featured several comments about a specific topic, and it was not uncommon for callers to respond to previous callers, with dialogues that could extend for days or weeks.

Because of their ease of use and their anonymous nature, call-in forums provided a far more egalitarian public discourse than was found in the stodgier letters-to-the-editor forums of the era. The language in call-in forums often was coarse and common, and the forums often attracted vitriolic condemnations from the upper crust, something that foreshadowed the similarly negative attitudes many professionals would later develop toward anonymous commentary online.

In newspapers, the forums were often separated from the LTE forums, usually appearing on different pages entirely—whereas the LTE forums were akin to dignified dinner parties, the anonymous forums were more akin to rowdy, working-class pubs. They were given names such as "30 Seconds" or "Sound Off" or "Zing!," and in that way emulated the old "complaint forums" some newspapers ran in the 1800s through the turn of the 20th century.

Jim Sachetti of the *Press-Enterprise* in Bloomsburg, Pennsylvania, launched his newspaper's "30 Seconds" column in 1992, and explained his rationale:

> "Obsessed since the early 1900s with fairness, accuracy and objectivity, journalism has driven opinion out of the news columns and corralled it on one or two pages . . . And a lot of what passes for opinion is like watered-down whiskey. It may look like, smell, even taste like the real thing. But it ain't got much kick. That has not been good, for the republic or for journalism."[43]

Sachetti explained that names would not be published, but callers should mention which town they lived in. "Because your comments will be published without your name, we will edit them to remove personal attacks, allegations of wrongdoing, political endorsement and the like. The actions of public officials are fair game for criticism. . . ."[44] A few years after launching the forum, Sachetti explained, "We caught a lot of hell about it, especially from the powers that be, like the local chamber of commerce and elected officials. And then I realized that, if anything, this gives a voice to people traditionally cut out of the loop in any community."[45]

The powers that be weren't the only critics of such forums. Anonymous call-in opinions also received harsh criticism from many professional journalists and media scholars at the time. One of the most scathing rebukes was from Charles Reinken of the *Observer-Times* of Fayetteville, North Carolina, who in 1993 called feedback in anonymous call-in forums "verbal Nerf Balls" submitted by "linguistic infidels," arguing: "Letters are readers' way of feeling connected, forming a bond with the paper. Open the phone lines and you'll have more to print. Undoubtedly true. Also, if you gather nuts in the autumn you'll boost the count by picking up the ones with worm holes and those half-gnawed by squirrels, if quantity is the only thing that matters."[46] A defense of the forums came from Arthur Hagopian of the Lawrence, Massachusetts, *Eagle-Tribune*, who argued that his newspaper's "Sound Off" column expanded local discourse in ways that signed letters to the editor did not: "Everyone reads Sound Off. No kidding. . . . [E]veryone from local politicians to hairdressers to librarians admitted they are addicted. They also acknowledged that they are discriminating enough to know that Sound Off is not the same as a letter to the editor. They told us they take the calls with the proverbial grain of salt—but that they read every one of them."[47]

Interestingly, the forums received little attention from media researchers. Perhaps the only serious analysis of the content of the forums was conducted by journalism professor James Aucoin of the University of Southern Alabama, who in the mid-1990s compared comments in one newspaper's call-in forum to its signed letters to the editor. [48] Aucoin found that comments to the call-in forum covered topics that were not reflected in signed LTEs, with more emphasis on public safety issues, local government, and local culture:

> "The data show considerable differences between some aspects of called-in comments and letters to the editor, suggesting that something is being contributed by the call-in column. It is not simply an oral version of letters to the editor. Callers seem to some extent to talk about different things than letter writers write about. They also seem to respond differently to items in the paper. Letter writers appear more involved in the considered opinions of editorialists and political columnists, whereas callers tend to be more interested in responding to the news stories, or at least to each other. In addition, callers seem to be more local in their interests. On the negative side, callers' comments are

presented in abbreviated sound-bite format, so what appears in print is rarely more than a brief sounding off. This contrasts with the more carefully developed reasoning of a letter."[49]

Even without such systematic analysis, many editors who ran such forums argued that they served that same function—not to replace signed LTEs, but rather to provide another channel for those who were uncomfortable with writing and signing letters to the editor.[50] In a late-1990s study that I did on the topic, in which I interviewed editors with different views of the practice, those who ran anonymous call-in features often discussed how it served such people. As one editor stated, "The benefit is to allow more of the people who would feel otherwise restricted, because of job security, fear of getting beaten up, fear of having graffiti sprayed on their houses, to speak up."[51] Other comments along those lines included, "People who call are not the kind who would write letters"; "This opens up the forum for people who have something to say but feel they'd lose their jobs if identified"; and, "It gives readers who feel disenfranchised from society a chance to sound off."[52]

Many papers still run such features, and cite them as among the most-read sections of their publications. Even in the age of email and social media, there seems to be a desire for the "quaint" practice of calling an opinion into a newspaper and then seeing it in print a few days later.

DEFENDING AND EXPANDING "OLD-FASHIONED LETTERS TO THE EDITOR"

As electronic media helped to create many new channels for audience feedback, the ink-on-paper press did not give up on traditional letters to the editor. Continuing and expanding the gentrification of those forums that occurred through the mid-20th century, many publications invested even more effort toward developing their LTE forums.

The late 1980s and 1990s saw the rise of "public journalism," also called "civic journalism," which was a movement by which news media tried to encourage broader public discourse and civic engagement. Civic journalism proponent Jay Rosen described it as an approach by which news media could serve "their communities in a different way, often by encouraging civic participation or regrounding the coverage of politics in the imperatives of public discussion and debate."[53] LTE forums were central to such efforts, as the primary goal of most civic journalism projects were aimed at helping resolve community conflicts, such as *The Charlotte Observer*'s effort to resolve differences in a local park between "cruisers" (young people driving their cars around for fun, mostly African Americans) and older, White residents who lived near the park. The newspaper used its editorial page to present a variety of opinions from all stakeholders—the young cruisers,

African American adults who defended the youth's legal use of the park, and the White families who initiated the complaints. The newspaper's effort of fostering a dialogue was largely credited in defusing a conflict with a strong subtext of racial tension.[54] One side effect of the civic journalism movement was that it made news media far more cognizant of the importance of gathering and presenting audience feedback.

Some editorial pages took additional steps to promote community discussions via their opinion pages, and a leading advocate for that was Ronald D. Clark of the *Pioneer Press* newspaper serving the Minneapolis-St. Paul region of Minnesota. Clark argued that "the forum function" of editorial pages was at least as important, if not more important, than the work of editorial writers and columnists. "This often runs counter to what we editorialists were taught, and certainly to tradition," Clark explained.[55] "No prizes honor expanding letters to the editor, forming community advisory boards or boards of contributors, convening forums on sensitive and difficult issues that divide the community. But if our audiences, not our peers, controlled the prizes, things might be different."[56] Clark noted that some newspapers had created forums for anonymous submissions despite condemnations from old-school opinion editors; that many editors were shifting their selection bias toward publishing more criticisms of their newspapers and more minority viewpoints; that many were rejecting letters "from outside your circulation or viewing area" to keep the conversation local; and above all else, trying to encourage more participation. Among the more notable efforts:

- The *Post-Register* of Idaho Falls, Idaho, began publishing at the top of its opinion page a tally of the LTEs it publishes, and marking each published letter with a "received" date. The page notes the number of letters in the "backlog" waiting to get published. It also makes note of letters that haven't run, and why (for example, how many letters were rejected due to "excessive lawsuit risk" or "letter violated policy guidelines." It is arguably the most transparent LTEs forum in publication.[57]
- *The News Sentinel* of Fort Wayne, Indiana, in the late 1990s produced a 42-page booklet titled "In a Pig's Eye: How to Argue with the Editorial Page," which it gave away to readers who were interested in writing letters to the editor or guest columns.[58] Many newspapers provide similar, if far more concise, suggestions for writers.
- Acknowledgements of letter-writers are now fairly common. Many newspapers keep tallies of how many letters they publish and make note of that each year (the *Express-Times* of Easton, Pennsylvania, published 1,607 letters in 2013;[59] *The North Scott Press* of Eldridge, Iowa, publishes an "honor roll" during the first week of January to thank all who wrote letters the previous year—225 of them in 2012, according to publisher Bill Tubbs[60]).
- Some newspapers include expanded space, with modified rules, for "election letters"—letters regarding political campaigns in the lead-up

to elections. Community newspaper consultant Jim Pumarlo assembled an entire chapter of best practices regarding election letters in his book, *Votes and Quotes: A Guide to Outstanding Election Campaign Coverage.* Some of those best practices include allowing candidates to write LTEs under the same restrictions as other writers, suspending publication of regular columns from incumbents (or giving challengers equal space), and setting election-letter deadlines that prevent eleventh-hour attacks to which campaigns cannot respond.[61]

- Some publications recognize exceptional LTEs by inviting particularly talented writers to the newspaper for a private tour or by taking them out to lunch. Clark was especially active in that vein: "My newspaper picks one outstanding letter a month and invites the writers and their guests to a semi-annual breakfast with the editorial page staff and publisher or senior newsroom executives. Then we reprint the letters."[62]

With increased encouragement for audiences to submit feedback came more problems for editors, however. One complication of the "must-sign" policies that became ubiquitous by the end of the 20th century was that they opened newspapers up to hoaxes in which writers would use false or fictitious names. A common practice of the "must-sign" era is for editors to require writers to include both names and daytime telephone numbers, but of course a writer seeking to use a false name need only answer the phone by using that false name—the editor of a North Dakota weekly reported just such a situation in July 2014 to the listserv of the International Society of Weekly Newspaper Editors, leading several editors to share similar anecdotes of how some letter-writers attempted to get their letters published under fake names.[63]

Organized letter-writing campaigns also were perceived to be a problem by many editors in the early 21st century. Editors dubbed such campaigns "astroturf" (an allusion to the "fake grass roots" nature of the activity). Many special-interest groups encouraged their supporters to write LTEs, and some went so far as to provide pre-written letters on their websites that their supporters could just sign and submit as their own opinions—essentially, creating LTE versions of greeting cards.[64] The tactic was widely used by the re-election campaign of U.S. President George W. Bush, especially the "astroturf" letter beginning with the phrase "When it comes to the economy, President Bush is demonstrating genuine leadership," which was published under different names in numerous newspapers, including *USA Today, The Boston Globe,* the *Atlanta Journal-Constitution, The International Herald Tribune,* and *The Financial Times of London.*[65] Other examples included a letter written by a U.S. military commander and "signed" by different soldiers under his command, published in at least 11 different newspapers,[66] and an LTE prepared by Planned Parenthood to commemorate the 30th anniversary of the landmark *Roe v. Wade* court decision on abortion rights for women, a letter that was published under different names in numerous newspapers.[67] A number of newspaper editorial boards excoriated readers who participated in such efforts as engaging in dishonest and unethical behavior—the *Democrat and Chronicle* of Rochester, New York, declared, "Fake letters are published lies"[68]—and stepped up efforts to catch and reject such "astroturf" letters. *The Denver Post* in July 2002 ran a notice that it would no longer publish such letters:

> "However well-meaning individual senders of astroturf may be, the Web pages that are stirring up this flood of unoriginal commentary know darned well that they're stealing space and credibility from real writers who are expressing their own concerns in their own words."[69]

Interestingly, the level of vitriol found in many "anti-astroturf" editorials and columns seemed to indicate that those journalists had an emotional bias against the practice—which, again, is not much different from such common communication practices as signing pre-written greeting cards, putting mass-produced bumper stickers on cars, singing the lyrics to a song someone else wrote, or the time-honored practice of signing petitions (what was the Declaration of Independence, after all, but just such a petition?). Editors often were less damning of the individuals who participated, but often characterized them as dupes rather than citizens trying to express views with which they agreed. The newspaper industry's leap to condemn and attempt to ban "astroturf" letters indicated that, despite all of the positive and socially beneficial advances made to LTE forums by the turn of the 21st century, many editors were still very much of the mindset that the forums were theirs to control and manipulate. Those professional attitudes were only hinted at in their public condemnations of "astroturf," however; with the advent of online comment forums, the journalistic penchant for controlling public discourse was on full display.[70]

BACK TO BASICS: THE WIDE-OPEN DISCOURSE OF ONLINE FORUMS

The late 20th century saw the dramatic expansion of public discourse thanks to two concurrent developments—the personal computer and the Internet. Online discussion forums date from the 1980s, most notably the 1980 launch of Usenet by two graduate students at Duke University[71] and the 1985 launch of The Whole Earth 'Lectric Link (aka "The WELL"), which inspired the term "virtual community."[72] Those and other online discussion forums led to the integration of mediated communication into the everyday lives of millions of tech-savvy people, people who came to be called "Netizens."[73] Early online discussion forums provided by nascent Internet service providers often were moderated not by professional staff, but rather by self-appointed volunteers who monitored discussions for inappropriate content. It was not long before professional news media started creating online-only forums as well via their own channels, but only in a limited way. It would take nearly two decades for established news media to move en masse to accommodate the robust nature of online discourse.

One of the early creators of such a forum was the weekly television magazine and directory *TV Guide*, which in 1994 arranged for an online version to be distributed via the Delphi ISP along with forums in which fans could discuss their favorite shows.[74] A number of different media made deals with the service-provider America Online to provide topic-specific forums, such as the American Broadcasting Corporation's "Careers for Kids" forum[75] and Time Warner[76] (which would be purchased by AOL in 2000). The public expansion of the all-access World Wide Web quickly denuded ISP-specific forums, but the basic topic-focused organization structure of forums remained for several years.

Legacy news media were slow to adapt to the forum functions of the Internet, however, with the exception of quickly adopting email and Web-based submission forms for standard letters to the editor. That reluctance may have had to do with the seemingly incompatible norms of virtual discussion forums (uncontrolled, unfettered, and largely anonymous) and the ideals of late–20th century media professionals (controlled, reserved, and strongly biased against anonymity). *The New York Times* began providing online forums for readers to interact with journalists only very late in the 1990s, for instance, and even with that relatively late start the newspaper was seen as a pioneer in how established, mainstream media outlets could adapt to the realities of an increasingly online world.[77] By the mid-2000s, most news media (both legacy media and new, online-only media) provided numerous spaces for audience feedback, including a "comments" forum at the bottom of each article.

In the United States, a federal law created an important loophole for news media interested in providing such comments forums. The 1996 Communication Decency Act gave news media broad immunity from being held responsible for libelous third-party comments posted to their websites, so long as the news outlet provided some kind of user agreement that said libelous comments would be removed when discovered and that the news outlet did not pre-screen submissions (that is, it was not actively involved in publishing an offending comment).[78]

At first, those comments forums were fairly simple affairs: Readers could type their comments into a text box on the Web page and hit "submit." At that point, the comment would enter a queue to be reviewed by a staff member or volunteer moderator before being posted. That was basically the same practice applied to anonymous call-in forums, just without the need to transcribe telephone messages. To save time, and especially to save money, a number of media outlets soon did away with the previewing process, and allowed readers to post their comments immediately, without prior review (in the U.S., to maintain the protections of the 1996 law).

The ensuing chaos did not sit well with many journalists who had been steeped in the 20th-century mythology of heavily controlled letters-to-the-editor forums. Pulitzer Prize–winning columnist Leonard Pitts Jr. summed up the disappointment and frustration many professional journalists exhibited toward the new, uncontrolled forums:

> "It must have seemed an inspiration kissed by the spirit of Jefferson: a free public space where each of us could have his or her say.
>
> "Unfortunately, the reality of the thing has proven to be something else entirely. For proof, see the message boards of pretty much any paper. Or just wade in the nearest cesspool. The experiences are equivalent."[79]

Pitts and many other industry leaders laid the blame for the perceived problem of "incivility" at the feet of anonymity. *American Journalism Review* editor Rem Rieder called for all news media to ban anonymous comments outright, arguing, "One good reason to end the practice of allowing unnamed comments is that it's flat-out wrong. Another is that it is causing headaches for news outlets, headaches they seriously don't need, and it will cause more in the future."[80] A number of media outlets felt the same and banned anonymity in their online forums, such as *The Buffalo News*,[81] *The Huffington Post*,[82] even all 300-or-so newspapers in the GateHouse Media chain.[83] Those bans came after those media had tried a number of measures to try to curb what they considered to be "incivility," such as automated language filters, the ability of readers to "flag" offensive comments for review and removal, requiring users to register accounts with the media websites, and the enlisting of third-party comment-management systems such as Facebook and Disqus.

The bans on anonymous comments generally failed—they resulted in greatly reduced participation in the forums and did not end the perceived problem of "incivility." A comparative study of 450 comments each in selected U.S. newspapers that allow anonymity and others that do not found that bans on anonymity slightly reduced, but certainly did not eliminate, uncivil discourse on the issue of immigration.[84] In the case of *The Buffalo News*, the announced ban on anonymous comments on the newspaper's website garnered more than 600 comments, many of them objecting to the move; after the ban, a column by the editor extolling the "success" of the ban received just 12 bland comments, a couple of which suggested the ban made the forums less interesting.[85] Similarly, the *Indianapolis Star* newspaper banned anonymous comments in 2011, and required writers to use their Facebook accounts, under their real names, to comment; three years later, the newspaper lamented the continued "incivility" in its "real-names" forums, noting, "Now, instead of anonymously hiding behind their comments, many simply own their virtual vitriol."[86] The evidence is clear: Perceived impoliteness in public discourse is not caused by anonymity, but by some other factors. Anonymity may embolden some commenters, but there appear to be many who don't mind signing their names to impolite, rude, even hostile comments.

Also missing from the "civility" discussion regarding online audience feedback have been concessions from media professionals that "must-sign" policies can have a chilling effect on legitimate participation by underrepresented groups, such as women and racial minorities, as well as those who fear retaliation[87]—not at all unlike the fears that led many people to participate in anonymous call-in forums before that, and to write anonymous LTEs for centuries before that. There also is a marked absence of any legitimate consideration among anti-anonymity journalists about the history of the "free expression" movement of the 18th century, and recognition that the right to anonymous speech has been at the core of democratic reforms and (in the U.S.) First Amendment law. Media law scholar Victoria Smith Ekstrand put it this way:

> "It has long been argued that anonymous speech is essential to the democratic process because it is often the only way for unpopular views to be heard. . . . Indeed, the United States Supreme Court has repeatedly upheld protections for anonymous speech, doing so most recently in *McIntyre v. Ohio Elections Commission* and *Watchtower Bible v. Village of Stratton.*"[88]

Ekstrand is among the seemingly small number of media scholars who are willing to acknowledge that anonymous speech is not inherently wrong (as Rem Rieder, Margaret Sullivan, and other industry elites seem to argue), but, rather, it is ethically neutral: "This faceless new medium not only offers unprecedented opportunities for anonymous speech, creating new methods for deception and illegal activity, but also opens positive new avenues of dialogue for marginalized groups."[89] Banning anonymous comments is just throwing the baby out with the bathwater.

The media industry's internal debate about anonymous comment forums in the early 21st century amounts to a clash of cultures. On the one side are the media elites who rose to prominence in the hyper-professional milieu of the late 20th century, who privilege authorship and, as such, tend to view the often rancorous and coarse rhetoric used by many Netizens as "uncivil." The Netizens make their preferences known, collectively, by being actively engaged in anonymous online forums, frequently defending anonymity when bans are proposed, and, for the most part, leading by example: Despite the bad-apple trolls, it seems large numbers of online commenters are serious about their participation and sincere in their opinions. Some may seem polite and reasonable, some stubborn and dogmatic, and a few outright hostile or out of touch. Although the media elites tended to make anonymity their straw man, what they really were objecting to was the very nature of public discourse in pluralistic societies. Calls to "restore civility" seem to be little more than calls to, once again, throw up barriers between news media forums and the public they ostensibly serve.

NOTES

1. Fred Blevens, "The Hutchins Commission Turns 50: Recurring Themes in Today's Public and Civic Journalism," paper presented to the Third Annual Conference on Intellectual Freedom (Montana State University, April 1997). Accessed August 21, 2014, from http://mtprof.msun.edu/Fall1997/Blevins. html.
2. The Commission on Freedom of the Press, *A Free and Responsible Press* (Chicago: University of Chicago Press, 1947), 1.
3. The Commission on Freedom of the Press, *A Free and Responsible Press*, 15.
4. The Commission on Freedom of the Press, *A Free and Responsible Press*, 15–16, 18.
5. The Commission on Freedom of the Press, *A Free and Responsible Press*, 23.
6. The Commission on Freedom of the Press, *A Free and Responsible Press*, 24.
7. Theodore Peterson, "The Social Responsibility Theory of the Press," in *Four Theories of the Press* (Urbana, Ill., and Chicago: University of Illinois Press, 1963), 87–92
8. Walter Lippmann, "How is Press to be Criticized?" *Nieman Reports*, July 1947. Accessed July 24, 2014, from www.nieman.harvard.edu/reports/ article/100552/1947-Press-Reaction-to-Hutchins-Report.aspx.
9. Barry Bingham, "Sensible but Inconclusive," *Nieman Reports*, July 1947. Accessed July 24, 2014, from www.nieman.harvard.edu/reports/ article/100552/1947-Press-Reaction-to-Hutchins-Report.aspx.
10. Frank Hughes, " 'A Free Press' (Hitler Style) Sought for U.S.," *The Chicago Tribune*, March 27, 1947, 38B.
11. George Sokolsky, "Dumb Professors," *Nieman Reports*, July 1947. Accessed July 24, 2014, from www.nieman.harvard.edu/reports/article/ 100552/1947-Press-Reaction-to-Hutchins-Report.aspx.
12. Victor Pickard, " 'Whether the Giants Should Be Slain or Persuaded to Be Good': Revisting the Hutchins Commission and the Role of Media in Democratic Society," *Critical Studies in Mass Communication* 27, 4 (2010), 391–411.
13. Elena Razlogova, *The Listener's Voice: Early Radio and the American Public* (Philadelphia: University of Pennsylvania Press, 2011), 15–16.
14. Razlogova, *The Listener's Voice: Early Radio and the American Public*, 15–16.
15. Razlogova, *The Listener's Voice: Early Radio and the American Public*, 16.
16. Kenneth Byerly, *Community Journalism* (Philadelphia: Chilton, 1961).
17. Razlogova, *The Listener's Voice: Early Radio and the American Public*.
18. Richard S. Salant, *Salant, CBS, and the Battle for the Soul of Broadcast Journalism: the Memoirs of Richard S. Salant*, ed. B. Buzenberg, S. Buzenber, and Mike Wallace, (Boulder, Colo.: Westview Press, 1999).
19. Salant, *Salant, CBS, and the Battle for the Soul of Broadcast Journalism*, 232.
20. Richard Campbell, *60 Minutes and the News: A Mythology for Middle America* (Urbana, Ill.: University of Illinois Press, 1991), 176.
21. Bill Reader, "Air Mail: NPR Sees 'Community' in Letters from Listeners," *Journal of Broadcasting & Electronic Media* 51, 4 (2007), 651–69.
22. BBC, "Section 6: Fairness, Contributors and Consent, Right of Reply," *BBC Editorial Guidelines*. Accessed August 21, 2014, from www.bbc.co.uk/ guidelines/editorialguidelines/page/guidelines-fairness-right-of-reply.

23. Minna Kassner, "Radio is Censored," in Ithiel de Sota Pool, ed., *Technologies of Freedom* (Cambridge, Mass.: Harvard University Press, 1983), 127.
24. Patricia Aufderheide, "After the Fairness Doctrine: Controversial Broadcast Programming and the Public Interest," *Journal of Communication*, 40, 3 (1990), 47–72; Timothy J. Brennan, "The Fairness Doctrine as Public Policy," *Journal of Broadcasting and Electronic Media*, 33, 4 (1989), 419–40; Adrian Cronauer, "The Fairness Doctrine: A Solution in Search of a Problem," *Federal Communications Law Journal*, 47, 1 (1994), 51–77.
25. Alan B. Albarran and Gregory G. Pitts, *The Radio Broadcasting Industry*. (Boston: Allyn and Bacon, 2001), 51–52
26. Lisa Gunders, "Local Talkback Radio and Political Engagement," *Media International Australia* 1, 142 (2012), 50–60.
27. Beatriz Lovo Reichman, Anand Pradhan, Sleiman El Bssawmai, Yuriy Zaliznyak, Carole Phiri-Chibbonta, and Bill Reader, "Cultural Relativism and Community Journalism: Snapshots of the State of Community Journalism in Five Developing Nations," *Community Journalism* 5, 1 (2015, in press).
28. Reichman et al., "Cultural Relativism and Community Journalism."
29. David Bauder, "NPR 'Car Talk' Duo Retiring; Reruns to Continue," The Associated Press, New York, N.Y., June 8, 2012. Accessed July 24, 2014, from www.webcitation.org/68djZLtRU.
30. David Hinckley, "Mag: Dr. Laura's Star Falling," *New York Daily News*, May 13, 2002. Accessed July 24, 2014, from www.nydailynews.com/archives/entertainment/mag-dr-laura-star-falling-article-1.477481.
31. Liz Gould, "Cash and Controversy: A Short History of Commercial Talkback Radio," *Media International Australia* 1, 122 (2007), 81–95.
32. Monika Bednarek, "Involvement in Australian Talkback Radio—A Corpus Linguistic Investigation," *Australian Journal of Linguistics*, 34, 1 (2014), 4–23.
33. Jacqui Ewart and Sidney Dekker, "Radio, Someone Still Loves You! Talkback Radio and Community Emergence During Disasters," *Continuum: Journal of Media & Cultural Studies* 27, 3 (2013), 365–81.
34. Graeme Turner, "Politics, Radio and Journalism in Australia: The Influence of 'Talkback," *Journalism* 10, 4 (2009), 411–30.
35. Graeme Turner, "Ethics, Entertainment, and the Tabloid: The Case of Talkback Radio in Australia," *Continuum: Journal of Media & Cultural Studies* 15, 3 (2001), 349–57.
36. John Shrader, "Folly of Outrage: Talk Radio's Unethical and Damaging Business Model," *Journal of Mass Media Ethics* 28, 4 (2013), 289–92.
37. Broadcasting staff, "Chancellor: 'Too Much Vox Populi,' *Broadcasting* 123, 5 (1993), 8.
38. Margaret Andreasen, "Listener Recall for Call-In Versus Structured Interview Radio Formats," *Journal of Broadcasting & Electronic Media* 29, 4 (1985), 421–30.
39. Stuart H. Surlin (1986) "Uses of Jamaican Talk Radio," *Journal of Broadcasting & Electronic Media* 30 (4), 459–66.
40. P.V. Ahern, "Talk Radio a Player in Presidential Campaign," *Broadcasting* 122, 25 (1992), 14.
41. Thomas Kelly of WHK 1420 AM, Cleveland, Ohio, personal communication, June 19, 2014.
42. Thomas Kelly, personal communication, June 19, 2014.
43. Jim Sachetti, "The Call: A New Way to Make Your Opinions Heard," Press-Enterprise, Bloomsburg, Pa., January 7, 1992. In Gerard Stropnicky, Tom Byrn, James Goode, and Jerry Matheny , *Letters to the Editor: Two Hundred Years in the Life of an American Town* (New York: Touchstone, 1998), 47.

44. Sachetti, "The Call: A New Way to Make Your Opinions Heard," 48.
45. Bill Reader, "Anonymity in Newspapers' Readers' Forums: Policies and Practices Applied to Letters to the Editor and Anonymous Call-In Forums," master's thesis, The Pennsylvania State University (2000), 48.
46. Charles Reinken, "Linguistic Infidels Hurl Verbal Nerf Balls," *The Masthead* 45, 1 (1993), 16–17.
47. Arthur Hagopian, "Sound Off Turns Readers into Participants," *The Masthead* 45, 1 (1993), 15–16.
48. James Aucoin, "Does Newspaper Call-In Line Expand Public Conversation?" *Newspaper Research Journal*, 18, 3&4 (1997), 122–40.
49. Aucoin, "Does Newspaper Call-In Line Expand Public Conversation?," 135.
50. Bill Reader, "An Ethical 'Blind Spot': Problems of Anonymous Letters to the Editor," *Journal of Mass Media Ethics* 20, 1 (2005), 62–76.
51. Reader, "An Ethical 'Blind Spot,'" 68.
52. Reader, "An Ethical 'Blind Spot,'" 68.
53. Jay Rosen, "Public Journalism: First Principles," in Jay Rosen and Davis Merritt Jr., *Public Journalism: Theory and Practice* (Dayton, Ohio: The Kettering Foundation, 1994), 6.
54. Lisa Austin, "Freedom Park Conversations," CPN.org (Waltham, Mass., Civic Practices Network). Accessed July 24, 2014, from www.cpn.org/topics/communication/charlotte4.html.
55. Ronald D. Clark, "The Forum Function," in Maura Casey and Michael Zuzel, eds., *Beyond Argument: A Handbook for Editorial Writers* (Rockville, Md.: National Conference of Editorial Writers, 2001), 52–62.
56. Clark, "The Forum Function," 52–53.
57. Post Register, "Whose Opinion is Getting Ink," *The Post Register*, Idaho Falls, Idaho, September 11, 2012, A6.
58. Clark, "The Forum Function," 56.
59. *Express-Times* opinion staff, "Thank You to the Writers Who Contributed Letters in 2013," *Express-Times*, Easton, Pa., January 1, 2014. Accessed July 24, 2014, from www.lehighvalleylive.com/opinion/index.ssf/2014/01/editorial_thanks_to_all_the_wr.html.
60. Bill Tubbs, personal communication, March 8, 2013.
61. Jim Pumarlo, *Votes and Quotes: A Guide to Outstanding Election Campaign Coverage* (Oak Park, Ill.: Marion Street Press, 2007), 44–59.
62. Clark, "The Forum Function," 59.
63. International Society of Weekly Newspaper Editors, "Hotline: How Far Do You Go in Confirming Letter Writer's Identity" [listserv thread], ISWNE Hotline, July 31, 2014.
64. Bill Reader, "Who's Really Writing Those 'Canned' Letters to the Editor?," *Newspaper Research Journal* 26, 2&3 (2005), 43–56.
65. Reader, "Who's Really Writing Those 'Canned' Letters to the Editor?"
66. Gannett News Service. "Many Soldiers, Same Letter," *The Portland Oregonian*, October 11, 2003, A1.
67. Reader, "Who's Really Writing Those 'Canned' Letters to the Editor?," 54.
68. James Lawrence, "Fake Letters are Published Lies," *Democrat and Chronicle*, Rochester, N.Y., August 25, 2004, A12.
69. Sue O'Brien, "Mowing Down the Astroturf," *The Denver Post*, July 16, 2002, E6.
70. Bill Reader, "Turf Wars? Rhetorical Struggle Over 'Prepared' Letters to the Editor," *Journalism* 9, 5 (2008): 606–23
71. Christopher Lueg and Danyel Fisher, *From Usenet to CoWebs: Interacting with Social Information Spaces* (New York: Springer, 2003).

72. Howard Rheingold, *The Virtual Community: Homesteading on the Electronic Frontier* [electronic book]. Accessed July 24, 2014, from www.rheingold.com/vc/book/intro.html.

73. Michael Hauben and Ronda Hauben, *Netizens: On the History and Impact of Usenet and the Internet* [electronic book]. Accessed July 24, 2014, from www.columbia.edu/~hauben/netbook/.

74. Mark Berniker, "'TV Guide' Going Online," *Broadcasting & Cable* 124, 24 (1994), 49.

75. Mark Hudis, "ABC's Forum Teaches More Than ABCs," *Media Week*, 5, 32 (1995), 28.

76. Advertising Age staff, "Bulletin Board," *Advertising Age* 65, 38 (1994), 20.

77. Tanjev Shultz, "Mass Media and the Concept of Interactivity: An Exploratory Study of Online Forums and Reader Email," *Media, Culture & Society* 22, 2 (2000), 205; Lauren Janis, "On Race, Online: The Digital Afterlife of a Powerful Series," *Columbia Journalism Review* 39, 3 (2000), 37.

78. Victoria Smith Ekstrand, "Unmasking Jane and John Doe: Online Anonymity and the First Amendment," *Communication Law & Policy* 8 (Fall 2003): 405–27.

79. Leonard Pitts Jr., "Anonymity Brings Out the Worst Instincts," *The Miami Herald*, March 31, 2010. Accessed July 1, 2010, from www.miamiherald.com/2010/03/31/1555967/anonymity-brings-out-the-worst.html.

80. Rem Rieder, "No Comment: It's Time for News Sites to Stop Allowing Anonymous Online Comments," *American Journalism Review* (June/July 2010). Accessed July 24, 2014, from http://ajr.org/Article.asp?id=4878.

81. Margaret Sullivan, "Seeking a Return to Civility in Online Comments," *The Buffalo News*, Buffalo, N.Y., June 20, 2010. Accessed July 24, 2014, from www.buffalonews.com/article/20100620/OPINION02/306209938.

82. Elizabeth Landers, "Huffington Post to Ban Anonymous Comments," CNN.com, August 22, 2013. Accessed July 24, 2014, from www.cnn.com/2013/08/22/tech/web/huffington-post-anonymous-comments/.

83. Dan Kennedy, "GateHouse Papers Ban Anonymous Comments," Media Nation, dankennedy.net, June 27, 2013. Accessed July 24, 2014, from http://dankennedy.net/2013/06/27/gatehouse-papers-ban-anonymous-comments/.

84. Arthur D. Santana, "Virtuous or Vitriolic: The Effect of Anonymity on Civility in Online Newspaper Reader Comment Boards," *Journalism Practice* 8, 1 (2014), 18–33.

85. Bill Reader, "Free Press vs. Free Speech? The Rhetoric of 'Civility' in Regard to Anonymous Online Comments," *Journalism & Mass Communication Quarterly* 89, 3 (2012), 495–513.

86. Amy Bartner, "Create a More Civil, Happier Internet for All Webkind With #ShareTheLove Week," *Indianapolis Star*, February 10, 2014. Accessed July 24, 2014, from www.indystar.com/story/life/2014/02/05/sharethelove/5228437/.

87. Bill Reader, Guido Stempel III, and Douglass K. Daniel, "Age, Wealth, Education Predict Letters to the Editor," *Newspaper Research Journal* 25, 4 (2004), 55–66.

88. Ekstrand, "Unmasking Jane and John Doe: Online Anonymity and the First Amendment," 407.

89. Ekstrand, "Unmasking Jane and John Doe: Online Anonymity and the First Amendment," 407–8.

6 Concerning "Crackpots"
The Media's Love-Hate Relationship with Feedback

"Every paper that amounts to anything makes people violently angry."

—William Allen White[1]

I have a small collection of letters to the editor—not the letters as they were published, but the original letters that were submitted for consideration. They were written in the late 1990s, just before email became ubiquitous, so many are handwritten, a few composed on typewriters. Most were submitted via the auspices of the U.S. Postal Service, but some were faxed, only a couple were emailed, and some were hand-delivered to the newspaper office. A few were handed to me personally. During my two-year stint as an opinion-page editor for a mid-sized daily in central Pennsylvania, I probably handled 5,000 or more letters to the editor. I printed the vast majority of those letters in the newspaper and on its website. But only about two dozen of those LTEs made it into my collection of keepers.

One of them is handwritten on both sides of a sheet of three-hole-punch paper. The penmanship appears shaky and coarse, and the awkwardly phrased message is crammed into single-spacing, with some additional scrawling along the margins. The topic? A lament about conservative Republicans in the U.S. Congress who were calling for broad budget cuts to social programs that aid the poor at the same time they "made it clear that they have an ADDICTION to Military Spending." Looking at that letter certainly brings back memories, as it was from one of my "regulars," a local man who consistently submitted a new letter to me every 30 days (that was the time limit my newspaper imposed on prolific writers). The top of the handwritten letter has a note, "Dear Bill—As Promised," and the envelope that was hand-delivered to the front desk of the newspaper reads "URGENT. Bill Reader, Editor, Opinion Page." The name of the newspaper is not mentioned; to Mike S., the only opinion page in the late 1990s was the one that would typeset and publish his hand-scrawled missives once every month.

Another letter in that collection was written in K'iche', which (I learned over time) is the second most-common language in Guatemala, after Spanish. I couldn't publish the letter because it was more than four pages long, single-spaced, and also because I could not find any contact information with which to verify the writer's identity (another requirement of my newspaper's LTE forum). The letter included a one-page English summary that I seriously considered printing but for the lack of verifiable contact information. It was a petition condemning alleged atrocities against Mayans by the infamous U.S. Army School of the Americas in Guatemala, also known as the "School of the Dictators."[2] The letter was co-signed by 48 different people, all self-identifying as clergy and lay-clergy, many of them also providing their inmate ID numbers and the locations of the U.S. federal penitentiaries where they were being held: Allenwood, Beckley, Lexington, Fort Worth. . . .

I have kept two envelopes that intrigue me, but for some reason lost to memory I did not keep the letters they contained. Both were sent to me by a Malcolm "Mac" K. Both were adorned with hand-drawn borders of overlapping red and blue lines, and "Mac" had affixed to each a plethora of stickers (the sort teachers put on the work of kindergarteners and first graders: foil stars, smiley faces and frowny faces, "SUPER!" and "NICE!" in series, and, my favorite, a Christmas gift tag written as "To: 'U!' From: 'Me!'"). I also kept the envelope of a letter protesting an increase in postage rates sent to me by a David H.—the envelope was mailed to me with nearly three dozen one-cent stamps on it (33, to be exact, which was the precise postage of the time; the cancellation stamps were also artfully applied by the local postmaster, who I gathered was equally amused by the philatelic excess). And (of course!) I kept an eight-page typed and collated pamphlet that purports to translate "the original Scriptures" from the Greek; the letter is a single-spaced, 5,500-word, comprehensive condemnation of just about any kind of sex that does not lead to reproduction by a married couple, and is signed "'amore (sexual love) vincit omnia' [Latin], Anonymous." I especially appreciated that the writer pointed out the use of Latin in brackets.

One of my very favorite keepsake LTEs, though, is the following handwritten comment:

> "Many believe that receding hair or baldness is a result of heredity. This is simply not so!
>
> It is caused by drawing energy off a spouse or your children instead of God. This extra energy is released by the scalp burning out the hair roots, causing the hair to fall away.
>
> There is only one way to avoid this loss of hair and that is to pray alone. When you pray, to believe your own prayers—that is when God will believe you and grant you His energy, the Power of the Holy Spirit.
>
> Seek out God's Kingdom and his Righteousness and all things will be added unto you. You may not get your hair back, but you will stop the process of losing it and have Eternal Life."[3]

Although that letter expressed an odd and arguably discomforting opinion, it was within our policy's length limit, included a valid signature, did not contain profanity or personal attacks, and in all other ways conformed to our letters-to-the-editor policy. So I published that letter. The day it appeared, several of my newsroom coworkers confronted me to question the ethics of publishing such a letter, arguing that its appearance in the newspaper harmed our credibility. One suggested that seeing such a letter in the same newspaper as his bylined articles was an affront to his professionalism. Many of those colleagues said the same things when I ran the outrageously homophobic screeds submitted every couple of months by a local research engineer, or the wickedly left-wing tirades of a feminist English professor, or the obtuse prose of a local advocate for legalizing marijuana, or any letter from a cadre of "regulars" whose names they recognized but whose sanity they questioned. Some readers also would call to complain, or write letters "not for publication" to take issue with my decision to publish the letters of (more than one suggested) the "mentally ill."

Even now, nearly two decades later, I will occasionally show the letters to a colleague or a student who expresses an interest in studying audience feedback. After looking at the first two or three, the most common reaction is nervous laughter, and a query along the lines of "is this for real?" And the laughter is almost always followed by the same comment: "That's crazy."

COMMENTS AND THE 'IDIOM OF INSANITY'

"Crazy" is not an uncommon word used by journalists when discussing audience feedback, and those attitudes also exist in the broader public and popular culture (as in the Joe Henry song "Short Man's Room": "He writes letters to the newspaper/And he'll dance to the talk radio"[4]). Journalism scholar Karin Wahl-Jorgensen of Cardiff University referred to the phenomenon as "the idiom of insanity"—in her groundbreaking study of LTE management at several daily newspapers in the San Francisco Bay area, she observed that one of the ways editors streamline the process of selecting LTE submissions for publications was to sort the letters into two broad categories: crazy and not crazy. Wahl-Jorgensen argued that editors "have developed a simple apparatus for classification of participants and their letters. The basic distinction of this apparatus is between the (clinically) insane and the rational, and it is one whose dichotomous poles are in constant use in the editor's everyday banter, to the exclusion of almost any other ways of talking about letter-writers. A description of a letter-writer as a rational person is rare and exceptional, whereas the label of 'crazy' is generously and frequently applied."[5] Wahl-Jorgensen further noted that the "idiom of insanity" was frequently and commonly invoked by journalists in the various newsrooms she visited.

The dichotomy of "insane" and "rational" could just as easily be applied to editors, pundits, journalists, or any others who put their opinions into the public sphere, and the idiom of insanity is certainly not reserved for those who provide feedback to the media. When *The American Way of Death* was published in 1963, a nonfiction book highly critical of the funeral home industry in the United States, author Jessica Mitford was attacked by defenders of the mortician industry with ad hominem attacks such as "crackpot" and "vicious and incompetent," despite widespread critical acclaim for Mitford's research (Mitford also was harangued for her Communist Party activities; during the Cold War, Western conservatives often used "communist" and "crazy" as synonyms).[6] Other examples include when *The New York Times* editorialized in 2005 that televangelist Pat Robertson was a "garden variety crackpot" for his calls that Venezuelan President Hugo Chávez be assassinated.[7] The idiom of insanity sometimes is applied to journalists themselves, often when considering the more colorful characters of the business. One might, for example, question the rationality of the late Jim "Shu" Shumaker (inspiration for the newspaper comic strip "Shoe"), a legendarily foul-mouthed curmudgeon who also was known to be at times extraordinarily charming and compassionate. Shumaker acknowledged a few years before his death in 2000 that when he was editor of *The Chapel Hill Weekly* in the 1970s, he did indeed express frustration one time by throwing his typewriter—although, contrary to legend, he did not throw it into the presses, but rather through a hole in the newsroom wall.[8] One might also wonder whether Tom and Pat Gish, renowned owners/editors of *The Mountain Eagle* in Whitesburg, Kentucky (motto: "It Screams"), were in their "right minds" in 1974 when, after their newspaper office was firebombed, they didn't pack up their kids and flee town, but instead produced the newspaper from their home, and on schedule—and to express their defiance of the corrupt local authorities behind the arson, they changed their newspaper's motto to "It Still Screams."[9] News managers are prone to talk lovingly about such eccentric, outspoken peers, and also to wax poetic about all manner of oddball politicians, quirky business owners, colorful civic leaders, and other colloquial characters whose newsworthy behaviors help to make the relatively routine aspects of news reporting that much more interesting. So the degree to which editors might use the "idiom of insanity" to discuss letter-writers, in general, is not necessarily beyond the pale, and really not all that surprising—"oddity" is, after all, one of the principle news values.

What is surprising, however, is that such rhetoric about other journalists or newsmakers is usually with a tone of admiration, but the rhetoric often takes a more disdainful tone toward such eccentricity from audience members. A former member of the U.S. Federal Communication Commission and longtime radio broadcaster in Detroit, James H. Quello, argued in 2007 against reinstating after three decades the agency's "right-to-respond" rule, the Fairness Doctrine, arguing that it forced stations to give air time to crackpots: "If you editorialized positively for God, country and motherhood, you would have to provide response time for Satan, treason and bastards. No thank you."[10] Mention those who post anonymously to online comment threads, and the disrespect from many journalists toward audience members is even more visceral.[11]

RARE EXAMPLES OF ACTUAL INSANITY

On balance, it should be noted that some communication to media does come from people struggling with mental illness. Examples can be stark, if rare. Syndicated columnist Bob Greene of the *Chicago Tribune* received letters around New Year's Day in 1980 in which a man threatened random killings in California, to which police said "We are treating . . . as though the author needs some help and we are doing everything to try [to] provide that help."[12] In March 2014, a newspaper in Utah filed for an injunction against a man who was allegedly harassing newspaper staffers at work and in their homes to publish his letters to the editor,[13] although a letter to the editor published by the *Standard-Examiner* in nearby Ogden, Utah, claimed it was the editor, not the letter-writer, who initiated hostilities.[14] A caller to the "Viewpoint" radio program in rural southeastern Ohio was arrested, once in 2009 and again in 2011, for allegedly making threats of violence against the show's host, and was involuntarily placed in a mental-health facility for evaluation.[15] And a Pennsylvania man was jailed in 2007 for writing threatening letters to local schools and newspapers, which the judge determined to be empty (but frightening) threats that were actually expressions of frustration and anger by the man over allegedly being racially profiled by local police.[16] A high-profile example from Europe involved an alleged neo-Nazi sending an LTE to a regional newspaper threatening to kidnap the 12-year-old princess of Belgium if King Phillipe did not end immigration to the country.[17]

More often, fears of letter-writers being dangerous turn out to be overly cautious reactions of the "better safe than sorry" variety. There was the 2013 case in Connecticut when *The Norwich Bulletin* went into lockdown after receiving a "suspicious letter" in which the writer self-described himself as suffering from a serious infection, Methicillin-resistant Staphylococcus aureus (commonly known by the acronym MRSA). The newspaper's publisher delivered the letter to police and was quarantined until the letter was determined to contain neither threats nor infectious material.[18] There also was the case of the deputy editor of *The Times Argus* of Barre, Vermont, who opened a letter to find it contained a white powder; the journalist immediately placed the letter in a plastic bag, without reading it, and notified police.[19] The newspaper subsequently filed a Freedom of Information Act request to obtain the letter, as neither local nor federal police would reveal the contents of the letter itself to the newspaper.[20] A more high-profile example of threatening feedback was in the U.S. state of Maine in 2013, when the governor of that state, Paul LePage, said from the cockpit of a jet-fighter simulator that he would like to blow up the largest newspaper in Maine, the *Portland Press Herald*—in that case, the governor's offhand remarks were dismissed as "a joke" by the governor's staff and as a "misguided sense of humor" by the newspaper's publisher.[21]

In the grand scheme of audience feedback throughout history and around the world, such examples can only reasonably be considered rare, isolated, and extraordinary. Yet it is understandable why journalists who experience such situations firsthand, or who can easily imagine themselves facing similar incidents, might project fear and anxiety onto the vast bulk of peaceful forum participants. The media-effects theory of "exemplification"[22] helps to explain the ways that news-media examples can lead to inaccurate assumptions by the audience—for example, coverage of bizarre murder in a movie theater may lead to public hysteria and fears of all movie theaters, or coverage of a burglary of the home of an elderly woman may lead others in the community to assume a crime wave is in progress. "Emotional exemplars"—specific incidents reported with strong emotional delivery by the media—can be especially powerful in leading audience members to exaggerate risks and overestimate the frequency of such incidents.[23] Media professionals are not immune from such psychological influence, and as such may point to anecdotes such as those mentioned above as justification for assuming that most who submit feedback to the news media are mentally unstable.

Likewise, disproportionate attention paid to such anecdotes over time may further exacerbate such exaggeration and overestimation.[24] That tendency may explain why the idiom of insanity is particularly evoked when journalists consider those who contribute to feedback forums with some frequency, typically called "regulars."

EDITORS' PERCEPTIONS OF 'REGULARS'

In her research, Wahl-Jorgensen found that editors at the publications she studied kept collections of "crazy letters," and she noted that "members of the editorial page staff stored letters and objects from crazy letter writers as a constant, institutionalized reminder that insanity was the paradigm for understanding letter writers."[25] Probing more deeply, she found that the "insanity" rhetoric was especially prominent in discussions about "regulars," or letter-writers who contributed frequently, usually writing about the same issues and making the same arguments. That meshes with my own experience, too—in our newsroom, a regular who consistently wrote in favor of private gun ownership would of course be labeled by my colleagues as a "gun nut," one who regularly quoted scripture would be labeled a "Bible thumper," one who always wrote in favor of strict preservation of natural spaces would be deemed a "tree hugger" or "hippy freak," and so on. Even regular writers whose comments were calm, measured, and well written were referred to with suspicion by many of my colleagues, as if habitual letter-writing was, in itself, indicative of abnormal behavior.

Such overt prejudice and armchair analysis may be both unfair and unkind, but at many publications such bias does not cross the line into outright rejection. Quite the opposite, in fact—despite the idiom of insanity, many journalists will hold their noses and publish letters from readers considered to be a little off. That's why serial letter-writers are called "regulars" in the first place, obviously. As Wahl-Jorgensen discovered, and many commentary editors would confirm anecdotally, regular writers and callers are often quite cognizant of the various rules and limits news outlets apply to forum participants, such as maximum word counts or on-air time, prohibitions of libel and profanity, frequency limits, reasons for comments to be removed online, and so forth. Regular writers and callers are also usually regular audience members who are quite familiar with the forum's rules and preferences, and tend to adhere to them—regulars often stick to length limits, time limits, and topics that are likely to get the favorable attention of editors and call-screeners. In a way, that makes regulars model citizens in the virtual village square. Is it just their frequency of visiting that leads so many journalists to question the sanity of regular letter-writers and callers?

The idiom of insanity journalists use to discuss commentators has taken its toll on modern journalistic practice. Assuming most commenters are "crazy" not only builds an accretion of disdain journalists have toward their audiences in general (Wahl-Jorgensen termed it "hating the public"), but also serves as a way for journalists to rationalize their unhealthy and anti-social detachment from the publics they serve.

'ECCENTRICS' AND 'FANATICS'

> "Last year, I had two letters published in *The Times* and I've been dining out on them ever since. They involved me in an exchange of letters of ever-increasing lunacy with other correspondents. I can bear witness that the prime qualifications you need to get letters published in *The Times* is eccentricity."
>
> —*Sylvia Margolis, letter to* The Times *of London, January 28, 1970.*[26]

The contempt many modern journalists express toward the "insane" feedback they get has been socialized into the profession, and is not so much a bias developed over years of personal experience than it is a prejudice that has been institutionalized and reinforced by teachers, mentors, and role models since at least the mid-20th century.

It is not hard to find the "idiom of insanity" expressed by previous generations of editors. In one of his memoirs, the late John Cutler, editor of the

Duxbury Clipper newspaper in a small Boston suburb on Cape Cod Bay,[27] had mostly positive things to say about the letters-to-the-editor forum provided by the *Clipper*: "Slowly but inexorably, the *Clipper* has become the mouthpiece for anyone in the community who has a complaint, a suggestion, an orchid to toss, a quip to share. No longer does Jonathan Q. Citizen have to wait until the moderator at Town Meeting gives him the floor. And that's how readers take over, making it their paper—that's a good thing."[28] And yet Cutler, clearly a champion of the egalitarianism of a good LTE section, also seemed to buy into the "idiom of insanity" bias—he explained that he frequently discouraged anonymous letters by telling readers about the time he showed an unsigned letter "to a psychiatrist friend. 'Obviously written by a dangerous psychopath,' he said."[29] Another noteworthy Massachusetts editor of that era, Henry Beetle Hough of the *Vineyard Gazette* on Martha's Vineyard, made similar allusions in his memoir, *Country Editor*, with regard to his reluctant accommodation of poetry submitted by a local retired military officer:

> "[His] poems were not among those which we liked, but a rejection carried with it the shadow of an added responsibility. The Colonel seemed always likely to blow up. As a matter of fact on those occasions when his scribblings were not published, he assumed an attitude of hurt superiority; but we never knew what might happen the next time."[30]

Aspiring journalists also have been exposed to the "idiom of insanity" in classroom lectures and textbooks. In his 1974 textbook about community journalism practice, Bruce M. Kennedy demonstrated a seemingly inconsistent message that an editor should be accommodating to "all the sincere letters you receive," but to draw the line for writers who are "nothing but crackpots"—"Don't turn your paper over to the fanatic. He'll take advantage of your patience and understanding. Give him his fair say, then cut him off. . . . National statistics show more letters come from fanatics and rabble-rousers than from all the rest of the writers together. You'll find your statistics are comparable."[31] (Kennedy did not reference or source those statistics, so it is unclear what data he was referring to). Another early champion of community-focused journalism, the late Kenneth R. Byerly of the University of North Carolina at Chapel Hill, wrote in 1961 about specific anecdotes from editors of that era, and although most seemed to take LTEs quite seriously, they also used a variety of terms to suggest they, too, perceived writers could be insane: "rabid writer," "rabble-rousing crackpot," "daily ration of 'nut' letters."[32] Editors to this day will question the mental state of some writers, especially those who participate in online discussion forums of large news outlets.

Media serving smaller communities are more likely to develop professional relationships with regular writers, not just the interestingly eccentric, but also those who exhibit ideological fanaticism. Bill Tubbs, publisher of the *North Scott Press* in Eldridge, Iowa, recalls quite a few regulars from his four decades as publisher of that weekly newspaper, including one from 2013 whom Tubbs described as "a high maintenance guy": "He writes [letters] out in manuscript, sometimes many pages at a time. He doesn't use email. . . . He signs off every letter with, 'For freedom, God, and country.'" Tubbs describe the writer as someone who often dresses up in military garb and dubiously (if not falsely) claims to be a college professor. The writer's rhetoric in letters is undeniably caustic, arrogant, self-righteous, and insulting toward any whose opinions are contrary to his own. Tubbs is often so exasperated by the man's submission that, he conceded, "it would be a relief" if the man would stop submitting letters. Yet Tubbs said he feels obligated to accommodate the writer: "I want to treat him with respect, even if I think he's a little bit off center."[33] I asked Tubbs if he thought the man was mentally ill, and the response was a quick and firm "No." The clear subtext was that Tubbs considered the man to be akin to a strange nuisance who lives in the neighborhood—a troublesome and annoying person, for sure, but still a member of the community who should neither be ignored nor dismissed. The antiquated, decidedly non-PC term that came to my mind as Tubbs described the man was "the village idiot," but I sensed that Tubbs felt enough compassion for all people, and a strong sense of obligation toward providing a relatively open forum, that he would tolerate such a marginalized person in his newspaper's virtual village square.

A former editor of the *Lunenberg County Progress Bulletin* in Nova Scotia, said he will also run letters from writers who seem a little unhinged. "I won't rewrite it to make it better, either," he explained. "It's their letter. It's my obligation to respect that so long as they meet my criteria. If it's a fair and open comment, then they have the same right as a university professor who writes on an issue."[34]

The degree to which any editor is willing or able to accommodate such a difficult regular may be inversely related to the size of the news operation. At a small, community newspaper such as the *North Scott Press* or *Lunenberg County Progress Bulletin*, run by editors who are passionate about publishing letters-to-the-editor, an obsessed fanatic in the community may find a patient, accommodating editor. But at a larger medium that may receive thousands upon thousands of submissions each week, such as the aforementioned *Huffington Post*, a fanatic may have little or no chance of getting published unless the message is so interesting as to get through the many filters big media use to process feedback. More populous areas would, by extension, have larger numbers of fanatics who might want to have their opinions published or broadcast; yet the media serving large audiences often are far less likely to accommodate "crackpots" in their LTE forums. It was not until the advent of less-regulated online forums that fringe opinions found more accommodating venues for their voices. Still, the more detached news media are from the people in their audiences, the more intolerant they seem to be toward letters and the people who write them. That can include extreme prejudice, such as Gawker.com's insulting headline "Brad Pitt's Mom Writes Excellent Crazy Person Letter to Local Paper"[35]—the 2012 letter by Jane Pitt stated a fairly common argument for why conservative Christians should vote for Republican presidential candidate Mitt Romney,[36] yet the Gawker.com writer called Ms. Pitt a "loon" and compared her to "family members prone to quasi-racist, half-coherent Thanksgiving dinner rants."

Journalists are not the only ones who perpetuate the idiom of insanity. Readers of the forums often continue the meme. For example, when *Orlando Sentinel* blogger Scott Maxwell wrote a snarky post in 2007 complaining about letters that are not "pithy and pointed and insightful," a number of readers responded via the online comments forum.[37] Maxwell did not evoke the idiom of insanity, but commenter "KT" did, writing: "Next, I hope you'll address some of the insanity people put on the forum threads attached to individual stories. . . . Where do these crazy people live? Nuts. . . ."[38] The assumption that there are "crazies" lurking in feedback forums may be a deterrent to participation.[39]

Some journalists openly ask for participation and encourage feedback, then secretly express disdain toward active participants. They may talk broadly and publicly about offering truly "public" forums, then go behind the scenes to ridicule and express hostility if that "public" does not fit their ideals, or to set up policies and roadblocks that they use to reject letters that they think are a bit "crazy." Interestingly, such behavior fits the criteria for "passive-aggressive" behavior, which the World Health Organization lists as a recognized personality disorder.[40] Yet the fact that feedback managers who are disdainful toward participants continue to provide such forums and encourage participation also suggests that their professional imperative to accommodate (maybe even tolerate) problematic writers invariably trumps their personal dislike toward such individuals. That professional imperative is summarized in the code of ethics of the Society of Professional Journalists, which encourages journalists to "[s]upport the open exchange of views, even views they find repugnant"[41]—or, perhaps, views from people they find unpleasant.

And yet there are many barriers that journalists routinely set up to block audience feedback. Overly long letters are rejected as "rants," fringe opinions regarding race or gender or religion may be rejected as "offensive," harsh criticisms of people in the news may be rejected as "attacks," and so on. I was just such a journalist in the 1990s, and so, when being given an opinion section to manage, I created a list of criteria for acceptable letter-writing behaviors that evoked the conventions developed throughout previous decades.[42] It was a ten-point list that set restrictions on length, frequency, topics and formats ("No poetry, please," for example). The intent of the policy was, quite obviously, for my convenience, so I could easily reject letters that didn't conform to the professional standards I had been taught by my mentors. But once I started interacting with letter-writers, I found it harder to say "no" and began to look for ways to say "yes." An overly long letter would get recommendations for tightening; a submission from a regular writer might get published a week earlier than normal if the topic were timely, on condition that the next submission be submitted that much later; portions of an anonymous letter might get published within the context of an editor's column; and so on. When I realized that participating in the forums was important to those people, especially the regular writers, I started to view the letters as more than just forms of personal expression. For many people, writing LTEs is a form of therapy, of catharsis. And that role of feedback forums is something that working professionals and scholars had noticed since at least the early 20th century.

FEARING TROLLS AND CRYING WOLF

The "crackpot" meme of the 20th century, of course, has given way to the "troll" meme of the 21st. In the context of audience feedback forums, a "troll" is a commenter, usually in an anonymous online forum, who intentionally and repeatedly posts inflammatory and insensitive comments. Media scholar Whitney Phillips, who has studied trolling behavior in online forums, describes why some people engaging in "trolling":

> "They do so to garner what many trolls refer to as 'lulz', a particular kind of aggressive, morally ambiguous laughter indicating the infliction of emotional distress. To the troll, the precise nature of this distress is secondary, if not downright inconsequential, to their enjoyment of its effects. In my experience, trolls are as likely to attack members of the Westboro Baptist Church (aka the 'God Hates Fags' church) as they are to torment gay rights activists, and would harass members of the KKK just as quickly as they would post racist messages on the National Association for the Advancement of Colored People's website. Put very simply, trolls are equal-opportunity offenders, primarily interested in lulz; this is what trolls refer to as 'the game' . . . trolling is unethical, it's not because trolls mean what they say—it's because they don't."[43]

Forum trolls are nothing new—"Cato's Letters" of the 1720s mentioned "monsters" who wrote "libels" in the press, but John Trenchard and Thomas Gordon also argued that society must tolerate such anti-social expressions to ensure freedom for thoughtful and beneficial opinions as well.[44] Newspaper editors of the mid-20th century often defended new bans on anonymous letters to the editor—and their retreat from the libertarian ideals that gave birth to the concept of freedom of the press—as reactions against uncivil submissions from "the haters and the hollerers."[45]

The phenomenon gained considerable attention in the early 21st century with the explosion of Web 2.0 and online discussion forums. Usually, the conversation about "trolls" falls along very stark philosophical lines—those who lean toward "freedom of expression" liberalism view crackpots and trolls as unavoidable byproducts of a free society, whereas those who lean toward the "social responsibility" brand of collectivism tend to view them as problems that have to be "addressed" rather than just an age-old symptom of society—people who are angry and hateful tend to express themselves in ways that also are angry and hateful. Even some defenders of more libertarian approaches to providing media forums will complain about such participants. Noted film and television critic Matt Zoller Seitz suggested in his essay for Salon.com, titled "Why I Like Vicious, Anonymous Online Comments," that such forums in U.S. news media "show us the American id in all its snaggletoothed, pustulent glory."[46] Seitz further argued:

> "It's impossible for anyone who reads unmoderated comments threads on large websites to argue that racism, sexism or anti-Semitism are no longer problems in America, or that the educational system is not as bad as people say or that deep down most people are good at heart. Unmoderated comments threads are X-rays of the reptilian brain—indicators of the dark stuff that rattles around in the id and that would get blurted out in the home or workplace routinely if the superego didn't intervene."[47]

Despite the new-media buzz about the phenomenon, the truth is that the frequent pronouncements against trolls by media elites is just a high-tech rehash of the idiom of insanity developed by 20th century journalism, and it tends to bring up the same questions of ethics and practice as well as the same cloaks of professional detachment and elitist hypocrisy.

I use the word "hypocrisy" because many times the journalists who complain about trolls engage in much the same behavior that they decry: Name calling, dehumanization, and denigration of legitimate (if harsh) opinions. In a 2012 study I conducted on the rhetoric of describing online forums, I found that journalists frequently used very harsh and dehumanizing language to refer to audience members they consider to be unworthy of feedback forums, such as "swine," "reptilian," and of course "troll" (itself a dehumanizing term; like them or not, "trolls" are people, too). And those journalists referred to entire forums that accommodate extreme opinions with the rhetoric of filth—"cesspools," "gutters," and "trash."[48] Much of the blame was placed on the anonymity of such forums, and indeed there is some research that suggests requiring signatures can reduce the number of "uncivil" submissions, but by no means does it eliminate submissions that journalists might consider out of bounds. A 2013 study by journalism scholar Arthur Santana found that 26 percent of the anonymous submissions related to immigration reform articles, posted to select newspaper forums, were deemed "uncivil" as he defined the term, compared to 14 percent of "signed" posts.[49] Such research shows that banning anonymity does not eliminate the perceived problem of "incivility," and, in fact, media professionals who are concerned about the tone of rhetoric in comments should not blame anonymity, but rather a growing incivility in politics and professional media.[50]

A conundrum for media professionals and media scholars alike is just how to define "civility" and "incivility." One study, attempting to discern if uncivil comments affected how readers perceived information in science articles, defined as uncivil a statement such as, "If you don't see the benefits of using nanotechnology in these products, you're an idiot."[51] That might be an overly restrictive and hypersensitive definition of "uncivil," especially compared to the widespread use of the word "idiot" in popular culture. Was Bob Dylan being uncivil in his song "Idiot Wind" when he used that same word repeatedly?[52] Or was Alpha Books being uncivil toward its customers with its popular "Complete Idiot's Guides" series of how-to books—or John Wiley & Sons' even more popular "For Dummies" series, for that matter? Or William Shakespeare for suggesting a "tale told by an idiot, full of sound and fury, signifying nothing"?[53] Although an extreme example, to be sure, the suggestion that the phrase "you're an idiot" rises to the level of "uncivil" in the early 21st century demonstrates the degree to which some critics may be overstating the issue.

The tendency for journalists to exaggerate the scope and influence of trolling is understandable. The work of screening and moderating such forums requires media professionals to review and monitor a lot of nasty verbiage, what Santana has referred to as "wading around in the muck."[54] *Chicago Tribune* columnist Eric Zorn explained in 2010 how he managed the discussion threads beneath his columns:

> "I edit with a pretty heavy hand here to get rid of the crude, mean, nasty bigots, snipers and simple provocateurs, while still giving a great deal of latitude for dissent and debate. I delete comments that cross the line, I ban people who persistently or flagrantly cross the line and I chide others to stay on point. Quite a bit still slips through—my inconsistency is more related to the time and patience I have at any given moment than to any fundamental hypocrisy—and ideally my editing hand would be even heavier."[55]

Just as police officers in troubled neighborhoods may develop a dim view of society because they see society's worst situations, so might journalists who regularly deal with opinions that they find offensive become cynical, frustrated, and, indeed, angry. A very large site, such as the *Huffington Post*, that moderates forums may delete far more comments than they receive (one estimate put the rejection rate at *HuffPo* at 75 percent[56]). Whether that high rejection rate reflects a high number of truly uncivil submissions or a sense of elitism on the part of the *HuffPo* moderators may never be known, but clearly the assumption of those doing the work is the former. When announcing that she was going to ban anonymous comments on her site, publisher Arianna Huffington said the goal was to "maintain a civil environment" and that banning anonymous comments would allegedly "evolve our platform . . . to meet the needs of the grown-up Internet."[57] That is code that, in the name of "civility" (as defined by, apparently, media elites such as Huffington), efforts will be made to create a sophisticated and mature dialogue and to block out those deemed to be unsophisticated, immature rabble. If only those deemed worthy should be allowed to participate in the dialogue, the public nature of the forum is greatly diminished, and the comments sections will look less like true public spheres and more like gated communities.

Juxtapose even the worst vitriol in an online feedback forum to what occurs in the front ends of the media and in real village squares. Maureen Dowd, the Pulitzer-winning *New York Times* columnist, persistently heaped insults onto those she disagrees with, especially former U.S. Vice President Dick Cheney, referring in a single column to Cheney's opinions as "demented scaremongering" and "bile," and referring to him, in a single column, as a "mountebank," as "the man without a pulse," and as "Darth Vader."[58] On the other end of the spectrum, neo-conservative darling Bill O'Reilly regularly reduces his arguments to name-calling and vitriol, and celebrates when it is done by others, such as when a military pundit referred to U.S. National Security Adviser Susan Rice as "aggressively stupid, immaculately clueless, and a disgrace to our system of government."[59] Public protests often also involve a great deal of offensive language, name-calling, racial and sexist slurs, and other hateful rhetoric. When there is so much incivility in the messages that media professionals and special-interest groups put forward, is it any wonder that audience feedback forums also contain such rhetoric? The trolls may just be emulating what they hear and read from the news media themselves—and, perhaps, they are using the forums to vent their frustrations rather than resorting to actual harassment or physical violence.

'THE SOCIAL SAFETY VALVE'

Scholarly study of audience feedback started in the early 1900s, and almost from the start, researchers surmised that feedback forums served more complex roles than simply giving citizens a way to talk back to the news media. One of those assumed roles was that feedback forums serve as an outlet for the frustrations inherent in living in pluralistic, complex societies. The basic assumption is this: A pluralistic society is going to necessarily result in a lot of disagreement and debate, often coupled with strong emotions. Emotional release is important to maintain the peace, so providing irritated or frustrated citizens with forums to vent in writing is far preferable to other forms of venting, such as harassment and violence.

At the turn of the 20th century, the accommodation of venting was formalized in many publications, which alluded to the practice in their calls for submissions. A 1937 article in *The American Political Science Review* noted, "So well known is the tendency of letters to the editor to be protests that in some newspapers the so-called 'Vox-Populi' column is known as the 'Safety Valve.'"[60] Several studies since have considered and explored that "social safety valve" function of audience feedback. In a 1950 study of those who wrote letters to the Louisville, Kentucky, *Courier Journal*, the author argued that "the Louisville Courier Journal 'Point of View' columns might be described as a 'social safety valve'" and that writers he interviewed "describe themselves as crusaders for this or that special cause, some stating that letter writing is a means for 'blowing off steam.'"[61] The metaphor of the "safety valve" was the focus of a 1972 study of letters in the *Kent Record-Courier* in northeastern Ohio after the infamous incident of May 4, 1970, in which National Guardsmen opened fire on anti-war protesters at Kent State University, killing four.[62] Journalism scholar Byron Lander found that most of the published LTEs about the shootings were supportive of the soldiers and disdainful toward the students, and he concluded that as such the forum "was not a harmless safety valve by emotional citizens . . . the open approval of the killings could encourage law enforcement officials to over respond in future encounters."[63] That role was understood even into the end of the century—media scholar Ernest Hynds surveyed newspaper editors circa 1990 and found that 50 percent of editors agreed that their LTE forums provided just such an outlet.[64]

There is some evidence that the "safety valve" assumption is supported by research into individual and social psychology, particularly when the topics are related to trauma: tragedy, loss, catastrophe, etc. Writing has long been viewed as a therapeutic tool in treating emotional trauma; an early 21st-century study of a ten-week group-writing project found that writing in a group setting could boost self-esteem and individual coping strategies while also cultivating supportive relationships—that is, "emotional catharsis."[65] However, writing is not the only means of catharsis, and other creative pursuits such as dancing, painting, and making music also might have that effect, although research in that regard has been inconclusive. Coupled with writing about their experiences, people who engage in those other activities may experience improvements in both mental and physical health: "The mere expression of a trauma is not sufficient to bring about long-term physiological changes. Health gains appear to require translating experiences into language."[66] However, much of that research has (necessarily) been conducted as experiments and usually assured participants that their writing would be kept anonymous and relatively confidential—a far cry from voluntarily submitting their thoughts to the news media and having them published along with their names, either screen names or real names.

What is fairly well documented, and obvious to anyone who spends any time studying audience feedback, is that many who contribute clearly have very strong emotional feelings about the topic at hand. I had been an editorial page editor for less than a year when I saw how important feedback forums are in times of crisis. On April 20, 1999, two teen students at Columbine High School in suburban Denver, Colorado, assaulted their school with guns and explosives, killing 12 students and a teacher, injuring 24 others, and then committing suicide. Before the day was over, my newspaper in far-off central Pennsylvania was getting a steady stream of LTE submissions about the "Columbine shootings," most focused on issues of the availability of guns in the U.S., lax security in public schools, and the glorification of violence in entertainment media such as action movies and video games. The intense public attention to the massacre, coupled with the huge volume of submissions to our forum, led the executive editor and publisher to agree with me that we should open up some additional space in the newspaper to accommodate as many letters as possible, rather than to just limit them to the dedicated space on the Opinion page. It took a page and a half of extra LTE space to accommodate the swell of signed letters; in keeping with our newspaper's policy, we rejected many letters that were submitted anonymously (although many of those were just as well written as those that were published; some were even better). Forum managers and talk-show producers regularly discuss similar spikes when something significant happens that increases their audiences' emotional state, most often tragedies or serious scandals, the onset of wars, or hard-fought elections.

During such times of intense public opinion, most people will never be invited to write an op-ed column for a newspaper. They will never be called by reporters seeking their opinions on the news of the day. They will not be asked to debate an issue on a TV talk show, and they will not be interviewed on national radio. They will not be profiled in either the magazines they read nor on the most important news websites of the day. And a great number of people are perfectly content with that, keeping their opinions to themselves and remaining relatively secure in the woodwork of the public sphere.

But many people want to have their opinions noted, their interpretations of the facts considered, and their voices heard. If invited to do so by professional news media, they would gladly accept; if called for a quote, they would gladly respond. However, reporters and editors only have so much time and so much space, and most news professionals would much rather get quotes from veteran pundits or academic experts than from people chosen at random on the street (except for, of course, the ubiquitous "person on the street" features). Most journalists certainly would not want to give time and space to people they consider to be crackpots.

So those frustrated people who want to engage in public discourse write letters to the editor, weekly or monthly, sometimes marking their calendars if newspapers limit prolific writers to just one letter per month. In between their turns on LTE pages, they voraciously read online news and post comments to news forums, and respond quickly to the comments of others. They listen to talk radio and hit "redial" over and over, week after week, trying to beat the busy signals to get the chance to speak on the air during their favorite call-in shows. And in the interim they may practice what they would say on the air if today were to be their lucky day, and they'd make it onto the air.

In many ways, the "crackpots" who regularly participate in audience feedback are the most loyal fans of the free press, because they have fully bought into the ideal that the media are, first and foremost, forums for public discourse. In a pluralistic society, that discourse will inevitably include nastiness, flashes of anger, and the occasional rant from somebody who comes back to the forum over and over and over. Feedback forums that purport to be conduits for public discourse are the most reflective of that public when they put up the fewest barriers; one of those barriers is the journalistic norm of hating the public and forgetting that "crackpots" are human beings, and that allowing those people to participate in feedback forums helps them deal with their very human emotions.

NOTES

1. William Allen White, "The Blessings of Amnesia," *The Emporia Gazette*, Emporia, Kans., October 21, 1901. Reprinted in Helen Ogden Mahin, ed., *The Editor and His People: Editorials by William Allen White* (New York: The MacMillan Company, 1924). 16.
2. *The New York Times*, "School of the Dictators," *The New York Times*, September 28, 1996. Accessed December 14, 2012, from www.nytimes.com/1996/09/28/opinion/school-of-the-dictators.html.
3. Unpublished letter to the editor to the *Centre Daily Times*, State College, Pa., March 15, 2000. From the personal collection of the author.
4. Joe Henry, "Short Man's Room," *Short Man's Room* [audio album] (Chapel Hill, N.C.: Mammoth Records, 1992).
5. Karin Wahl-Jorgensen, *Journalists and the Public: Newsroom Culture, Letters to the Editor, and Democracy* (Cresskill, N.J.: Hampton Press, 2007).
6. Sharon Crook West and Joseph P. McKerns, "Death and Communists: The Funeral Industry's Attack on Jessica Mitford's *The American Way of Death*," *American Journalism* 26, 1 (2009), 31–52.
7. Justin Delacour, "The Op-Ed Assassination of Hugo Chávez," *Extra!* 18, 6 (2005), 24–27.
8. Perry Dean Young, "Shu: The Late Great Jim Shumaker in His Own D*%# Words," *IndyWeek*, Raleigh, N.C., January 31, 2001. Accessed December 14, 2012, from www.indyweek.com/indyweek/shu/Content?oid=1183018.
9. Andy Mead, "Letcher Journalist Was 'Watchdog for the People,'" *Lexington Herald-Leader*, Lexington, Ky., November 22, 2008. Accessed December 14, 2012, from www.kentucky.com/2008/11/22/600788/letcher-journalist-was-watchdog.html.
10. James H. Quello, "Don't Bring Back the Fairness Doctrine," *Broadcasting & Cable*, New York, September 10, 2007, 32.
11. Bill Reader, "Free Press vs. Free Speech? The Rhetoric of 'Civility' in Regard to Anonymous Online Comments," *Journalism & Mass Communication Quarterly* 89, 3 (2012), 495–513.
12. UPI, "Letter Writer Threatens Slayings," *The Hour*, Norwalk, Conn., January 2, 1908, 46.

13. Associated Press, "Newspaper Seeks Stalking Injunction Against Reader," *The Washington Times*, Washington, D.C., March 19, 2014. Accessed August 21, 2014, from www.washingtontimes.com/news/2014/mar/19/newspaper-seeks-stalking-injunction-against-reader/.
14. Dakota Tuck, "Letter Writer Cordial, Non-Threatening" [letter to the editor], *The Standard-Examiner*, Ogden, Utah, March 24, 2014. Accessed August 21, 2014, from http://e.standard.net/stories/2014/03/24/letter-writer-cordial-non-threatening.
15. Staff report, "Local Activist Jailed Once Again for Alleged Threats," *The Athens News*, Athens, Ohio, July 31, 2011. Accessed August 21, 2014, from www.athensnews.com/ohio/article-34492-local-activist-jailed-once-again-for-alleged-threats.html.
16. Patrick Lester, "Bucks Letter Writer Gets 2 Years for Threats," *The Morning Call*, Allentown, Pa., June 19, 2007. Accessed August 21, 2014, from http://articles.mcall.com/2007–06–19/news/3725299_1_james-t-weed-letters-amish-schoolhouse.
17. Palash Ghosh, "Neo-Nazi Threatens to Kidnap Elisabeth, Crown Princess of Belgium, Blaming Her Father, King Philippe, for Influx of Immigrants," *International Business Times*, New York, December 3, 2013. Accessed August 21, 2014, from www.ibtimes.com/neo-nazi-threatens-kidnap-elisabeth-crown-princess-belgium-blaming-her-father-king-philippe-influx.
18. Robert Rizzuto, "Lockdown Lifted at Norwich Bulletin Newspaper in Connecticut After Letter Threatens to Spread MRSA," MassLive.com, Worcester, Mass., November 20, 2013. Accessed August 21, 2014, from www.masslive.com/news/index.ssf/2013/11/lockdown_lifted_at_norwich_bul.html.
19. John Dillon, "Newspaper at Odds with Police over Threatening Letter," Vermont Public Radio, Colchester, Vt., December 29, 2004. Accessed August 21, 2014, from www.vpr.net/news_detail/72430/newspaper-at-odds-police-over-threatening-letter/.
20. Dillon, "Newspaper at Odds with Police over Threatening Letter."
21. Eric Russell, "LePage Says He'd Like to Blow Up the Press Herald," *Portland Press Herald*, Portland, Maine, August 9, 2013. Accessed August 21, 2014, from www.pressherald.com/2013/08/09/lepage-threatens-to-blow-up-press-herald-building/.
22. Dolf Zillman, "Exemplification Theory of Media Influence," in Jennings Bryant and Dolf Zillman, eds., *Media Effects: Advances in Theory and Research* (Mahwah, N.J.: Lawrence Erlbaum Associates), 19–41.
23. Zillman, "Exemplification Theory of Media Influence," 34–37.
24. Zillman, "Exemplification Theory of Media Influence," 38.
25. Wahl-Jorgensen, *Journalists and the Public*, 139.
26. Sylvia Margolis, "First and Foremost" [letter to the editor], *The Times*, London, January 28, 1970. Reprinted in *Your Obedient Servant: A Selection of the Most Witty, Amusing and Memorable Letters to The Times of London, 1900–1975*, ed. Kenneth Gregory (Toronto: Metheun, 1976), 335.
27. Elizabeth W. Crowley, "John H. Cutler Dead at 88," *The Patriot Ledger*, Quincy, Mass., September 17, 1998. Accessed December 14, 2012, from http://theduxburyfile.wikispaces.com/file/view/John+H.+Cutler+dead+at+88,+September+1998.pdf.
28. John Henry Cutler, *Cancel My Subscription, Please!* (New York: Ives Washburn, 1965), 80.
29. Cutler, *Cancel My Subscription, Please!*, 84.
30. Henry Beetle Hough, *Country Editor* (Riverside, Conn.: Chatham Press, 1974), 127–28.

31. Bruce M. Kennedy, *Community Journalism: A Way of Life* (Ames, Iowa: Iowa State University Press, 1974), 45–46.
32. Kenneth R. Byerly, *Community Journalism* (Philadelphia, Pa.: Chilton, 1961), 310–18.
33. Personal communication, March 8, 2013.
34. Personal communication, March 13, 2013.
35. Taylor Berman, "Brad Pitt's Mom Writes Excellent Crazy Person Letter to Local Paper," Gawker.com, July 5, 2012. Accessed December 14, 2012, from http://gawker.com/5923827/brad-pitts-mom-writes-excellent-crazy-person-letter-to-local-paper.
36. Jane Pitt, "Election-Casting Ballot Deserves Prayerful Consideration," *The News-Leader*, Springfield, Mo., July 3, 2012. Accessed December 14, 2012, from www.news-leader.com/article/20120703/OPINIONS03/307030043/Election-Casting-ballot-deserves-prayerful-consideration?gcheck=1.
37. Scott Maxwell, "Don't Write a Letter to the Editor if . . .," *The Orlando Sentinel*, Orlando, Fla., November 30, 2007. Accessed December 14, 2012, from http://blogs.orlandosentinel.com/news_local_namesblog/2007/11/dont-write-a-le.html.
38. Maxwell, "Don't Write a Letter to the Editor if. . . ."
39. Hans Meyer and Michael Clay Carey, "In Moderation: Examining How Journalists' Attitudes Toward Online Comments Affect Participation and the Creation of Community," *Journalism Practice* 8, 2 (2014), 213–28.
40. World Health Organization, "Other Specific Personality Disorders," *International Statistical Classification of Diseases and Related Health Problems, 10th Revision* (Geneva: World Health Organization, 2010). Accessed July 1, 2014, from http://apps.who.int/classifications/icd10/browse/2010/en#/F60.8.
41. Society of Professional Journalists, "SPJ Code of Ethics," SPJ.org (Indianapolis, Ind.: Society of Professional Journalists, 1996). Accessed July 1, 2014, from www.spj.org/ethicscode.asp.
42. Bill Reader, "Letters to the Editor Policy," in Jock Lauterer, *Community Journalism, Relentlessly Local* (Chapel Hill, N.C.: University of North Carolina Press, 2005), 151–53.
43. Whitney Phillips, "Meet The Trolls," *Index on Censorship* 40, 68 (2011), 68–76: 69.
44. John Trenchard and Thomas Gordon, "Reflections upon Libelling," in Ronald Hamowy, ed., *Cato's Letters, or, Essays on Liberty, Civil and Religious, and other Important Subjects, Volume One* (Indianapolis, Ind.: Liberty Fund, 1995), 228.
45. J. Craig, "Priming a Balky Pump," *The Masthead* 20, 3 (1968), 26–27.
46. Matt Zoller Seitz, "Why I Like Vicious, Anonymous Online Comments," Salon.com, August 3, 2010. Accessed August 21, 2014, from www.salon.com/life/feature/2010/08/03/in_defense_of_anonymous_commenting.
47. Seitz, "Why I Like Vicious, Anonymous Online Comments."
48. Bill Reader, "Free Press vs. Free Speech?"
49. Arthur D. Santana, "Virtuous or Vitriolic: The Effect of Anonymity on Civility in Online Newspaper Reader Comment Boards," *Journalism Practice* 8, 1 (2014), 18–33.
50. Ashley A. Anderson, Dominique Brossard, Dietram A. Scheufele, Michael A. Xenos, and Peter Ladwig, "The 'Nasty Effect:' Online Incivility and Risk Perceptions of Emerging Technology," *Journal of Computer-Mediated Communication* 19 (2014), 373–87.
51. Anderson et al., "The 'Nasty Effect.'"
52. Bob Dylan, "Idiot Wind," *Blood on the Tracks* [audio album] (New York: Columbia Records, 1975).

53. William Shakespeare, *The Tragedy of Macbeth*. Accessed August 21, 2014, from http://shakespeare.mit.edu/macbeth/full.html.
54. Andrew Beaujon, "Huffington Post Deletes 75 Percent of Incoming Comments," Poynter.org, St. Petersburg, Fla., August 27, 2013. Accessed July 3, 2014, from www.poynter.org/latest-news/mediawire/222059/huffington-post-deletes-75-percent-of-incoming-comments/.
55. Eric Zorn, "Pseudonymity Can Battle the Scourge of Comment Anonymity," *The Chicago Tribune*, April 1, 2010. Accessed August 21, 2014, from http://blogs.chicagotribune.com/news_columnists_ezorn/2010/04/pseudonymity-can-battle-the-scourge-of-comment-anonymity.html.
56. Beaujon, "Huffington Post Deletes 75 Percent of Incoming Comments."
57. Elizabeth Landers, "Huffington Post to Ban Anonymous Comments," CNNTech, August 22, 2013. Accessed July 3, 2014, from www.cnn.com/2013/08/22/tech/web/huffington-post-anonymous-comments/.
58. Maureen Dowd, "My Head's Exploding: Is That The Iraq Drumbeat from Cheney & Co. Again?" *The New York Times*, July 1, 2014. Accessed July 11, 2014, from www.nytimes.com/2014/07/02/opinion/maureen-dowd-is-that-the-iraq-drumbeat-from-cheney-co-again.html.
59. Bill O'Reilly, "A Deal with the Devil," BillOReilly.com, New York, June 12, 2014. Accessed July 11, 2014, from www.billoreilly.com/column/A-Deal-with-the-Devil?pid=43234.
60. H. Schuyler Foster Jr. and Carl J. Friedrich, "Letters to the Editor as a Means of Measuring the Effectiveness of Propaganda," *The American Political Science Review* 31, 1 (1937), 71–79: 74.
61. Sidney A. Forsythe, "An Exploratory Study of Letters to the Editor and Their Contributors," *Public Opinion Quarterly* 14, 1 (1950), 143–44.
62. Byron Lander, "Functions of Letters to the Editor: A Re-Examination," *Journalism Quarterly* 49, 1 (1972), 142–43.
63. Lander, "Functions of Letters to the Editor: A Re-Examination," 143
64. Ernest C. Hynds, "Editorial Page Editors Discuss Use of Letters," *Newspaper Research Journal* 13, 1&2 (1992), 124–36; Ernest C. Hynds, "Editors at Most U.S. Dailies See Vital Roles for Editorial Page," *Journalism Quarterly* 71, 3 (1994), 573–82.
65. Genevieve Chandler, "An Evaluation of College and Low-Income Youth Writing Together: Self-Discovery and Cultural Connection," *Issues in Comprehensive Pediatric Nursing* 25, 4 (2002), 255–69.
66. James W. Pennebaker and Janel D. Seagal, "Forming a Story: The Health Benefits of Narrative," *Journal of Clinical Psychology* 55, 10 (1999), 1243–54.

7 "In My Opinion . . ."
Commenting as Individual Agency

The late Ruth H. Shirt-Porter was a prolific writer of letters to the editor in central Pennsylvania from the 1990s until shortly before her death in 2010.[1] During my time as opinion-page editor of the *Centre Daily Times* in the late 1990s, I published about one letter per month from her, usually something related to her advocacy for improved health-care policies. James "Jim" McClure wrote less frequently, but was still a "regular" on those pages until his death in 2013[2]—the retired art editor for Penn State University's College of Agriculture was a water-conservation advocate, and often illustrated his letters with clever sketches and editorial cartoons. I published numerous letters and op-eds from Gary L. Morella, now a retired researcher from Pennsylvania State University, whose published essays usually expressed very strong views opposing homosexuality from a strict Catholic perspective (which would receive many similarly strong responses challenging his opinions, as well many more letters and phone calls challenging me for publishing them). Retirees Miriam and Malcolm Klein, about the sweetest retired couple I've ever met, would hand-deliver Miriam's handwritten letters to my office every few months. We would visit briefly while I reviewed each letter to ensure it was suitable for publication and suggested some edits to improve its clarity. Miriam suffered from sight-loss, and that topic was often central to her letters and related volunteer work until her death in late 2011 (Malcolm passed away just a few months later).[3]

To me, they were not just names on the page, but real people, each interesting in her or his own way, and each getting a great deal of satisfaction from having his or her individual opinions published in my newspaper. At the *Centre Daily Times*, we restricted prolific writers to one letter per month—Ruth Shirt-Porter once told me that she actually marked her calendar to make sure she didn't miss what she called her "deadline," and she sometimes complained if one of her letters wasn't published within a week of submission. Jim McClure was a gifted artist, as well as a good writer, so publishing his illustrated letters was a pleasure; he appreciated the opportunity so much that he gave me a generous farewell gift when I left the newspaper, and that framed print of one of his editorial cartoons hangs prominently in my living room. Gary Morella's homophobic essays were about the most offensive opinions I ever published, yet in my telephone conversations with him, I found him to be a soft-spoken and sincere individual with a genuine concern about the spiritual well-being of his fellow human beings. When I left the newspaper, he gave me a gift of a Bible with my name embossed on the front (as a way to perhaps save my soul). Miriam and Malcolm Klein were so grateful for the time I took to meet with them and to help Miriam edit her letters that, one day, they surprised me with an autographed copy of the breakout novel by their son, *Primary Colors*, which Joe Klein signed (appropriately) "Anonymous"—Miriam and Malcolm also gifted me over the years with signed copies of their son's later books, *The Running Mate* and *Woody Guthrie: A Life*. Until they gave me the first gift, I had no idea that their son was the famous and respected columnist and author, and I didn't treat them any differently after the revelation. Our relationship remained very firmly on the basis that Miriam had things to say, and that I ran the forum in which she wanted to say them.

Journalists who take the time to get to know their regular writers usually do not regret the effort. Bill Tubbs has been publisher of the *North Scott Press* in Eldridge, Iowa, since 1971, and he knows a great deal about many of his regular letter-writers.[4] Tubbs is so committed to his newspaper's letters-to-the-editor section that each January he runs a half-page "honor roll" that lists each person who submitted an opinion, along with a column thanking them for their collective contributions. In January 2013, for example, Tubbs wrote: "Our annual salute to letter writers . . . recognizes 225 of you who believed The NSP was a good way to engage in conversations in the greater rural Scott County community."[5] Those 225 people wrote approximately 340 letters and op-eds that were published, Tubbs estimated, which suggests that a number of those writers were published more than once. Tubbs said there are many who write two or three times a year, but there also are a handful who write more frequently, nearly always with very strong ideological biases. One of them who submits about 15 letters a year is known for his strident, ultra-conservative opinions that might make him seem like a grumpy old crank. "He's a wonderful guy," Tubbs explained. "But his mindset was set through World War II and the writings of the John Birch Society. He's 93." Another regular is an accountant and demographer who writes frequently. "He may be kind of an egghead, but everything he says is right," Tubbs remarked. "He just has a quick way of cutting to the core of an issue." That writer also "turns in clean copy," which the small-town editor appreciates greatly.

Talk-radio host Pete Price of Liverpool, England, was so familiar with a regular late-night caller named "Terry" that he became concerned when the caller's phone signal went silent in the middle of a call in 2006. According to the BBC, the DJ was so concerned that he "abandoned the show and rushed to the man's house," where he was found dead of an apparent heart attack.[6] "Terry was a regular caller to the show and I knew something was wrong when the line went silent. I just had a gut instinct," Price told the BBC. Price asked his listeners to help over the air; a neighbor reportedly responded, but was too late to help the man. "I'm just glad he died doing something he enjoyed doing," Price told the BBC. "We all heard his last words."

At *The Los Angeles Times*, one of the most renowned regulars has been Trent D. Sanders, a retired wildlife biologist. From 1985 to early 2013, the suburban Los Angeles man had 54 letters to the editor published in the *Times*, and about 150 others published in a variety of other local and regional newspapers.[7] Self-described as "right wing," Sanders frequently espoused conservative views on political issues such as immigration reform,[8] animal rights,[9] interpreting the U.S. Constitution,[10] and government over-spending.[11] In a column about Sanders, the *Times* reader representative asked why he wrote so many LTEs: "Letters to the editor are one of the few ways an individual can influence public debate," Sanders explained.[12]

Unlike private messages, telephone calls, in-person meetings, and other forms of interpersonal communication, the public nature of audience feedback necessarily puts the issues and people discussed in such messages into the spotlight. Public officials often respond to such public criticisms, and sometimes those individual letters can spark ongoing discussions. That was the case in early 2014 on Bainbridge Island, Washington, off of Seattle's west shore, when a letter to the hyper-local website InsideBainbridge.com complained about a perceived lack of public input into renovations to a ferry terminal.[13] The very next day, Mayor Steven Bonkowski responded with a letter of his own, stating that in response to the letter, a public meeting would be scheduled to discuss the upgrades, which "are primarily structural modifications to meet seismic requirements and some minor cosmetic changes including upgrading the bathrooms and windows."[14] A different case in rural Rushville, Indiana, illustrates how such letters also can help public officials defend against unfair criticism in feedback forums. The mayor of Rushville, responding to an LTE in the local newspaper alleging unprofessional behavior by the local police during a minor traffic stop,[15] provided a detailed explanation of the incident, along with links to the police reports and supporting evidence, to defend his officers' conduct, concluding: "It has been my desire to not respond publicly to complaints such as this as some complaints are proven to be totally unfounded. This situation deserves my response as the accusations made and the picture it portrayed of the Rushville Police Department did not accurately illustrate the incident. The perception being portrayed was incorrect and it needs to be stated as such."[16]

Whether correcting an error, raising a concern, blowing the whistle on local corruption, or simply venting, those who participate in audience feedback most often need a catalyst to do so. As with most aspects of audience feedback, the individual agency dimension is complicated and multi-faceted, but it is perhaps the least understood (and least considered) dimension within professional journalism and journalism studies.

'I COULD NO LONGER STAY SILENT'

Journalists often view audience feedback in a predominantly collective sense—as feedback from "the public" or "the audience" who are collectively engaged in discourse in virtual "village squares." For feedback writers, however, the practice is highly idiosyncratic. Although it results in public expressions, the motivations often are deeply personal. That is especially true for people who write infrequently or only once.

Individuals who write just one letter or make one call to a talkback show in a lifetime usually are moved by a specific event or circumstance. It is quite common for such feedback to include some variation on the statement, "This is my first letter to the editor" or the radio call-in show equivalent, "First-time caller, longtime listener." The meme is often followed with an explanation of why the person has decided to write, most often due to some feelings of moral outrage or deep-seated concern, but also sometimes out of an unusually strong desire simply to participate in the public sphere. An example of the latter is when Cat Paulk of suburban Los Angeles wrote an endorsement letter for a local candidate to the *Glendale News-Press*, explaining, "This is my first letter to the editor, but I feel the upcoming City Council election is quite important and, as citizens, we should voice our opinions."[17] Far more common are examples of first letters inspired by anger. In *The Ely Times* of central Nevada, a first-time LTE writer complained about the local courts not allowing her to fully represent herself in court without an attorney by refusing to let her enter evidence in her traffic-accident case; the woman wrote, "This is my first 'letter to the editor.' I have a personal interest. I am hurt and I am mad so I must tell of a recent injustice. It is a sad day in the Ely community when a person is in court representing themselves to prove their innocence and justices and unprepared attorneys will not permit their pictorial and diagrammed evidence to be presented during the court session."[18] In another example, a village council member in Ruidoso, New Mexico, wrote a letter to correct allege misrepresentations of his public statements, starting with "This is my first letter to the editor ever, but I feel I must clarify and correct of couple of things written in the paper. . . ."[19] In Maysville, California, a protest by local Sikhs against having to remove their ceremonial kirpan swords to enter a county courthouse for jury duty prompted Priscilla Miller to write in defense of prohibiting the swords: "This is my first letter to the editor in my 78 years; however, I feel I must speak to the idiocy occurring in Sutter County. . . ."[20] And Janis Garland of Centralia, Washington, began her letter supporting a local school-funding referendum with, "This is my first letter to the editor. I have lived in Centralia my entire life. After I read the 'Our Readers' Opinions' recently, I could no longer stay silent. . . ."[21] Those and countless other examples of "first letters" include a subtext that the "first letter" is an act of significance to the writers, important enough to mention up front (and important enough for editors to retain in the published versions of such letters).

For Libbey Aly of Blanco, Texas, the motivation to write her first LTE was the increased automobile and pedestrian traffic in the center of her town; after nearly being hit by cars twice, she wrote the local *Blanco County News*, "This is my first letter to the editor in all the 18 years I've lived in Blanco, but for the first time, I feel very much compelled to write."[22] Almost two months after she wrote her first letter, I called Libbey Aly at the Blanco Chamber of Commerce, where she serves as director. Although she has been interviewed many times by the *Blanco County News* in that role, and even though the editor is a friend of hers, Aly said she had previously been uncomfortable about submitting her opinions for public scrutiny. "There were a few things that bothered me" that she would have liked to comment on, "but nothing I felt comfortable putting my name to. It was more controversial stuff than I was comfortable writing about for fear of, well, of retaliation."[23] The small town is just north of San Antonio and just west of Austin, and the sprawl of those cities has reached toward Blanco, significantly increasing development, tourism, and traffic. Aly explained in greater detail the two near-misses in the town center as she walked to the post office to pick up the chamber's mail. "When I almost got hit the second time, I figured, 'OK, that's it." Aly said she actually was more concerned about some of the elderly ladies who volunteer at the chamber, including an 86-year-old who carries her tiny dog with her when she gets the mail. "If it had been her at that place and time, she likely wouldn't have been able to respond as quickly," Aly said. "She would have been struck."

Asked if she might write again, Aly said "I just might," because, overall, she had a positive experience. "I had a lot of people say 'I'm so glad you wrote about that,' and people stopped by office, talked to me about at the bank, and so on." She also reads letters in the *Blanco County News*, and said she thinks the forum is inviting because the letters published in the paper tend to be pretty low-key and respectful. "Because this is a small town, chances are, unless you sign it 'anonymous,' people will see you at the grocery store or church, and if you're too inflammatory, they'll let you know it."

First-time and one-time LTE writers often face the same trepidations Aly explained. Concerns about offending neighbors, retaliation, or simply embarrassing oneself are all aspects of the social phenomenon known as "the spiral of silence." The theory was put forward in the early 1970s by German sociologist Elisabeth Noelle-Nuemann, who postulated that individuals who want to publicly express opinions may refrain from doing so out of fear of social isolation—for example, fear about expressing a minority opinion that could reduce one's acceptance by the majority or lead to taunting, harassment, rejection, etc.[24] The emphasis of the theory is on the fear people have about expressing their opinions publicly, regardless of whether that fear is warranted. Those fears often involve (potentially erroneous) assumptions about how the "majority" might react, along with other factors, such as a fear of appearing uninformed[25] or not conforming to diverse cultural norms.[26] With letters to the editor, which typically require people to include their names, the spiral of silence theory is very much in play. In feedback forums that allow for anonymity, the effect has been found to be reduced somewhat, but not eliminated completely.[27]

The nature of the forum itself can also have a deterrent factor along the lines of Aly's perceptions of "small-town" dynamics, which increases the likelihood of in-person interactions after an opinion is published compared to LTEs published in large-circulation national media, where the size of the audience is so large that a writer can enjoy a sort of relative anonymity, a single face lost in the virtual crowd. Moderated forums, such as letters to the editor and talk radio, also can be perceived as "safer" forums than many of the online free-for-all forums, where first-time commenters may encounter more personal insults, inflammatory responses, derogatory statements, and other forms of incivility, albeit all of that within the relative safety of anonymity. Even then, there can be some trepidation—a "longtime listener, first-time caller" to a radio talk show may justifiably become nervous through the screening process and also while waiting in the queue, and use the meme as a common (if cliché) salutation to the host. The phrase is so common that it is often used ironically in popular media, and it is a running joke in the recurring "Mr. Obvious" skit on "The Bob & Tom Show" (in which the caller is very obviously the same voice actor over and over again).

With a signed letter to the editor, the writer's name is literally on the line, and that can lead to concerns about protecting one's reputation and not exposing oneself to more individualized criticism. The stakes can be even higher when the person's job is on the line or when that writer's opinion gets close to or crosses the line of defamation.

INDIVIDUAL RIGHTS OF LETTER-WRITERS

In October 2012, an anti-tobacco activist was fired from his job at a Glendale, California, hospital, after he wrote a letter to the local newspaper condemning the Glendale City Council's decision to loosen restrictions on smoking in outdoor seating areas of certain restaurants.[28] An official from the hospital sent a follow-up letter to the *News-Press* newspaper a few weeks later, claiming that two employees of the hospital's Tobacco Control Program showed a "lack of professionalism" in criticizing the city council: "Their passion got away from them and their communication did not reflect their roles as professional outreach workers representing the hospital."[29] The fired employee filed a wrongful termination against the hospital in 2013, alleging hospital officials were coerced into firing him by city officials who did not like the public criticism.[30]

In 1977, a Veterans Affairs worker in Conecuh County, Alabama, was fired after writing a letter to the *Montgomery Advertiser* that was critical of a recent action by the county government; he was later reinstated if he agreed to drop a wrongful termination lawsuit.[31] In 2006, the administration of Brigham Young University in Utah fired a student-leadership coordinator after he wrote a letter to the campus newspaper that was critical of recent student-government elections.[32] That same year, an oil-rig worker was fired by the drilling company he worked for after publication of his LTE that was critical of the company deciding to incorporate overseas to avoid U.S. corporate taxes; that same worker had previously testified that the company had falsified tests of crucial safety equipment that would prevent "blowouts" of oil wells, similar to the equipment that failed during the 2010 Deepwater Horizon disaster in the Gulf of Mexico.[33] In 2008, a mid-level administrator at the University of Toledo in Ohio was fired for an op-ed she had written to the *Toledo Free Press* that suggested homosexuality is a choice, and as such the gay-rights movement should not be compared to the Civil Rights movement that advocated for an end to race-based discrimination—the administrator lost her lawsuit against the university because, according to a federal appeals court, her views were expressed in violation of the anti-discrimination policies she was required to enforce as a university official.[34] And in 2013, a tenured high-school Spanish teacher in western Kentucky was fired for helping a student write a letter to *The Paducah Sun* raising concerns about alleged threats made at the school, which resulted in the school being closed for a day while local authorities investigated the claims.[35]

All of those letters have two things in common. First, each was written (in whole or in part) by a person who had insider knowledge of a particular practice or policy agenda. Second, each was written by a citizen of the United States, and as such had, ostensibly, broad protections under the First Amendment. Their use of news media forums to express their criticisms tested the limits of First Amendment protections in the employer-employee relationship, for certain. They also tested the ethics of the news media that agreed to publish those controversial comments.

If feedback-forum managers are concerned about one potential danger more than any other, it is regarding letters that make allegations of wrongdoing. That is especially true in countries that have criminal libel statutes, but it is also true in countries such as the United States in which libel is a civil matter only. Faced with the potential for lawsuits from aggrieved individuals—even frivolous lawsuits that have no hope of advancing beyond preliminary hearings—many news media have very strict policies and procedures aimed at preventing the publication of libelous comments. Personal attacks are systematically rejected at most news outlets, and great caution is made to evaluate claims of wrongdoing against public officials (for whom the standard of proving libel is far more rigorous than for private individuals). In the above examples, the newspapers that published the controversial opinions were not held legally responsible, but from an ethical standpoint their decisions to publish put them in the middle of local and even national controversies. That is especially true when the letters result in the writers getting fired from their jobs.

People who criticize their employers or make claims of wrongdoing via the news media, either in news reports or via audience feedback forums, may or may not enjoy legal protections against retaliation by their employers. Most democratic countries have whistleblower-protection laws that were established to protect employees who report criminal or ethical misconduct by their employers, particularly employees of government agencies, but many of those require the reporting be done to a designated government office. Legal protections for writers of whistleblower letters are less clear in most jurisdictions, primarily because the majority of those laws are relatively new. The United Kingdom issued its landmark whistleblower law in 1998 via the Public Interest Disclosure Act,[36] and it is a measure that is slowly being replicated in a number of Commonwealth nations; India's parliament approved the Whistleblowers Protection Act in early 2014 after a protracted political process,[37] and Jamaica's 2011 Protected Disclosures Act has led to a slow change toward a "whistleblowing culture" in that country's government and corporate offices.[38] Ireland's Protected Disclosure Act went into effect in 2014.[39] Australia enacted its Public Interest Disclosure Act in 2013,[40] an effort built upon a decentralized precedent through which each state has its own whistleblower-protection law (alternately called "public-interest disclosure" laws), as well as provisions of the Fair Work Australia Act of 2009 and a common-law precedent stemming from a case in New South Wales, *Wheadon v. State of New South Wales*, 2001.[41] Canada has protections for most employees of the federal government via the Public Servants Disclosure Protection Act of 2007, but does not extend to provincial or municipal governments, not to the private sector;[42] despite very narrow provincial laws in New Brunswick, Ontario, and Saskatchewan, a watchdog group has argued that "[f]or the most part, however, whistleblowers in Canada are unprotected by statute."[43] In the United States, whistle blower legislation predates the U.S. Constitution, with the ad hoc Continental Congress unanimously approving such a law in 1778.[44] The False Claims Act of 1863 was enacted as an effort to crack down on fraud by defense contractors for the Union armies during the Civil War of the United States; the law was amended during World War II to curtail penalties paid to whistleblowers via civil lawsuits, but was strengthened in 1986 and again in 2009 in response to unscrupulous practices by some defense contractors.[45] Overall, though, whistleblower protection in the United States is covered by a complex array of state and federal laws that often lack consistency in terms of jurisdiction, reporting procedures, and levels of protection—the National Whistleblower Center, an advocacy group based in Washington, D.C., explains that in the U.S., "[a] case may be covered under more than one whistleblower protection provision. Depending upon whom one works for and in which state one is employed, the nature and scope of whistleblower protection are varied.

In addition to explicit whistleblower protection laws, employees may also be protected under traditional tort or contract for damages resulting from retaliation for whistleblowing."[46]

Protections for writers of whistleblower letters-to-the-editor also depend a lot upon jurisdiction. The strongest precedent for such protection in the United States is a 1968 Supreme Court Case, *Pickering v. Board of Education of Township High School District 205, Wills County*.[47] The case involved an Illinois high-school teacher, Marvin L. Pickering, who was fired after sending an LTE to his local newspaper that was critical of the fiscal practices of the school board and school administration. Pickering concluded the letter with this statement: "I must sign this letter as a citizen, taxpayer and voter, not as a teacher, since that freedom has been taken from teachers by the administration."[48] The school board had claimed the LTE had been "detrimental to the efficient operation and administration of the school district," and that "the teacher by virtue of his public employment has a duty of loyalty to support his superiors."[49] Writing for the majority, Justice Thurgood Marshall argued:

> "We have already noted our disinclination to make an across-the-board equation of dismissal from public employment for remarks critical of superiors with awarding damages in a libel suit by a public official for similar criticism. However, in a case such as the present one, in which the fact of employment is only tangentially and insubstantially involved in the subject matter of the public communication made by a teacher, we conclude that it is necessary to regard the teacher as the member of the general public he seeks to be."[50]

The *Pickering* decision was concerned with a vary narrow issue, which is the distinction between the First Amendment rights of a citizen and the supervisory rights of an employer, and it established the generalized standard in the United States that public employees who participate in news media forums should make it clear that they are expressing their opinions as private citizens and not as public servants. The *Pickering* precedent was not ironclad, however, nor did it cover the broader issue of whether individual citizens have an unassailable right to express their opinions so long as they are not libelous. Despite broad protections afforded to opinions via some contemporary decisions under and after the Warren Court—most notably *Brandenburg v. Ohio*,[51] *Times v. Sullivan*,[52] and *Gertz v. Welch*[53]—the First Amendment status of letters to the editor, specifically, remained murky and parochial. In New Jersey, the state supreme court ruled that allegations of "conspiracy" and "cover up" in a letter to the editor were not specific allegations but rather simply rhetoric, and as such was not defamatory.[54] A long legal battle in the 1980s resulted in the New York Court of Appeals decision in *Immuno A.G. v. Moor-Jankowski*, which found that an LTE published in a scientific journal also was protected opinion.[55] In regard to the latter case, legal scholar Donna R. Euben (now associate council for the American Association of University Professors) argued that the United States should extend "absolute privilege" to letters to the editor, similar to the legal immunity of speech uttered in official debates of legislatures:

> "[E]ditorial choices are shaped by fear of libel, thus undermining the free speech purposes served by letters to the editor. Furthermore, even the ultimate victory in letter to the editor libel suits by a journal or newspaper does not encourage the media to publish letters to the editor. When the choice is between publishing a controversial letter that raises the possibility of libel litigation or reprinting a 'safe' letter, editors will 'steer clear' of risk and practice editorial caution. An absolute privilege for the media to reprint letters to the editor can effectively reduce the free speech chill created by potential libel litigation, notwithstanding the potential dangers posed by such a privilege."[56]

Although no such protection has been extended to print media forums, the *Communications Decency Act* of 1996, via its Section 230, did extend some immunity to the providers of online forums, including news media. So long as they post general rules of conduct and act in good faith to remove comments that could be libelous, the providers of such forums are not considered "publishers" of the content, and thus are not legally responsible for their publication.[57] Individuals who post comments to the forums, however, can be and have been held responsible for what the post online, even if they do so anonymously.

As of late 2014, when this book is being written, individuals who participate in news media forums can be held responsible for their statements both in libel litigation or in the workplace, unless they exercise great caution to avoid making libelous statements and to ensure that their comments cannot be seen as related to their employment. Assumptions about "freedom of speech" in general, "whistleblower" protections specifically, and (in the U.S.) beliefs about the First Amendment are not reliable or strong defenses for individual forum participants, no matter who they are. News media policies against publishing personal attacks and unsubstantiated claims in audience forums therefore are protecting not just the news media from possible litigation, but also the forum participants, whether they like it or not.

WHO IS THE 'TYPICAL' WRITER?

Several early studies tried to answer the question, "Who writes letters to the editor?," and from the mid-1940s through 1970 the pattern was that typical writers in the U.S. "are older, wealthier, better educated, more rooted in their communities and more conservative than the general population."[58] A

2003 telephone survey of a random U.S. population found essentially the same pattern, and added that those who read their newspaper often (four to seven days a week) were far more likely to submit LTEs than infrequent readers.[59] But overall, only a relatively small portion of media audiences even try to participate—those so-called "lurkers" can make up 90 percent or more of a feedback forum's audience.[60] For online forums especially, the "1/10/90 rule" is often assumed to be in play: less than 1 percent of people create online content, 10 percent react/respond to it, and the rest (almost 90 percent) simply observe.[61] However, the rise of social media online has made contributing feedback easier than ever before; a study in the United Kingdom estimated that 77 percent of that country's population was active online, although that report did not specify how many were active in terms of providing feedback to news media.[62]

There are a number of practical barriers to getting good, reliable data about who is more likely to participate in news-media forums. Early studies contacted writers whose signed letters appeared in newspapers, which of course left out information from people who wrote letters that were not selected for publication. Broader surveys overcame that limitation, but often encountered the "1/10/90" effect by finding that only relatively small percentages of people surveyed had contributed feedback—the 2003 survey mentioned above, for example, found participation rates no higher than 50 percent in even the most active demographic groups, participation closer to 20 or 30 percent in most groups, and some below 10 percent.[63] More and more diverse participation occurs in anonymous online forums, especially when the forums are moderated (moderated forums saw increase participation by about 12 percentage points, one study found).[64]

Given the many barriers to getting reliable data about "who writes/calls," a number of studies focus on the content of published/broadcasted comments to develop typologies of participants. One such attempt looked at political talk-radio callers in the U.S. and Israel, and discerned five types of callers: "anonymous, regular, returning, first-time, and unmarked standard caller."[65] Earlier scholarship also typified talk-show callers by behaviors when speaking on the air, such as "expressive callers" who focus on expressing personal opinions, or "confessing callers" who share personal details in an effort to seek individualized advice.[66] A 1990s study in Ireland found similar groupings among callers to the Irish "tabloid" radio program "The Gerry Ryan Show".[67] And a study of Australian talk-show callers found that callers often use rhetoric that suggests they view themselves as part of a community of listeners, rather than just part of an audience.[68]

Considered in the aggregate, the one consistent finding across all "who participates" research is that those who contribute feedback to news media tend to be, not surprisingly, avid consumers of those news media. To call them "fans" might be misleading, given that many comments to news media are negative toward those media, but the typical feedback contributor is someone who spends considerable time with those media. That may help explain the phenomenon of "the regular," or the person who writes/calls with considerable frequency.

'LET YOUR SOULS SING'

Beyond the inspirations, legal responsibilities, and demographic considerations of individual forum participants, there is the matter of motives. In that regard, it is worth considering once again those who contribute to forums with some regularity.

Nick Bianchi, a frequent LTE writer to the 5,500-circulation *Bracebridge* (Ontario) *Examiner*, explained his motives for writing LTEs in (what else?) a letter to that newspaper:

> "The reasons why I write my letters are many, and they are all important . . . Writing and clicking 'send' on the email is a bit unnerving as doing so exposes oneself. We make known our inner thoughts and emotions, our biases and opinions, our likes and dislikes. 'What will our friends think? The impact on my family and business? Why am I doing this, anyway?' These are questions of the fearful part of our consciousness. There is, however, another part of us that encourages and indeed compels us to write. 'We must do this;' our souls sing out, 'it is for the greater good! . . . Native American traditions focused on seven generations—the choices I make today affect my community seven generations from now. Letters-to-the-editor, columns, opinions, news stories—these are all seeds being planted to create a new forest that will exist sometime in the future. Keep writing those letters, keep putting yourself out there, and be the leader that we all need. And let your souls sing."[69]

Writing to *The Daily Mining Gazette* of Houghton, Michigan, another frequent LTE writer, Tony Gertsberger, provided an even more personal explanation for his motives: "Someone recently asked why I write letters to the editor when most don't read them or care about the opinions of others. I told him it was my parents' fault," Gerstberger wrote.[70] He explained that his parents fled war-torn Czechoslovakia in 1949 and moved to the United States, where he and his brother experienced taunting and bullying in school for being foreigners, but they overcame that adversity to adapt to American culture. "Our story isn't significantly different from others who came here for political or economic reasons," he continued. "My parents understood how the loss of individual freedom can consume an entire nation, particularly when citizens are detached and reluctant to express themselves. . . . Given the opportunity, events will repeat themselves. That is why I write letters to the editor."

Jessee Tabor of West Yanceyville, North Carolina, explained in a 2013 letter to the local *Caswell Messenger* that "I have no qualms with anyone protesting or demonstrating for issues that are near and dear to them. In fact, that is why I write letters to the editor."[71] In *The Advertiser-Tribune* of Tiffin, Ohio, another frequent LTE writer, Joe Robenalt, explained, "Some people ask me why I write letters to the editor and my answer is because some people ask me. Also, our city fathers seem to put out an endless stream of subject matter."[72] A reader writing as "cathylynn" on WrongPlanet.net, an online forum for those with autism and Asperger's syndrome, commented on a post about responding to homophobic "bigots" with "[T]hat's why I write letters to the editor. It's hard to leave 'stupid' alone."[73] Brendan Buschi of Magnolia, Delaware, has had letters published in a variety of Delaware newspapers, and shared on his personal blog a letter he sent to *The Delaware State News* in 2006, in which he wrote, "People have asked either my wife or me why I write letters to the editor. The simple answer is I write because it meets my need. . . . I write because I am angry. I write because I am afraid of what is happening to our country. I write because I am alive and kicking. I write because I am not too old to do so."[74] A post from "bufordtpisser" on Rider-Info.com, an online forum for motorcycle enthusiasts, explained his anger toward the greed of large corporations: "I refuse to buy gas at Exxon, or buy lumber at Home Depot. Even if their prices are better. . . . I write letters to the editor asking others to join me in this endeavor. Do I make a difference? Probably not. But I do get some peace of mind knowing that in my own little bufordland, I can make a personal statement."[75]

Strong personal feelings, often blending political views with strong religious or cultural beliefs, are often very evident in audience feedback. The motivation of religious fervor was explicit in Joe Hobson's letter in *The Longview* (Washington) *Daily News*, titled "Baptismal Calling": "Many people around Longview ask me why I write letters to the editor and why I seem so angry in my letters," he wrote.[76] "For me, voting down a jobs bill that would empower millions of Americans and voting 37 times to overturn Obamacare, which would insure many millions of uninsured, low income Americans, is a social sin. By speaking out against institutional and social injustice, by speaking for the excluded and the voiceless, I risk being misunderstood. So be it. But until each of us who call ourselves Christians and followers of Jesus takes our baptismal calling seriously, we will continue to be followers and accept the status quo."

Lifelong LTE writer Peggy Brayfield mused that her drive to write stems from her upbringing. Her family owned a small-town grocery store and also published a "little hometown paper," not only to advertise the store's wares but also to provide news about local schools, churches, and civic organizations. Her mother wrote a weekly column for the paper, which Brayfield said was published for only five or six years before her parents retired. Brayfield herself is retired now, a professor emerita in English at Eastern Illinois University. She cannot estimate how many LTEs she has written. "I have been sending letters since my teens, so it would be hard to estimate how many I have written over my lifetime," she wrote in an email.

"Since 2008, 35 of my LTE's have been published. . . . I'd say a ballpark figure over my lifetime might be, about 200 sent, and maybe 150 published."[77] She said her first published letter was in a California newspaper when she was 18, and she wrote a few to the campus newspaper while a student at Southern Illinois University. "Since 1970 I have mostly sent my letters to the local papers, the *Coles County Times-Courier* and the *Mattoon Journal Gazette*," she continued. "I have also published in the *Decatur Herald* and the *Champaign Gazette* a few times. While teaching, I often wrote letters to the student paper, the *Daily Eastern News*. I have also sent a few letters to bigger, non-local papers but don't recall any being published."

I asked Brayfield to recall her most poignant experience as a frequent letter-writer, and she said it was the very first experience she had:

"The first time one of my letters appeared in print and my friends, whom I knew read it, said nothing. (I was a college student at the time.) I knew that they did not support my views, and it was a lonely and vulnerable feeling. I realized then why writers ask to have their names withheld (as a rule I have never done this). It was a feeling I had to overcome (and did) in order to continue to put my opinions out there for public scrutiny. It's easy when one knows there are a lot of supporters out there, but not so easy when you know your views are at odds with most of those likely to read them. And publishing locally, in small towns such as Carterville, Carbondale, Charleston and Mattoon, makes one all the more aware of peer pressure. Over the years, some of my letters have provoked unkind replies, but I don't think any of those caused as much discomfort as that first time. I have also received a lot of appreciative comments but however gratifying, they aren't as 'poignant' as that instance."[78]

Brayfield wrote about her LTE-writing for her department's online journal, *Agora*, in 2010.[79] In that essay, she explained that after her retirement in 1997, she withdrew from writing for a few years, but the angry rhetoric she saw during the run up to the 2008 U.S. presidential election prompted her to start writing again. She explained that mostly she felt compelled to try to demonstrate civil discourse. "This has become my reason for sending letters to the newspapers: 'If you don't like the ugly, cynical, unreasonable, or hostile tone of what you see on the opinions page, try to get something more constructive published there. If the blogsters attack your letter, don't get baited into incivility yourself. "A soft answer turneth away wrath." Don't let the angry and the cynical dominate and set the tone. Be the change you want to see.'"[80]

CONCLUSION

Being one among millions can be an intimidating realization, and being just a single person in a world dominated by huge institutions and corporations can make it seem almost impossible that one can have her voice heard. Democratic elections have tallies that can total thousands, hundreds of thousands, even millions at the national level; most people will never meet their elected officials, let alone get a chance to express their opinions to them. The sheer scale of the human world is overwhelming, and being just one person in that world comes with an inherent degree of powerlessness.

Audience feedback forums are one of the most enduring ways for individuals to engage in that world. They provide channels through which individuals can have their opinions entered into the historical record (and, for those who sign their work, their names entered as well). The forums allow individuals to vent their frustrations against the seemingly unresponsive behemoths that are governments, corporations, and major institutions, and to also find fellowship with people who share their same interests, if not their same opinions.

By engaging in audience feedback forums, individuals are collaborating in a number of phenomena, but one of the most noteworthy is that of "imagined community." The concept, put forward by historian Benedict Anderson,[81] suggests that individuals in large collectives often must imagine themselves to be parts of those communities: "[T]he members of even the smallest nation will never know most of their fellow members, meet them, or even hear of them, yet in the minds of each lives the image of their community."[82] Contributing to the shared dialogue of feedback forums is a means be which individuals can reach out to their communities, to attempt to be known by them; by reading other submissions to those forums, individuals can also develop nuanced and complicated ideas about the nature of the communities they share with others. Put another way, William Hedgepeth and Dennis Stock contend that "[a] community . . . is a gathering of individuals whose certain shared goals and values create, for each, a real feeling of personal involvement for the common good."[83]

In previous research, my colleague Kevin Moist and I noted that one of the functions of a letter to the editor (or a call to a radio talkback show, or a comment to an online forum) is to serve as an avatar of the writer. The comment is, in itself, representative of the person who writes it. The choice of words, the phrasing, the cultural references, all provide not just an expression of opinion, but also an expression of self. One can read an LTE and learn a lot about the writer, often from subtle cues that reveal gender, age, socio-economic class, and education levels: "Writers use the LTEs to position themselves within the context of the community. . . . LTEs are a means by which community members maintain and express their individuality within the collective."[84] When media professionals become so detached from their feedback forums that they no longer consider participants to be individuals, but rather a faceless mob, those professionals also can lose credibility within their community. Forum managers face very real pitfalls in their work, from figuring out how best to handle seemingly impossible volumes of submissions to navigating the various legal and ethical issues presented by the untrained writers hitting "submit." It is certainly not possible for a forum manager to get to know every participant, or even to have one-on-one exchanges with each person who contributes—and in the case of a controversial or "red flag" submission, the easiest thing might be to just hit "delete" and move on. But there is no question that the forums provided by news media do not exist for "the audience" en masse, but for all of the countless humans who use those forums for different purposes and to achieve their personal goals.

NOTES

1. "Obituary of Ruth H. Shirt-Porter, 86," StateCollege.com, State College, Pa., September 7, 2010. Accessed May 28, 2014, from www.statecollege.com/obituary/detail/obituary-of-ruth-h—shirt-porter—86,994/.
2. "James Joseph McClure" [obituary], *Centre Daily Times*, State College, Pa., February 20, 2013. Accessed May 28, 2014, from www.legacy.com/obituaries/centredaily/obituary-preview.aspx?n=james-j-mcclure&pid=163188989&referrer=1406.
3. "Malcolm and Miriam Klein" [obituary], *The New York Times*, February 5, 2012. Accessed May 28, 2014, from www.legacy.com/obituaries/nytimes/obituary.aspx?n=malcolm-and-miriam-klein&pid=155767014.
4. Personal communication, March 8, 2013.
5. Bill Tubbs, "An Invitation for Morley Safer to Come to North Scott: We'll Show You That Newspapers Aren't Dying!," *The North Scott Press*, Eldridge, Iowa, January 16, 2013, 12A.
6. BBC News, "Radio Talkshow Caller Dies on Air," BBC News, January 6, 2006. Accessed May 25, 2014, from http://news.bbc.co.uk/2/hi/uk_news/england/merseyside/4587550.stm.
7. Deirdre Edgar, "A Man of Many Letters, Though Sometimes Few Words," *The Los Angeles Times*, January 29, 2013. Accessed May 28, 2014, from http://articles.latimes.com/2013/jan/29/local/la-me-rr-a-man-of-letters-in-the-times-20130129.
8. Trent Sanders, "It's Not Their Dream Act" [letter to the editor], *The Los Angeles Times*, September 30, 2011. Accessed May 28, 2014, from http://articles.latimes.com/2011/sep/30/opinion/la-le-0930-friday-20110930.
9. Trent D. Sanders, "California's Lion-Protection Law Ought to be Caged" [op-ed], The *Christian Science Monitor*, Boston, August 7, 1995. Accessed May 28, 2014, from www.csmonitor.com/1995/0807/07192.html.
10. Trent D. Sanders, "Thomas' Literal Interpretations" [letter to the editor], *The Los Angeles Times*, June 21, 2004. Accessed May 28, 2014, from http://articles.latimes.com/2004/jun/21/opinion/le-thomas21.
11. Trent D. Sanders (2006) "Bills Come Due" [letter to the editor], *The Los Angeles Times*, December 13, 2006. Accessed May 28, 2014, from www.csmonitor.com/1995/0807/07192.html.
12. Edgar, "A Man of Many Letters, Though Sometimes Few Words."
13. Dana Berg, "Letter to the Editor: Dear Mayor, Please Give Citizens a Say in Ferry Terminal Upgrade" [letter to the editor], InsideBainbridge.com, Bainbridge Island, Wash., January 2, 2014. Accessed May 27, 2014, from www.insidebainbridge.com/2014/01/02/letter-to-the-editor-dear-mayor-please-give-citizens-a-say-in-the-ferry-terminal-upgrade.

14. Steven Bonkowski , "Letter to the Editor: Mayor Bonkowski Responds to Request for Public Input on Ferry Terminal Upgrade" [letter to the editor] InsideBainbridge.com, Bainbridge Island, Wash., January 3, 2014. Accessed May 27, 2014, from www.insidebainbridge.com/2014/01/03/letter-to-the-editor-mayor-bonkowski-responds-to-request-for-public-input-on-ferry-terminal-upgrade.

15. Amanda Phillips, "Upset About Traffic Stop Treatment" [letter to the editor], *Rushville Republican*, Rushville, Ind., July 30, 2013. Accessed May 27, 2014, from www.rushvillerepublican.com/letters/x710301685/Upset-about-traffic-stop-treatment?zc_p=1.

16. Mike Pavey (2013) "Mayor Responds to Recent Letter" [letter to the editor], *Rushville Republican*, Rushville, Ind., August 13, 2013. Accessed May 27, 2014, from www.rushvillerepublican.com/letters/x1750260247/Mayor-responds-to-recent-letter/print.

17. Cat Paulk, "Letter: A Personal Tale of Vartan Gharpetian" [letter to the editor], *Glendale News-Press*, Glendale, Calif., May 27, 2014. Accessed May 30, 2014, from www.glendalenewspress.com/opinion/tn-gnp-letter-a-personal-tale-of-vartan-gharpetian-20140527,0,3653688.story.

18. Virginia Hays, "Dear Editor" [letter to the editor], *The Ely Times*, Ely, Nev., March 21, 2014. Accessed May 30, 2014, from www.elynews.com/2014/03/21/letter-editor-2/.

19. Joe Eby, "The Vote on Mayor Alborn's Nominee Clarified" [letter to the editor], *The Ruidoso News*, Ruidoso, N.Mex., September 12, 2013. Accessed May 30, 2014, from www.ruidosonews.com/ci_24082471/ruidoso-news.

20. Priscilla Miller, "Letter: Re: Kirpas" [letter to the editor]. *The Appeal-Democrat*, Maysville, Calif., May 20, 2014. Accessed May 30, 2014, from www.appeal-democrat.com/opinion/letter-re-kirpans/article_283a5a60-dfdc-11e3-8d53-001a4bcf6878.html.

21. Janis Garland, "Those Opposed to Centralia Bond Issue Should Visit Schools" [letter to the editor], *The Chronicle*, Centralia, Wash., May 20, 2003. Accessed May 30, 2014, from www.chronline.com/editorial/article_3490a525-50fb-57f5-8b3c-eee1223e4c7f.html?mode=jqm.

22. Libbey Aly, "Dear Editor" [untitled letter to the editor], *Blanco County News*, Blanco, Tex., April 9, 2014. Accessed May 30, 2014, from www.blanconews.com/news/115756/.

23. Personal communication, May 30, 2014.

24. Elisabeth Noelle-Nuemann, *The Spiral of Silence: Public Opinion—Our Social Skin* (Chicago: University of Chicago Press, 1993).

25. Charles T. Salmon and Gerald F. Kline, "Perception of Opinion 'Climates' and Willingness to Discuss the Issue of Abortion," *Journalism Quarterly* 67, 3 (1990), 567–77.

26. Dietram A. Scheufele and Patricia Moy, "Twenty-Five Years of the Spiral of Silence: A Conceptual Review and Empirical Outlook," *International Journal of Public Opinion Research* 12, 1 (2000), 3–28

27. Gi Woong Yun and Sung-Yeon Park, "Selective Posting: Willingness to Post a Message Online," *Journal of Computer-Mediated Communication* 16, 2 (2011), 201–27.

28. Steven Gallegos, "Secondhand Smoke Drifts Regardless of Scale," *The Glendale News-Press*, Glendale, Calif.: Los Angeles Times Co., October 5, 2012. Accessed August 30, 2014, from www.glendalenewspress.com/opinion/tn-gnp-1006-secondhand-smoke-drifts-regardless-of-scale,0,709664.story.

29. Bruce Nelson, "Outreach Workers Spoke Out of Turn," *The Glendale News-Press*, Glendale, Calif.: Los Angeles Times Co., October 22, 2012. Accessed August 30, 2014, from www.glendalenewspress.com/opinion/tn-gnp-1022-outreach-workers-spoke-out-of-turn,0,5446824.story.

30. Brittany Levin, "Courts OKs 1st Amendment Complaint Against Najarian," *The Glendale News-Press*, Glendale, Calif.: Los Angeles Times Co., September 12, 2013. Accessed August 30, 2014, from www.glendale newspress.com/news/tn-gnp-court-oks-1st-amendment-complaint-against-najarian-20130912,0,920630.story.
31. The Associated Press, "Phillippi Regains Post," *The Tuscaloosa News*, Tuscaloosa, Ala., June 18, 1977, 3.
32. Stephanie Sonntag, "BYUSA Employee Terminated," *The Daily Universe*, Salt Lake City, Utah, March 24, 2006. Accessed August 30, 2014, from http://universe.byu.edu/2006/03/24/byusa-employee-terminated/.
33. Marcus Baram, "Whistleblower Claims That BP Was Aware of Cheating on Blowout Preventer Tests," *The Huffington Post*, May 12, 2010. Accessed August 30, 2014, from www.huffingtonpost.com/2010/05/12/bp-whistleblower-claimed_n_573839.html.
34. Scott Jaschik, "A Dismissal Upheld," *Inside Higher Ed*, Washington, D.C., February 10, 2012. Accessed August 30, 2014, from https://www.insidehighered.com/news/2012/02/10/court-finds-hr-directors-free-speech-rights-were-limited.
35. WestKyStar staff, "Fired Teacher Files Court Motion," *West Kentucky Star*, Paducah, Ky.: Bristol Broadcasting Co., February 7, 2013. Accessed August 30, 2014, from www.westkentuckystar.com/News/Local-Regional/McCracken-County/Fired-Teacher-Files-Court-Motion.aspx.
36. Parliament of the United Kingdom, "Public Interest Disclosure Act 1998" (London: The National Archives, July 2, 1998). Accessed August 30, 2014, from www.legislation.gov.uk/ukpga/1998/23/introduction/enacted.
37. TNN, "After 2 Years and No Changes, Whistleblowers Bill Cleared," *The Times of India*, Mumbai, India, February 22, 2014. Accessed August 30, 2014, from http://timesofindia.indiatimes.com/india/After-2-years-and-no-changes-Whistleblowers-Bill-cleared/articleshow/30815449.cms.
38. Stephanie Sterling, "Developing a Whistle-Blower Culture," *Jamaica Observer*, Kingston, Jamaica, April 17, 2013. Accessed August 30, 2014, from www.jamaicaobserver.com/business/Developing-a-whistle-blowing-culture_14082685.
39. RTÉ News staff, "New Legislation to Protect Whistleblowers," RTÉ News, Dublin, Ireland: RTÉ Commercial Enterprises, July 15, 2014. Accessed August 30, 2014, from www.rte.ie/news/2014/0715/630799-whistleblowers-legislation/.
40. Commonwealth Ombudsman, "Public Interest Disclosure Scheme," ombudsman.gov.au. Accessed August 31, 2014, from www.ombudsman.gov.au/pages/pid/.
41. Whistleblowers Australia, "Civil Remedies," Whistleblowers.org.au, undated. Accessed August 30, 2014, from www.whistleblowers.org.au/civilremedies.html.
42. Office of the Public Sector Integrity Commissioner of Canada, "The Public Servants Disclosure Protection Act," PSIC.gc.ca, October 25, 2013. Accessed August 30, 2014, from www.psic.gc.ca/eng/aboutus/psdpa.
43. Canadians for Accountability, "About Accountability & Whistleblowing," Canadians4Accountability.org, Ottawa, Ontario: Canadians for Accountability, September 11, 2008. Accessed August 30, 2014, from http://canadians4accountability.org/accountability-and-whistleblowing/#stat.
44. Stephen Martin Kohn, *The Whistleblower's Handbook* (Lanham, Md.: Rowman & Littlefield, 2011), 199.
45. David L. Haron, Mercedes Varasteh Dordeski, and Larry D. Lahman, "Bad Mules: A Primer on the Federal and Michigan False Claims Act," *Michigan Bar Journal* 88, 11 (2009), 22–25.
46. National Whistleblowers Center, "Know Your Rights FAQ," Whistleblowers.org, Washington, D.C.: National Whistleblowers Center, undated. Accessed

August 31, 2014, from www.whistleblowers.org/index.php?option=com_con
tent&task=view&id=34&Itemid=63.

47. *Pickering v. Board of Education of Township High School District 205, Wills
County*, 391 U.S. 563 (1968).

48. 391 U.S., 578

49. 391 U.S., 568.

50. 391 U.S., 574.

51. *Brandenburg v. Ohio*, 395 U.S. 444 (1969).

52. *New York Times Co. v. Sullivan*, 376 U.S. 254 (1964).

53. *Gertz v. Robert Welch, Inc.*, 418 U.S. 323 (1974).

54. *Kotlikoff v. Community News*, Supreme Court of New Jersey, 444 A.2d 1086
(1982)

55. *Immuno A.G. v. Moor-Jankowski*, Court of Appeals of New York, 77 N.Y.2d
235 (1991).

56. Donna R. Euben, "Comment: An Argument for an Absolute Privilege for Letters to the Editor," *Brooklyn Law Review* 58 (1993), 1439–1501: 1482.

57. *Communications Decency Act of 1996*, 47 U.S.C. §§ 230.

58. David L. Grey and Trevor R. Brown, "Letters to the Editor: Hazy Reflections
of Public Opinion," *Journalism Quarterly* 47, 3 (1970), 450–56, 471: 454.

59. Bill Reader, Guido H. Stempel III, and Douglass K. Daniel, "Age, Wealth,
Education Predict Letters to the Editor," *Newspaper Research Journal* 25, 4
(2004), 55–66.

60. Jon Katz, "Luring the Lurkers," Slashdot.org, December 29, 1998. Accessed
June 4, 2014, from http://news.slashdot.org/story/98/12/28/1745252/
luring-the-lurkers.

61. Charles Arthur, "What is the 1% rule?" *The Guardian*, London, July 19,
2006. Accessed June 4, 2014, from www.theguardian.com/technology/2006/
jul/20/guardianweeklytechnologysection2.

62. Holly Goodier, "BBC Online Briefing Spring 2012: The Participation Choice,"
BBC Internet Blog, May 4, 2012. Accessed June 4, 2014, from www.bbc.
co.uk/blogs/legacy/bbcinternet/2012/05/bbc_online_briefing_spring_201_1.
html.

63. Reader, et al., "Age, Wealth, Education Predict Letters to the Editor."

64. Hans Meyer and Michael Clay Carey, "Cranks or Community? Describing
Those Who Comment on News Stories," paper presented at the annual conference of the Association for Education in Journalism and Mass Communication (Washington, D.C., August 2013).

65. Gonen Dori-Hacohen, "With Whom Do I Have the Pleasure?": Callers' Categories in Political Talk Radio Programs," *Journal of Pragmatics* 44, 3 (2012),
280–97.

66. Andrew Crisell, *Understanding Radio* (London: Routledge, 1994).

67. Sara O'Sullivan, "'The Whole Nation Is Listening to You': The Presentation
of the Self on a Tabloid Talk Radio Show," *Media Culture & Society* 27, 5
(2005), 719–38.

68. Richard Fitzgerald and William Housley, "Talkback, Community and the
Public Sphere," *Media International Australia* 122 (2007), 150–63.

69. Nick Bianchi, "A Letter of Encouragement to Letter Writers" [letter to the edi-
tor], *Bracebridge Examiner*, Bracebridge, Ontario, May 29, 2014. Accessed
May 30, 2014, from www.muskokaregion.com/opinion-story/4546581-a-let
ter-of-encouragement-to-letter-writers.

70. Tony Gerstberger, "Events Will Repeat Themselves" [letter to the editor],
The Daily Mining Gazette, Houghton, Mich., September 17, 2011. Accessed
May 30, 2014, from www.mininggazette.com/page/content.detail/id/522000/
Events-will-repeat-themselves.html.

71. Jessee Tabor, "Solve Overspending" [letter to the editor], *The Caswell Messenger*, Caswell, N.C., November 6, 2013. Accessed May 30, 2014, from www.caswellmessenger.com/opinion/article_80ffbf72–467c-11e3-bf42–001a 4bcf887a.html.

72. Joe Robenalt, "Put Street Before the Scape" [letter to the editor], *The Advertiser-Tribune*, Tiffin, Ohio, January 25, 2010. Accessed May 30, 2014, from www.advertiser-tribune.com/page/content.detail/id/520694.html.

73. cathylynn, untitled online comment, WrongPlanet.net, February 24, 2013. Accessed May 30, 2014, from https://www.wrongplanet.net/postp5284524. html.

74. Brendan Buschi, "Why I Write Letters—This Is Where I'm Coming From Mr. Skocik" [blog post], Brendan Buschi's Blog, September 17, 2007. Accessed May 30, 2014, from http://brendanbuschi.blogspot.com/2007/09/why-i-write-letters-this-is-where-im.html.

75. bufordtpisser, untitled online comment, RiderInfo.com, February 6, 2007. Accessed May 30, 2014, from http://riderinfo.com/forums/archive/index. php/t-5536.html.

76. Joe Hobson, "Baptismal calling" [letter to the editor], *The Longview Daily News*, Longview, Wash., June 27, 2013. Accessed May 30, 2014, from http://tdn. com/news/opinion/letters-american-values/article_d6b3fa22-de9f-11e2-b12e-001a4bcf887a.html.

77. Personal communication, June 2, 2014.

78. Personal communication, June 2, 2014.

79. Peggy Brayfield, "Why I Write Letters to the Editor," *Agora*, Charleston, Ill., February 2010. Accessed May 29, 2014, from http://castle.eiu.edu/agora/1002/Peggyall.htm.

80. Brayfield, "Why I Write Letters to the Editor."

81. Benedict Anderson, *Imagined Communities: Reflections on the Origins and Spread of Nationalism* (New York: Verso, 1991).

82. Anderson, *Imagined Communities*, 6.

83. William Hedgepeth and Dennis Stock, *The Alternative: Communal Life in New America* (New York: Collier Books, 1970), 18.

84. Bill Reader and Kevin Moist, "Letters as Indicators of Community Values: Two Case Studies of Alternative Magazines," *Journalism & Mass Communication Quarterly* 85, 4 (2008), 823–40: 834.

8 "We, the People . . ."
Commenting as Collective Action

In August 2014, many high-profile civic leaders and celebrities were caught up in the "Ice Bucket Challenge," a fundraising initiative aimed at generating donations for research into treatment of amyotrophic lateral sclerosis, or "Lou Gehrig's disease." The fundraiser was enacted by people agreeing to have buckets of ice water dumped over their heads, at which point they would give a donation (typically US$100) and then "nominate" another person to take the challenge. The effort gained participation from public figures at all levels, from small-town mayors and high-school teachers on up to international star athletes, media celebrities, and even former heads of state.[1]

One such challenge was made by Ohio University President Roderick McDavis, who, after playfully getting "iced" himself, nominated the president of the university's undergraduate student senate to take the challenge. Instead of engaging in the playful, light-hearted approach most used, the student leader instead made a video of herself dumping a bucket of fake blood on herself as a protest against the Israeli occupation of the Gaza Strip, and called on the university to divest itself of investments tied to Israeli corporations.[2] The video stirred a firestorm of debate on the rural college campus: Initial reactions to the video were highly critical of the student leader, mostly from other students and campus leaders with strong pro-Israeli views, and those were followed by numerous public statements of support either for the student's pro-Palestinian views or for her right to free expression. A number of other statements, both critical and supportive, came into the community from alumni of the university and larger special-interest groups.

What was most interesting about those responses is that they were submitted to the student newspaper, *The Post*, which published most of them in its printed edition.

That was rare for *The Post*, which can go many weeks without getting more than a handful of LTEs from students on campus—it received more than 16 letters within the first few days of the "blood bucket" controversy, and multiple responses to those letters in subsequent days.[3] Although hardly a huge number, 16-plus LTEs is far more feedback than *The Post* receives in a typical month. The assumption is that students at the university—as with college students everywhere—simply do not read ink-on-paper newspapers, and as such would rather use social networking sites such as Facebook and Twitter to exchange their views. A much more likely explanation is that it takes a big controversy to stir activity in the feedback forums of college newspapers, and it is in times when a campus community is bitterly divided over such controversy that such forums become important to that community. Readership of the newspaper at that time also was noticeably increased, as racks around campus that usually remained full through most days were emptied by noon in the days after the controversy erupted, and the coverage triggered numerous conversations about a host of issues, from the Israeli-Palestinian conflict to the very issue of freedom of speech, throughout the campus—most of it documented in the primary forum for public discourse on the campus, the independent student newspaper.

One of the letter-writers, an international graduate student,[4] explained that he had written LTEs in his home country, but never in the United States. Responding to the "blood-bucket" controversy, he first wrote his comments on social media platforms, "but I chose to write to *The Post* because it is widespread on campus, and much of my target audience read it. Therefore, it is an effective tool to get my voice heard as wide as possible."[5] The student explained the value of printed discussion forums compared to online social networks this way:

> "We should not marginalize and ignore those who still prefer or hold to reading print newspapers, [such] as elderly people or those who may have no access to online services . . . There is also another value in writing for print newspapers, which is the idea of documentation and archiving. Online services are always prone to service downfalls or other technical issues, so print is a good way to keep the records of one's personal support of any issue."[6]

Another letter-writer, an undergraduate student, also suggested that social media are more limited forums than even printed forums in newspapers: "I felt [my opinion] would reach a wider scope of people than just posting on my Facebook page, where many of my friends express the same opinion as I do . . . it is one thing to have an opinion about something and to brood over it, to desire for people to see it your way, but when you allow yourself to use your resources (newspapers, magazines, etc.) to express your opinion in, hopefully, a respectful manner, you are opening up and declaring your own voice, as well as bringing a unique viewpoint into the public's scope."[7]

Both students said they received a lot of positive feedback themselves after their letters were published. The graduate student explained, "I got wild support and thumbs up from my friends and colleagues. More importantly, its publication inspired others to write and join in the cause. In short, it helped spread the awareness on the issue in question."[8] The undergraduate (who said she had never before written an LTE) stated: "I noticed that a

lot of people shared it on Facebook and Twitter in agreement with my sentiments. There was a comment on *The Post*'s webpage that was disagreeing
with me, but it was respectful. All in all, I felt that the response I received
was a positive one, and I look forward to continuing writing letters. It has
been empowering."[9]

In the 21st century, audience feedback forums do not stand alone. Readers and media professionals use the forums in dynamic ways that cut across
various forums. Letters to the editor prompt discussion in online forums;
online comments can be shared and further discussed via social platforms;
individual comments (especially when made by celebrities or public figures)
can become newsworthy themselves, and the topics of additional threads
via multiple channels. That kind of crossover effect is not new—LTEs were
often reprinted in numerous newspapers in the early 1700s and sparked
more localized discussion via those papers. However, the breadth, depth,
and speed of online communication greatly expands such crossover and
expansion of dialogue; the inability of media professionals to manage the
volume and speed of collective feedback also allows the discussions to be
far less controlled and far more fractal. Whereas, in the past, much of the
discussion focused on issues (or, more accurately, were edited to focus on
issues), the modern feedback forums quite often move past the primary topic
and branch off into discussions about tangential matters, often into debates
about the purpose of such forums, even the very nature of discourse itself.

THE COLLECTIVE NATURE OF FEEDBACK FORUMS

To most media professionals, the idealized audience feedback forum serves
as a space where one person can express his or her personal opinions to the
masses. The emphasis of most forum management practices and policies are
geared toward the one-person-one-opinion philosophy, a clear extension of
the Enlightenment ideals of individualism that evolved concurrently with
the Enlightenment ideals of freedom of speech and freedom of the press.

But audience-feedback forums also, obviously, serve as spaces for collective action. Whether through genuine groundswells of public interest in
a specific issue or through organized letter-writing campaigns run by huge
special-interest groups, countless people each year write or call the news
media to participate collectively in various political and social campaigns.
In the process, they can construct virtual communities that can be just as
rewarding, contentious, cohesive, or divisive as any other community. Even
a wide-open, anonymous online forum that may seem to be riddled with vitriol and discord forms its own collective identity, reflecting diversity of opinion and a diversity of rhetorical styles. Those are forums where the polite
and the serious intermix with the rude and the sarcastic. Optimists interact
with pessimists, dogmatists debate with reformers. Side conversations break
off from the dominant thread, sometimes tackling the nuances of semantics

and rhetorical tactics, even discussing what should or should not be acceptable practice within each forum. What emerges from those diverse, individual expressions is not just a narrative of disagreement and divisiveness, but rather a narrative of coming together, of learning and adapting, and ultimately of participants figuring out how to agree to disagree. There certainly is a lot of virtual shouting past one another, but far more often there is legitimate argument and debate and a construction of community—not the kind of fanciful, "everybody gets along" community of dreams, but the complicated, sometimes inharmonious collectivism found in genuine communities.

The power of that collective discourse is not lost on the powers that be. Politicians and special-interest groups often respond to criticisms in LTEs, and their supporters write plenty of letters and comments on behalf of their candidates and causes (as was the case in the "blood-bucket" controversy at Ohio University discussed earlier). Some campaigns go so far as to write "sample letters" that their supporters can simply copy and sign with their own names, a controversial practice in both journalism and public-relations circles.[10] An even more ethically challenged tactic is for a campaign to have volunteers write LTEs under a variety of alternate identities or generic letters that supporters can use as their own. Such tactics tend to be self-defeating, as many editors will reject pre-written or ghost-written letters as "astroturf" (or "fake grass roots"), and also will editorialize against campaigns that use the practice.[11] In fact, many forum editors are reluctant to accommodate even legitimate letter-writing campaigns, and have set up internal policies that obstruct publication of more than one letter per campaign per issue; some even charge a fee to publish election-related letters, which takes the commodification of feedback to a whole new level.

Despite considerable anti-forum sentiment among media elites, particularly aimed at anonymous online discussion forums that are difficult for media gatekeepers to control, the news media of the 21st century have created more and more varied forums for audience feedback than in any time in history. Part of the challenge facing news media as the 21st century approaches its third decade is making sure that their forum policies and procedures accommodate various channels and don't permanently drive away people who want to use existing news media as public spaces for collective discourse.

AUDIENCE FEEDBACK AND 'VIRTUAL COMMUNITY'

When Howard Rheingold coined the term "virtual community" in the mid-1980s,[12] he was clearly focused on the potential for collective discourse found on the nascent Internet. But the creation of virtual community is by no means an Internet-age phenomenon, as legacy media—broadcasting and print—also could be conduits for mediated community. Certainly, the communities formed via those older media were not as dynamic, nor could

members of the communities interact in real time with little or no moderation. But that does not mean virtual communities were not possible before
the Internet, or even before electronic communication technology.

One excellent example of a low-tech virtual community is *The Budget*
newspaper, published since 1890 in Ohio's Amish country. *The Budget*
started—and remains—as a way for members of the Amish and Mennonite faiths[13] to keep informed about what is happening in their religious
diaspora, with volunteers from each settlement, called "scribes," submitting
handwritten or typed summaries of news from their various communities
across North America.[14] The "news" is often little more than simple reports
about weather conditions, the progress of crops, and notes about births,
deaths, marriages, and the like. The weekly newspaper, still printed and
circulated to some 18,000 families worldwide as of mid-2014,[15] continues
to rely on low-tech communication for the bulk of its submissions, although
some scribes are from modernized sects of Amish and Mennonites, who use
fax or email to submit their entries; the newspaper itself, however, remained
a strictly ink-on-paper publication.

The process of constructing mediated collectives has been especially
noticeable in niche and local media, whether print, electronic, or both.
North Carolina journalist Joy Franklin, who was editorial-page editor of
the *Asheville Citizen-Times* through much of the early 2000s, put it this
way: "We are the voice through which the community talks to itself."[16]
Community journalism scholar Jock Lauterer points out that very large
newspapers and magazines simply lack the "human scale" to provide feedback forums that are truly reflective of a sense of community. He pointed
out that a major metro daily might "receive an average of 400 letters to the
editor each day; it has room to publish about four to six. The other 394
don't get run . . . How do you think that makes all those folks feel? The
[small town newspaper] will receive about four to six letters a week and
run each and every one. How do you think that makes *those* writers feel?
The human scale is again at work in favor of community newspapers."[17]
The same is true of alternative magazines, some of which rely heavily, some
exclusively, on submissions from readers as the source of content.[18]

It also is possible for large media to use their feedback features to construct narratives of community, even when they can only share a very small
sampling of the dozens or hundreds of submissions they receive each day.[19]
That was found by media scholar Karin Wahl-Jorgensen in her study of
LTE-handling practices at daily newspapers in the San Francisco Bay area,
who concluded:

> "As individuals tell their stories, characterized by their partiality, they
> also see the connections between their own interests and the society in
> which they live. . . . Though the embarrassing, the painful, the wonder-
> ful, the funny, and the beautiful textures of our lives may be grounded
> in experiences of a deeply personal nature, perhaps they are also the

only experiences we can truly share with others, and speaking about them the only way to link us together in an empathic pursuit of the elusive common good."[20]

One cannot fully understand the social importance of audience feedback forums without accepting a generous "warts and all" appreciation for the collectives that use those forums. The value of a heavily edited, gentrified forum is largely self-serving and isolationist, not unlike the comfortable isolation provided by exclusive social clubs or gated residential neighborhoods. *The Atlantic* magazine's website, for example, was heavily moderated by senior editor Ta-Nehisi Coates, who said he strived to construct a forum that's "like a dinner party, and I try to host it that way. I try to keep the conversation interesting, in terms of what is the bane of all comments sections, and that is, you know, rude commentary, people going over the line, trolling, that sort of thing."[21] The radio journalist who interviewed Coates, "On the Media" co-host Bob Garfield, heralded *The Atlantic*'s forum as an "intellectual treasure" because "the jerks are invited to leave, the grownups to stay and chime in."[22] Garfield, on balance, did mention that some might criticize such a controlling approach as "un-democratic" that "somehow undermines the diversity of opinion and thoughts . . . and so forth," to which Coates agreed, but said the Web has plenty of other forums for the more rancorous: "It's only in this particular corner that it is, in fact, totalitarian, anti-democratic . . . The diversity of opinion is rather small. I would certainly cop to that."[23]

A few media celebrities embrace the richness of more wide-open discourse. Film and television critic Matt Zoller Seitz, writing for Salon.com, suggested in 2010 that as news outlets try to block and ostracize commenters they consider to be "trolls," they also are whitewashing their forums and obscuring the realities of modern society. Un-moderated forums, Seitz argued, are more genuine reflections of society than heavily managed forums: "They show us what the species is really like: the full spectrum of human behavior, not just the part that we find reassuring and enlightening."[24]

The problem with much of the professional commentary on feedback forums is that the conversation is almost always framed from the perspective of those who work in the media, and not from the perspective of the writers for whom those forums are, ostensibly, provided. Most participants in such forums aren't necessarily happy with bona fide trolling behavior, either, but they seem much more willing to tolerate a little mischief in exchange for being able to post anonymously or under pseudonyms so that they can be more frank in their opinions and less susceptible to "real-world" harassment.[25] After *The Buffalo News* announced it would ban anonymous comments on its website in 2010, many readers condemned the move, with arguments such as, "What you are doing will eliminate the vulgar and racist from the debate [but many] of us who are not vulgar and racist will choose to no longer participate, either,"[26] and, "The changeover to the use of real names and locations will happen around Aug. 1st, and the harassment of people who dare to speak out against the status quo will begin on Aug. 2nd."[27] Another critic of the proposed ban likened the move to a form of censorship and suppression of unpopular speech: "If the *News* is really so concerned about so-called 'civility,' then there are other ways of accomplishing it than to put people's lives and livelihoods at risk by requiring them to plaster their names and other private information on the Internet."[28] The collective sentiment from the writers of audience feedback seems to be that it is they, and not the authors of the professional news media, who should have the most control over feedback forums, and that includes giving participants the choice to post anonymously if they so choose.[29]

There certainly are individuals who participate in such forums simply to cause trouble (discussion of "trolls," as they are called, is covered in Chapter 6). In many ways, however, "trolls" add to the richness of the online forums by performing the role of the devil's advocate and as challengers of the status quo, much like stand-up comedians who are prone to speaking uncomfortable truths. In that way, forum trolls also form a community—as one self-describing troll put it:

> "The purpose of the [troll] community . . . is to exchange ideas and techniques, and to plan co-ordinated trolling. The underlying philosophical purpose or shared goal, anyway, would be to disrupt people's rosy vision of the internet as their own personal emotional safe place that serves as a proxy for real-life interactions they are lacking (i.e. going online to demonstrate one's grief over a public disaster . . . with total strangers who have no real connection to the event). This latter point can be said of trolls, too. There's a kind of interaction, in-your-face and disrespectful, that trolls would like to but can't do in real life (for various reasons), so they do it online."[30]

Too often, the word "community" is used to suggest an idealistic notion of a harmonious, homogeneous group, whereas most communities are far from being either thing. The classic example of a community—the rural small town—is, in reality, often marred by political divisiveness, feuds between neighbors and families, tensions between longtime residents and newcomers, mistrust toward outsiders, and so forth. Virtual communities are no different. Given over to their own devices, however, true virtual communities that are built upon broad audience participation can be messy and fascinatingly dynamic—and, for the most part, they also become self-policing and self-regulatory as they undertake the endless, fluctuating work of adapting to new challenges. Studies of unmediated discussion forums have found that the communities themselves tend to do a good job of setting agreeable ground rules for participation and of challenging/chastising "trolls" and other disruptive participants.[31] That kind of messy discourse is, as a result, no more important in democratic societies than when the issue is about the

enactment of actual, enforceable rules and policies, and the forum threads
are focused on political campaigns and governmental elections.

ELECTION LETTERS: 'THE HEART OF NEWSPAPERS'

In democracies around the world, election season is typically a busy time for
all journalists, and that is especially true for opinion editors and forum managers. Heaped upon the increased workload of interviewing candidates for
endorsement editorials, managing op-ed columns from candidates and their
surrogates, fact-checking claims made in stump speeches and campaign lit-
erature, and critiquing the performance of officials charged with overseeing
the elections themselves, those editors also have to deal with a significant
increase of activity in their audience forums. Radio talkback shows get more
callers, online comment forums get more traffic, and newspapers get more
letters. Lots more.

The Frederick News-Post in eastern Maryland, for example, received
a self-describe "avalanche" of campaign letters in advance of that state's
June 2014 primary. Opinion editor Clifford G. Cumber didn't tally all of
the letters he received and published in those months, but explained in a
column that:

> "[A]s we crept toward the primary, we found we needed more and more
> space to run election-related correspondence . . . From June 17 on, we
> were choc-a-bloc, filling the page from stem to stern. Even earlier than
> that, the uptick in campaigning-by-letter-to-the-editor was becoming
> noticeable. I made my first request for an extra half-page on Sunday,
> May 11, to fit a couple of longer letters. The next week, I asked for
> an open third page. That continued every Sunday right up to June 22,
> when I squeezed in perhaps the most letters we've ever run on a single
> day, 22."[32]

Cumber described editing all of those letters as "headache-inducing. But
it was worth it." A colleague of his described getting that many election
LTEs as "a good problem to have."[33] That is a common sentiment in professional journalism—increased volume of audience feedback tends to signify
increased engagement by the voting public.

Because of the increased volume of submissions, many newspapers have
special policies for handling audience comments during elections. A typical
technique is to set deadlines for election-related LTEs that fall a week or so
in advance of election day, as a means to stifle eleventh-hour attacks and
to give each side a chance to respond to allegations or attacks. Many also
prohibit the candidates from writing their own letters, but will give them
a chance to respond to comments made about them by others. When I ran
an opinion page, I gave space to each candidate so that each could have a

"last word" in the newspaper (candidates who chose not to respond were given the space anyway—it was just left blank with a note that they did not respond). Even with such restrictions and accommodations, most editors will tell you that they get more letters from readers in the run-up to elections than at any other time.

Not all forums are so inviting to audience participation during election season. Some newspapers will not publish more than one letter per day endorsing each campaign; others might not publish any endorsement letters at all (but will publish letters about broader election issues). The publisher of the rural *Proctor Journal* in Minnesota gained some notoriety in 2006 when he announced his newspaper would charge five cents per word to publish endorsement letters ("I just got tired of spending space and time and not getting any sort of advertising," he explained[34]). The *Santa Clarita Valley Signal* of California started charging ten cents per word in 2012; the *Columbia Daily Tribune* in Missouri for many years charged $25 for endorsement letters of 100 words or fewer, with a charge of 50 cents per additional word.[35] The *Rapid City Journal* of South Dakota announced in 2012 that it would charge a fee of $15 per letter pertaining to elections, noting:

> "The extra crush of letters that are related to an upcoming election takes up staff time and requires the use of extra newsprint. In past years, the *Journal* has printed the additional letters without charge, diverting additional staff to the effort and printing extra pages to meet the demand. . . . Election-related letters essentially are unpaid political advertising, which candidates have taken advantage of. If election letters are going to be used as a form of political advertising, political supporters should bear the expense of their publication, not the *Journal*. We note that in any other form of media, there would be a charge for political testimonials."[36]

The newspaper's announcement drew four comments from readers, three of whom panned the idea. "People who are already ponying up their hard earned cash for a *Journal* subscription may get a little ticked off at being asked to pay another $15 just for the privilege of submitting a letter," one wrote; another wrote, "The last gasp of a dying industry! I expect to hear no more complaining from the *Journal* editorial board about campaign finance reform, since you will now only provide access to those with the means to pay."[37]

Community newspaper consultant Jim Pumarlo calls election-season LTEs "the lifeblood of editorial pages and the heart of newspapers."[38] Pumarlo supports an aggressive, diligent approach to handling election-season feedback, particularly letters to the editor. But he suggests that editors not reject or limit such letters simply because the volume creates more work. "As a general rule, editors say letters that simply repeat the ideas of another writer will not be published. At best, that's a subjective decision. At worst, it's telling a lot of local readers that their letters didn't make the grade, and might well deter them from writing at any time of the year. It leaves a bad taste in their mouths."[39]

Pumarlo's point is well made—if news media provide forums primarily to serve the democratic traditions of public discourse, than they should live up to that obligation by finding more ways to accommodate election-related commentary and institute fewer deterrents.

ORGANIZED CAMPAIGNS: FROM GRASSROOTS TO 'ASTROTURF'

One of the more common obstacles set up by forum managers are prohibitions of duplicate LTEs from organized campaigns. Recognizing the value of supportive LTEs, many special-interest groups encourage their supporters to write letters to the editor, even in the era of social networking and online-only communication.

The promotion of LTE-writing spans the ideological spectrum. Consider this call to action from the National Organization for the Reform of Marijuana Laws, a U.S.-based advocacy group that has been working since 1970 to overturn legal prohibitions against the growing and smoking of marijuana:

> "One of the most effective, cost-efficient ways to educate the voters and influence public officials is to consistently publish letters to the editor in national and regional newspapers. The opinion page is typically the most widely read section of the newspaper, and letters to the editor are usually clipped and saved by politicians. Moreover, letters to the editor show editors, reporters, and local representatives what the 'hot' issues are, thereby encouraging both greater news coverage and political debate of those topics."[40]

Here is a similar LTE-writing plea from Winning Progressive, a political action group that supports liberal causes:

> "One of the best ways to make your voice heard in support of progressive values is to write a letter to your local newspaper editor. If your letter gets published, you will be sending the progressive message to thousands or more people in your community. And even if it is not published, letters from progressives will help newspaper editors—who also dictate what the newspapers' editorial slant will be—to realize that the majority shares our progressive values."[41]

Most special-interest groups that promote LTE writing provide tips and suggestions for would-be writers, but nothing more. Some, however, provide pre-written LTEs, which journalists often refer to derisively as "astroturf."

A content analysis of special-interest group websites found that less than one-third of the groups that encouraged LTE writing provided such sample letters, whereas the majority of such groups only encouraged letter-writing, and many provided the same recommended guidelines as found in the "letters policies" of most newspapers—keep it short, sign your name, be respectful, and above all else write original letters.[42]

The problem with "astroturf" submissions is that they are often counterproductive. Although they may help organized campaigns maintain control over their messages—to the point of absurdity, in some cases—the negative publicity of getting caught far outweighs the potential benefits. The re-election campaign of U.S. President George W. Bush was embarrassed in 2003 when one of its astroturf LTEs, which claimed that Bush was "demonstrating genuine leadership on the economy," was published in more than 100 newspapers, including major daily newspapers such as *USA Today* and *The Boston Globe*.[43] The tactic also was used in the 2008 presidential campaign of U.S. Senator John McCain—one former volunteer for the campaign claimed to have been part of a handful of volunteers who were instructed to write LTEs under a variety of false identities: "The assignment is simple: We are going to write letters to the editor and we are allowed to make up whatever we want—as long as it adds to the campaign. After today we are supposed to use our free moments at home to create a flow of fictional fan mail for McCain."[44] Likewise, The Democratic Congressional Campaign Committee, at this writing, had a number of pre-written LTEs that supporters could choose from via a dynamic form on the DCCC website: Users just had to enter their names, addresses, and telephone numbers into the Web form, then check the boxes of the newspapers the letter should be sent to (including local newspapers identified by the supporter's address information). The form even indicated whether the letter had already been published with a note next to the newspaper's name reading, "letter limit reached."[45]

Forum managers have a number of legitimate concerns about the astroturf phenomenon, particularly the very shady tactic of having volunteers write letters under fake identities. But it seems that many professionals exaggerate the extent of the problem and, as they have with anonymity, taken the most draconian approach by publicly denouncing the practice and instituting bans on such letters, or even letters from organized campaigns. There seems to be little consideration among journalists that, to the campaign supporters, prepared LTEs aren't much different from prepared greeting cards, bumper stickers, political T-shirts, and other socially acceptable forms of ready-made expression. An easy accommodation would be for each forum to publish just one copy of the letter on a first-come, first-serve basis; a not-much-harder approach would be to run the prepared letter once along with the names of all of the individuals who submitted it, and to include an editor's note explaining that the letter was prepared by the campaign but signed by local supporters of the effort. But few modern editors would even consider such an approach, based upon the aura of authorship that so pervades professional journalism. The professional preference for original, one-of-a-kind opinions is very much at the root of journalists' anger and resentment toward organized letter-writing campaigns in general and astro-turf in particular. From the perspective of broader society, each is a harmless way for campaigns to motivate their supporters to get involved in civic life.

Even if an editor feels strongly opposed to astroturf, it also may be a practice that editors cannot stop. In 2014, there was a free website called PublishaLetter.com that was filled with ready-to-copy LTEs on almost any topic imaginable. Its motto: "Letters to the Editor Made Easy."[46]

AUDIENCE FEEDBACK AND SOCIAL REFORM

Beyond organized letter-writing campaigns, however, are the slow-burn causes that appear in feedback forums over many years, even decades. Long-fought campaigns against racial and gender inequality, poverty and hunger, environmental degradation, violent crime, and other social ills all have relied heavily on media forums as channels to keep those causes alive and moving forward. Although that use of the forums is laudable, it is also important to recognize that they also have served as conduits for backlash, retrenchment, and intimidation of those causes.

Returning to the story that opened this chapter, the "blood-bucket" pro-test created by a student leader on a college campus, it is helpful to consider how the conversation about the incident unfolded via the student news-paper, *The Post*. The editor was a senior named Jim Ryan, who the previ-ous year had been a senior editor involved in the editorial page. "*The Post* received a significant uptick in reader interaction, both on social media and in the form of letters to the editor, in the week following our first report about the 'blood bucket' video," Ryan explained.[47] "The story [had] gained significant traction on Facebook, where commenters [had] been using our posts as a forum to discuss the topic, and on Twitter." A week later, Ryan said that the newspaper received far more comments online than any other story in the previous six weeks.

I asked Ryan if he had noticed any changes in the dialogue over that week. "The tone of conversation has shifted several times since the video was released," he said. "At first, the conversation was dominated by those speaking out against [the student leader]. Her supporters then began to chime in, coming to her defense and evening out the dialogue. We have also heard from a number of readers who are speaking both for and against [her] free-speech rights; that has become a parallel discussion of sorts that was bred from the initial 'blood bucket' video dialogue."[48]

In most cases, the dialogue about an issue will dissipate in time, whether in a few hours in an online forum or over several weeks or months in a weekly print newspaper or monthly magazine. Over that time, the conver-sation naturally will advance and change, much like any other spontaneous argument one might encounter on a public street. There is initial hostility and anger and confrontational rhetoric, met with much the same from the other party. The argument then will either escalate into violence (which cannot happen via news media forums) or more talking (which can). For many, the additional talking will get calmer over time, sometimes even to the point of friendly reconciliation. Some won't let go of their hostility, but likely will move on in time. Because physical violence is not possible within feedback forums themselves, they allow people to confront one another and blow off steam, which is why so many forums have been called, in the past, social safety valves (as discussed in Chapter 5).

But for some communities, many issues are timeless. For example, the problems of racial bias in news coverage has been and remains a perennial concern in many countries, and as such become social movements that continue to be argued in media feedback forums. Racial bias clearly was an issue broached in 1897 in a letter published in the *Southwestern Christian Advertiser* of New Orleans:

> "There was an attempt to commit an outrage upon a respectable colored married lady in the vicinity of Aberdeen . . . I see that there is no note of the fact through the Southern press that boasts so loudly of the Southern chivalry in the protection of the virtue of women, to the death of the culprit, by swinging him to a limb of a tree or beneath the girders of the railroad trestle, then perforating the poor wretch's body with bullets. But it was not so in this instance. Why? In the first place, the aggressor was a white man and the assaulted, woman, colored. In the second place, the negroes that were offended are loyal to the laws of their country and are willing to abide by their just decision."[49]

Compare that the following letter published in August 1963 by the *Chicago Tribune*, pertaining to the U.S. Civil Rights Act that had been proposed about two months earlier by President John F. Kennedy:

> "I am against the granting of any special privileges to any group because of race, creed, or color, whether the people be black or white, Protestant or Catholic, or of Chinese or German descent, just because some people think it is 'the right thing to do.' Negroes have no rights. Whites have no rights. Catholics, Protestants, and Jews have no rights. Only individuals have rights. I hope we can keep that in mind in the coming weeks."[50]

And this example, from the *Times Leader* newspaper of Wilkes-Barre, Pennsylvania, in June 2014:

> "Blacks commit 85 percent of homicides in Wilkes-Barre while comprising only 10 percent of the population. You can say 'diversity is our

strength' until your throat is hoarse, but it doesn't change the fact that Wilkes-Barre was a much safer city when it was nearly all white."[51]

That letter was excoriated in another LTE published the following week:

"I am stunned and horrified that *The Times Leader* printed the racist garbage masquerading as a letter to the editor . . . Substitute 'Italians' or 'Jews' or 'Poles' or any other ethnicity to the letter writer's assertions and I'm sure such hatred would not have appeared in your paper. While the writer is entitled to his hate, responsible journalists wouldn't have spread it."[52]

Social-progress efforts invariably attract backlash and vitriol from all sides. Letters containing racist comments pose a particularly dicey dilemma for forum managers. On the one hand, they know such language would be offensive to many of their readers; on the other, they want to live up to their promises to provide truly public forums.[53] The Society of Professional Journalists' code of ethics, a commonly cited set of guidelines in the industry, for years encouraged journalists to "Support the open . . . exchange of views, even views they find repugnant."[54] Editors who oppose publishing racist language in LTEs argue that doing so undermines efforts to promote tolerance and "lowers the level of the edit-page conversation," but those who are willing to (begrudgingly) publish such letters argue that doing so does more good in the long run: It exposes that racism exists in communities, and such letters usually get many more responses condemning the writer's view. That is, publishing the occasional racist, sexist, or homophobic LTE can spark collective action from other writers to denounce such views—as one editor explained it, "The antidote to offensive, bigoted or just plain unreasonable speech is more speech, more dialogue, and more debate."[55]

An interesting case study of that phenomenon occurred in the Vancouver Island community of Nanaimo in 2013, when the local newspaper, the *Nanaimo Daily News*, published a letter titled, "Educate First Nations to be modern citizens." The letter-writer argued for ending government subsidies to First Nation tribes and to "bring them into society as equals."[56] Before that call for equal treatment, however, the letter-writer provided a list of technological advantages that Europeans had over indigenous North Americans, leading to a claim that First Nations people "[h]ave a history that is notable only for underachievement." The overall letter was, objectively, racist. The letter generated an immediate backlash against the newspaper for publishing it, including a Facebook campaign against the letter and protests in front of the newspaper office.[57] The next day, the letter was removed from the newspaper's website, and an executive with the newspaper wrote a message to readers stating, "The letter should not have run. We apologize for any distress this may have caused our readers."[58] On the website of the local alternative newspaper *Straight*, scores of comments were posted about the publication of the letter, with a nearly even split between those who believed the newspaper was wrong to publish such a letter and those who argued for the right to publish such opinions (a few even defended the opinion of the original letter).

Such cases illustrate a key schism in the realm of journalism ethics between the classic "libertarian" model that dominated until the mid-20th century and the "social-responsibility" model that has grown in influence in the decades since. It also exhibits a fatal flaw in the social-responsibility approach to freedom of expression—that approach gives collective power to the "moral majority" that allows them to effectively silence unpopular minority voices. When news media purge their forums of unpopular, politically incorrect minority views simply to avoid offending their audiences—or, more likely, to avoid dealing with collective backlash—they are surrendering their roles as referees and blatantly choosing sides. Media forums that do not accommodate discriminatory statements because of majority opinion are akin to referees who are biased against the visiting team simply because most fans in the stands favor the home team. In the short run, it may be easy for forum managers to just keep bigoted comments out of the discussion, but that negates the long-run benefits of giving bigots the ability to vent with words, not weapons, and also to expose themselves to broader public scrutiny and condemnation. The libertarian approach is harder, uncomfortable, and tasking, but it is far more effective in the long run of helping cultures purge negative prejudices and advance socially.

CONCLUSION

So many times, the great debates of the day are framed in terms of "both sides," usually with very powerful individuals and organizations marshaling their supporters to take firm, unwavering stands on either end of the issue. News media certainly play the "both sides" game in covering such issues, trying to strike a sense of journalistic balance by making sure the more prominent, vocal representatives of each side gets quoted in news copy. Politicians leverage the "both sides" mythos with incredible crassness in an attempt to divide the electorate just in time for election day.

The reality of course is that there are very few dilemmas facing the world that can be tidily divided into just two "sides." Issues that are big enough to capture the public's attention for extended periods of time are too big and too complex to be so easily described. For instance, the schism many cultures suffer over the issue of abortion is too often framed as "pro choice" or "pro life," yet many people support some moderate compromise in the middle, such as the oft-cited position that abortion procedures should be "legal, safe, and rare." That middle-road rarely gets mentioned in political rhetoric, and as a result it rarely gets mentioned in news copy, either.

Communications scholar Celeste Condit suggested a theoretical explanation for that phenomenon, something she called "hegemonic concordance." Rejecting the simplistic critical theory that hegemony is projected in a top-down manner from the most powerful institutions, Condit argued that cultural hegemony is more often constructed by the most powerful opposing sides.[59] The "both sides" approach to rhetoric privileges the most powerful contestants but largely ignores other, more nuanced positions. Condit argued that "good public policy must incorporate, hence accommodate, all agents, rather than representing a single interest," and noted that "Concord is neither harmonious nor inevitably fair or equitable; it is simply the best that can be done under the circumstances."[60] Concordance is not perfect, just a better approach than the "both sides" dichotomy.

If the news media is going to focus so much on "both sides" in its news coverage, then perhaps it should turn over the work of debating both the fringes and the middle ground to their audiences. Viewed as collectives, the communities constructed via audience feedback forums are decidedly poly-vocal, and the opinions therein nuanced and malleable. What is folly is for media professionals, politicians, or anybody else to believe that the opinions expressed in those forums are permanent and inflexible. Nobody can say for certain that a person who writes a letter to the editor or calls a talkback radio show will not change his or her views in the aftermath; perhaps not changing her overall position on the issue, but certainly modifying it to adjust to new information and insights gained through the exchange. Nor should anyone assume that any comments made in such forums have direct, demonstrable effects on the people who read them—a racist letter, for example, isn't going to convince tolerant readers that they, too, should be racist.

A superficial review of present-day feedback forums might lead one to believe that the participants are only talking past one another, when in fact they are doing the most important task of democratic society. They're communicating with one another.

NOTES

1. *New York Daily News*, "Stars Take on The Ice Bucket Challenge," *New York Daily News*, September 9, 2014. Accessed September 9, 2014, from www.nydai lynews.com/entertainment/stars-ice-bucket-challenge-gallery-1.1909004.
2. Maria Devito, "Video draws 'blood,'" *The Post*, Athens, Ohio, September 4, 2014. Accessed September 9, 2014, from www.thepostathens.com/news/article_191ad8ba-33de-11e4-98fb-0017a43b2370.html.
3. *The Post* editorial board, "Editor's Note," *The Post*, Athens, Ohio, September 8, 2014. Accessed September 9, 2014, from www.thepostathens.com/opinion/article_eaa258ec-36de-11e4-93fe-001a4bcf6878.html
4. The names of students who participated in the forum discussion about the "bucket of blood" incident are being withheld due to privacy concerns amid the volatile nature of the controversy in question.
5. Personal communication, September 9, 2014.

162   *"We, the People . . ."*

6. Personal communication, September 9, 2014.
7. Personal communication, September 9, 2014.
8. Personal communication, September 9, 2014.
9. Personal communication, September 9, 2014.
10. Bill Reader, "Turf Wars? Rhetorical Struggle over 'Prepared' Letters to the Editor," *Journalism* 9, 5 (2008): 606–23; Bill Reader, "Who's Really Writing Those 'Canned' Letters to the Editor?," *Newspaper Research Journal* 26, 2&3 (2005), 43–56.
11. Reader, "Turf Wars? Rhetorical Struggle over 'Prepared' Letters to the Editor."
12. Howard Rheingold, *The Virtual Community: Homesteading on the Electronic Frontier* [electronic book]. Accessed July 24, 2014, from www.rheingold.com/vc/book/intro.html.
13. The Amish and Mennonites are branches of Anabaptist Christianity who do not have a centralized religious structure, but rather follow a more anarchist approach with local autonomy for each settlement. They are most often known for eschewing most modern technology, such as motor vehicles and home electronics, and for being deeply religious people who adhere to strict codes of modesty and nonviolence.
14. M. Clay Carey, "A Plain Circle: Imagining Amish and Mennonite Community Through the National Edition of The Budget," master's thesis, Ohio University (2012). Accessed June 24, 2014, from https://etd.ohiolink.edu/!etd.send_file?accession=ohiou1337286843&disposition=inline.
15. Carey, "A Plain Circle: Imagining Amish and Mennonite Community Through the National Edition of The Budget."
16. Jock Lauterer, *Community Journalism: Relentlessly Local* (Chapel Hill, N.C.: University of North Carolina Press, 2006), 151.
17. Lauterer, *Community Journalism: Relentlessly Local*, 150.
18. Bill Reader and Kevin Moist, "Letters as Indicators of Community Values: Two Case Studies of Alternative Magazines," *Journalism & Mass Communication Quarterly* 85, 4 (2008), 823–40; Carey, "A Plain Circle: Imagining Amish and Mennonite Community Through the National Edition of The Budget."
19. Bill Reader, "Air Mail: NPR Sees 'Community' in Letters from Listeners," *Journal of Broadcasting & Electronic Media* 51, 4 (2007), 651–69.
20. Karin Wahl-Jorgensen, *Journalists and the Public: Newsroom Culture, Letters to the Editor, and Democracy* (Cresskill, N.J.: Hampton Press, 2007), 116–17.
21. Ta-Nehisis Coates, "How to Create an Engaging Comments Section," On the Media [radio interview transcript], May 31, 2013. Accessed July 24, 2014, from www.onthemedia.org/story/296318-how-create-engaging-comments-section/transcript/.
22. Bob Garfield, "How to Create an Engaging Comments Section," On the Media [radio interview transcript], May 31, 2013. Accessed July 24, 2014, from www.onthemedia.org/story/296318-how-create-engaging-comments-section/transcript/
23. Coates, "How to Create an Engaging Comments Section."
24. Matt Zoller Seitz, "Why I Like Vicious, Anonymous Online Comments," Salon.com, August 3, 2010. Accessed July 24, 2014, from www.salon.com/2010/08/03/in_defense_of_anonymous_commenting/.
25. Bill Reader, "Free Press vs. Free Speech? The Rhetoric of 'Civility' in Regard to Anonymous Online Comments," *Journalism & Mass Communication Quarterly* 89, 3 (2012), 495–513.
26. Anonymous untitled comment, Buffalonews.com, July 24, 2010, 9:18 a.m. Accessed July 1, 2010, from www.buffalonews.com/2010/06/20/1088283/seeking-a-return-to-civility-in.html#comment.

27. Anonymous untitled comment, Buffalonews.com, July 24, 2010, 9:18 a.m. Accessed July 1, 2010, from www.buffalonews.com/2010/06/20/1088283/seeking-a-return-to-civility-in.html#comment.
28. Anonymous untitled comment, Buffalonews.com, July 24, 2010, 9:18 a.m. Accessed July 1, 2010, from www.buffalonews.com/2010/06/20/1088283/seeking-a-return-to-civility-in.html#comment.
29. Bill Reader, "Free Press vs. Free Speech?"
30. Whitney Phillips, "Meet The Trolls," *Index on Censorship* 40, 68 (2011), 68–76: 71.
31. Scott Wright and John Street, "Democracy, Deliberation and Design: The Case of Online Discussion Forums," *New Media & Society* 9, 5 (2007), 849–69; Muneo Kaigo and Isao Watanabe, "Ethos in Chaos? Reaction to Video Files Depicting Socially Harmful Images in the Channel 2 Japanese Internet Forum," *Journal of Computer-Mediated Communication* 12, 4 (2007): 1248–68; Martin Tanis, "Health-Related On-Line Forums: What's the Big Attraction?," *Journal of Health Communication* 13, 7 (2008), 698–714; Eliza Tanner, "Chilean Conversations: Internet Forum Participants Debate Augusto Pinochet's Detention," *Journal of Communication* 51, 2 (2001), 383–403.
32. Clifford G. Cumber, "Ask the Editor: Campaign Letter Avalanche," *The Frederick News-Post*, Frederick, Md., July 5, 2014. Accessed July 24, 2014, from www.fredericknewspost.com/news/politics_and_government/governmental_and_political_topics/elections/ask-the-editor-campaign-letter-avalanche/article_a5143daf-2346–5abc-8aad-379e5383c637.html.
33. Cumber, "Ask the Editor: Campaign Letter Avalanche."
34. Jim Pumarlo, *Votes and Quotes: A Guide to Outstanding Election Campaign Coverage* (Oak Park, Ill.: Marion Street Press, 2007), 57.
35. Jim Romenesko, "Editor: Why We're Charging for Endorsement Letters," JimRomenesko.com, May 7, 2012. Accessed July 24, 2014, from http://jimromenesko.com/2012/05/07/editor-why-were-charging-for-endorsement-letters/.
36. Randall Rasmussen, "Editorial: Charge for Election Letters," *Rapid City Journal*, Rapid City, S.Dak., September 25, 2012. Accessed July 24, 2014, from http://rapidcityjournal.com/news/opinion/editorial-charge-for-election-letters/article_db5c2ada-74f4–5097-a44b-9d9d3e2fab21.html.
37. Comments posted to Rasmussen, "Editorial: Charge for Election Letters."
38. Pumarlo, *Votes and Quotes: A Guide to Outstanding Election Campaign Coverage*, 44.
39. Pumarlo, *Votes and Quotes: A Guide to Outstanding Election Campaign Coverage*, 44.
40. NORML staff, "How to Mount and Effective Letter Writing Campaign," norml.org, undated. Accessed July 24, 2014, from http://norml.org/join-norml/item/how-to-mount-an-effective-letter-writing-campaign.
41. Winning Progressive staff, "Send a Letter to the Editor," winningprogressive.org, undated. Accessed July 24, 2014, from www.winningprogressive.org/letters-to-the-editor-campaign
42. Reader, "Who's Really Writing Those 'Canned' Letters to the Editor?"
43. Mark Glaser, "Letters Editors Flummoxed Over Weed-like 'Astroturf' Growth," Online Journalism Review [website], August 24, 2004. Accessed July 24, 2014, from http://carapace.weblogs.us/archives/017332.html.
44. Margriet Costveen, "I Ghost-Wrote Letters to the Editor for the McCain Campaign," Salon.com, September 24, 2008. Accessed July 24, 2014, from www.salon.com/2008/09/24/mccain_letters/.
45. Democratic Congressional Campaign Committee, "Health Care Letters-to-the-Editor," www.dccc.org, undated. Accessed June 24, 2014, from www.dccc.org/page/speakout/healthcare.

46. PublishaLetter.com, "What is PublishaLetter.com," Publishaletter.com [website]. Accessed July 24, 2014, from www.publishaletter.com/what_is_publishaletter.jsp.
47. Personal communication, September 9, 2014.
48. Personal communication, September 9, 2014.
49. N.H. Whitlock, "Editor Southwestern" [letter to the editor], *Southwestern Christian Advocate*, New Orleans, La., April 15, 1897, 7.
50. Robert S. La Brant, "Whose Rights?" [letter to the editor], *Chicago Tribune*, August 23, 1963, A14.
51. Steve Smith, "Rep. Matt Cartwright Called a 'Hypocrite' on Sherman Hills Situation," *The Times Leader*, Wilkes-Barre, Pa., May 31, 2014. Accessed July 24, 2014, from http://timesleader.com/news/letters/1433023/Rep.-Cartwright-hypocritical-on-diversity.
52. Paula Chaiken, 'Racist Garbage' Didn't Belong Among The Times Leader's Letters to the Editor" [letter to the editor], *The Times Leader*, Wilkes-Barre, Pa., June 7, 2014. Accessed July 24, 2014, from http://timesleader.com/news/letters/1446633/Hateful-letter-didnt-belong-in-newspaper.
53. Richard Prince, "Publishing Racist Letters," Maynard Institute [website], Oakland, Calif., May 26, 2005. Accessed July 24, 2014, from http://mije.org/richardprince/publishing-racist-letters.
54. Society of Professional Ethics, "SPJ Code of Ethics," SPJ.org, September 6, 2014. Accessed September 9, 2014, from www.spj.org/ethicscode.asp.
55. Prince, "Publishing Racist Letters."
56. Travis Lupick, "Letters Titled 'Educate First Nations to Be Modern Citizens' Sparks Debate on Racism," straight.com, March 28, 2013. Accessed July 24, 2014, from www.straight.com/blogra/366901/letter-titled-educate-first-nations-be-modern-citizens-sparks-debate-racism.
57. Ginny Whitehouse, "Op-ed: How the Nanaimo Daily News Should Have Dealt With the Racist Letter to the Editor," The Canadian Journalism Project [website], April 4, 2013. Accessed July 24, 2014, from http://j-source.ca/article/op-ed-how-nanaimo-daily-news-should-have-dealt-racist-letter-editor.
58. Lupick, "Letters Titled 'Educate First Nations to Be Modern Citizens' Sparks Debate on Racism."
59. Celeste Condit, "Hegemony in a Mass-Mediated Society: Concordance About Reproductive Technologies," *Critical Studies in Mass Communication* 11, 3 (1994), 205–30.
60. Condit, "Hegemony in a Mass-Mediated Society," 210.

9 Conclusion
Gatekeeping in an Age without Fences

The partisan press era often is viewed as a crucible of innovation and experimentation, out of which emerged the professionalized industry of journalism. Judging the news publications of that era against 21st-century standards can lead to the unfair perception that the "better" journalism practices of today replaced the "worse" journalism of that earlier period. With regard to the handling of audience submissions, I disagree—a modern reflection upon audience feedback of previous centuries does more to illustrate not what has been gained, but rather what has been lost.

The early 21st century is, in many ways, a new Age of Enlightenment. It is a period of great social upheaval, popular revolt and revolution, and expanding public discourse, all carried on a relatively new communication technology. The 18th-century Age of Enlightenment had the printing press and the frontier of the New World; the 21st century has the Internet and the frontiers of the Information Age. Zeal for individualism and personal rights, disdain for entrenched economic and cultural institutions, dissatisfaction with government, fierce partisanship, and the poly-vocal nature of public discourse are all things that the two time periods have in common. Some might reject the analogy under false assumptions that the 18th-century Age of Enlightenment was dominated by educated, polite discourse, when in fact the discourse in salons and coffee houses and debating societies of the era could be just as rancorous and divisive, perhaps more so, than the discourse of the current age. A forum thread on Salon.com might get tetchy and vitriolic, for example, but it is highly unlikely to devolve into fisticuffs or pistols at ten paces; as disconcerting as the 21st-century "culture wars" can be to those desiring peace and harmony, the culture wars are relatively free of violence compared to the actual wars in nations without freedom of speech, and freedom of the press.

One notable aspect of the 18th-century Age of Enlightenment was the popular rejection of massive, entrenched institutions—in the West, those included the monarchy, the centralized church, and the mercantile economic system. Today, the targets of popular disdain are also massive and entrenched: professional political parties, powerful special-interest organizations, and large multinational corporations. That list also includes, quite often, "the media." A 2011 study by The Pew Research Center found that large majorities of U.S. residents viewed the news media as inaccurate (66 percent), biased (77 percent), and in the pockets of powerful organizations and people (80 percent).[1] That study found the press was trusted a bit more than government agencies and corporations, but it showed a relatively steady decline in public trust toward the news media over a period of nearly 30 years. That 30 years, perhaps not coincidentally, also saw increased gatekeeping in the media with regard to audience feedback—less space for feedback, more restrictions on submissions, reduced accommodation of perceived "incivility" and increased preference for submissions that met with journalists' professional standards of quality. An interesting comparison can be made from the Pew survey findings—57 percent of respondents agreed that the news media in 2011 was "highly professional," but only 26 percent agreed that news media "care about the people they report on."[2] The news media was seen as highly professional, and largely out of touch.

On balance, the 21st-century news media provide more channels for audience feedback than in any time in history, particularly in the form of online discussion forums on their websites and social-media platforms. Some have invested considerably in developing their commenting systems to take full advantage of computer-mediated communication. But much of the effort has been very clearly focused on automation and commodification, the goal of which is primarily to minimize personnel costs and maximize profits. High-traffic comment forums increase page views and advertising revenue for media companies; it is less certain how much those forums influence editorial decisions, help journalists keep their fingers on the pulse of public sentiment, or otherwise keep them in touch with the communities and individuals they ostensibly serve.

Adapting to the 21st-century realities of audience feedback is clearly one of those serious challenges, and in that regard, the mainstream news media seems to be retreating, not advancing.

The evidence of retreat is plentiful:

- *The New York Times* in 2007 reduced, not increased, the amount of space it provides for printed letters to the editor, opting instead to give more of its prime space to intellectual elites via guest columns and op-eds.[3] The space for printed LTEs was cut by about a third; the newspaper's concession was to expand the number of letters it published in the much less expensive (and, as such, less prestigious) online spaces.
- NPR in 2013 cancelled its long-running, popular talkback program, "Talk of the Nation," and replaced it with another scripted, edited news program ("Here and Now") that was not much different from its "Morning Edition" and "All Things Considered" programs.[4] At the time of its cancellation, "Talk of the Nation" was considered the top-ranked call-in show on U.S. public radio, but the network's content chief argued that

"there's been a proliferation of other call-in talk shows"—as if that was a problem, rather than a strength.[5]

- *Popular Science* in 2013 shut off its online comments completely. "A politically motivated, decades-long war on expertise has eroded the popular consensus on a wide variety of scientifically validated topics," the magazine's online director, Suzanne LaBarre, wrote in a column titled, "Why We're Shutting Off Our Comments."[6] She continued: "Scientific certainty is just another thing for two people to 'debate' on television. And because comments sections tend to be a grotesque reflection of the media culture surrounding them, the cynical work of undermining bedrock scientific doctrine is now being done beneath our own stories, within a website devoted to championing science."

The industry is moving away from allowing anonymous comments online. That particular retrenchment of access has snowballed since 2010, driven largely by anecdotal and unsubstantiated claims that anonymous online forums had "scared off" some readers. More accurately, the tone of unregulated discourse often offended the sensibilities of the control-obsessed media elites, many of them still pining for the "good old days" of 20th-century-style gatekeeping. The reporting on the trend has been overwhelmingly one-sided—for example, media watcher Rem Rieder railed against anonymity when he was editor of *American Journalism Review*,[7] and again three years later when he was media critic for *USAToday*. [8] In both columns, Rieder provided no empirical evidence—none—to support allegations that there was a groundswell of popular support for such bans. Empirical research actually suggests that the reading public is far more tolerant of vitriol and so-called "trolling" in forums than are professional journalists.[9] One study found that the more comments a news site receives, the more negativity journalists have toward such forums, while the more journalists got involved in moderating such forums, the better participants felt about the forums.[10]

It has been suggested by some that my own views—advocating for more anonymity and "uncivil" expression in news forums, not less—also are dismissive of evidence. Actually, those views are the product of a long, focused changing of the mind. I once was just as dogmatic as Rieder and others with regard to anonymous forums, and felt back then that they were woefully, inherently unethical. It was not a short and easy path for me to give up those very strong, almost visceral beliefs against anonymity and in favor of more editorial control. Those beliefs also guided my time as an opinion-page editor who was directly responsible for handling letters to the editor—although I still am proud of the openness of the forum I provided, in retrospect I could have been much more accommodating and forward thinking. Now, after having spent more than 15 years studying the historical, ethical, and practical dimensions of audience feedback to the media, along with multiple essays and presentations and producing more than a dozen research articles (and having read several dozen more studies by other scholars), I had no choice but to change my mind. Historical fact, empirical research, and critical analysis have all led me to conclude that professional journalism is on the wrong path with regard to forum management. It would have been intellectually dishonest to conclude otherwise.

The long, vibrant, and beneficial tradition of audience feedback in the media is in serious jeopardy of losing ground to the bubbles of self-reinforcement found in social media and topic-specific online forums. What the news-media forums offer that those other forums do not is the intermixing of views from a variety of public sectors. That public dialogue may not be accurately reflective of broader public opinion, but it is far closer to giving such a reflection that the discussions among "friends" in a relatively closed loop on Facebook or a carefully edited "dinner party" on the editorial page. Since the early to mid-20th century, the news media have collectively, if unwittingly, constructed forums that are welcoming only to the educated middle class. Journalists also have increasingly focused only on publishing opinions about themselves and their work, rather than letting the public drive the conversation.

That trend has been much to the detriment of the journalism profession, although few in the profession seem willing or able to see the harm such gentrification has done. As the saying goes, the path to hell is paved with good intentions, and the good intentions of professional journalists to control audience feedback in a manner that satisfies their personal and professional tastes is backfiring. It has driven more and more people away from the cold, detached mainstream media and into the warm embrace of social networking. The news outlets that are "keeping it real" in regard to audience feedback—allowing broad discourse, and investing staff resources and time in moderating and engaging with audiences—are the ones who will not lose audience participation (and, along with it, audience loyalty and trust) as the new Age of Enlightenment continues to unfold. It's the old-school myopia of 20th-century journalism that imperils legacy media more than anything else—the fallacious dogma that somehow editorial control of public discourse is somehow ethically correct, that vitriol is somehow un-democratic, and that the right to speak anonymously is inherently bad.

To adapt to the new era of audience participation, news media have to reject the dogma of late-20th-century gatekeeping and the trendy, early 21st-century dogma of political correctness. Forward-thinking journalists and media executives must re-think the myths upon which such dogma was built. There are three such myths. First, the myth that controlled and regulated feedback forums are "virtual village squares." Second, the myth that more efforts at control and regulation will somehow "restore civility" where no such civility really existed in the past. And, third, the myth that "banning anonymity" is somehow a step forward rather than a very serious and detrimental step backward in encouraging public participation in social discourse.

THE MYTH OF 'THE VIRTUAL VILLAGE SQUARE'

In 1972, *The New York Times* letters editor Kalman Seigel extolled upon the great tradition of audience feedback to his storied newspaper:

> "The letter to the editor is more than idle epistolary chatter. It is the reader's lance as he tilts with City Hall. It is his passport to a community of interest with his fellow man, or an arena of controversy in which he can test his thinking with those who differ. It is his town meeting in print, his approach to a purer form of participatory democracy."[11]

Siegel was not the first nor the last to evoke the mythos of audience feedback serving as a "town meeting" or a "virtual village square," nor to wax poetic and whimsical about the most idealized version of the tradition. Former *Buffalo News* editor Margaret Sullivan used the "village square" metaphor in describing her ideals for that newspaper's online forums in 2010: "The aim of publishing reader comments, all along, has been to have a free-flowing discussion of stimulating and worthwhile ideas—something of a virtual village square."[12] The metaphor has been used in reference to alternative media outlets as well, sometimes using the nomenclature directly: For example, the citizen-journalism site *Nigerian Village Square* tried to approximate Nigerian culture in which "people from all corners meet at the Village Square after a hard day's work to sip unadulterated palm-wine, share news, gossip, jokes, music, dance, events and opinions. Visitors to the square are warmly welcomed and can get directions, information and clarify misconceptions."[13]

Elsewhere in the introduction to his collection of LTEs to the *Times*, Siegel acknowledged that submissions to his forum also included obscenities, letters from "cranks," and that his forum was "a target for propagandists and special pleaders, for trial balloons from government officials and for unorthodox ideas from everyone who sees himself as the possessor of the world's residual wisdom."[14] The derision with which Siegel held such submissions made it clear that he considered them to be unsuitable for publication. Yet they still deserved to be read and considered, he argued, even if they were not published. Such was the norm of the time—editors read every letter, but only shared a relative few with the broader public.

At the same time, a common mantra of late-20th-century journalism was that news media existed primarily to just "report the facts" in a manner that was as fair and balanced as humanly possible, such that—as the professional meme often goes—"the readers can make up their own minds." Not so with audience feedback; only editors got to see the raw, unfiltered nature of true public discourse, including comments that could be argued to be rude, crude, offensive, racist/sexist/homophobic, scary, anti-social, etc. The editors made up the public's mind for it about what was suitable for publication in the "public forums," and in the process greatly removed the narrative of their forums from reality.

Go to a true town meeting, especially one during which a local controversy is to be discussed, and despite the trappings of decorum, one will still see and hear statements that could be considered rude, crude, and offensive. That happens at the highest levels of government as well. Former Australian Prime Minister Julia Gillard's celebrated "Misogyny Speech" in 2012 is a very high-profile example, as she was responding to a pattern of allegedly sexist public statements and actions by the opposition leader of the time, Tony Abbott (who was elected prime minister about a year later).[15] Similar claims of racism, sexism, and anti-social rhetoric also is not uncommon in the halls of the British Parliament, the U.S. Congress, or other national legislatures, not to mention the many state and provincial legislatures and, indeed, actual town meetings of local governments around the globe.

The myth of the "virtual village square" is built upon an elitist ideal that society should aspire toward intellectual and cultural sophistication. Such an ideal is untenable and unreasonable for truly democratic societies. Here it might be useful to think less about the comfortable debates that people have with their friends and colleagues, and think more about what it would be like to debate the issues of the day with the people who haul their trash, who operate their sewers, who wait on them in restaurants, and who clean up their hotel rooms while they are on vacation. They might also think about the customer-service employees to whom they might rudely complain or arrogantly demand this-or-that preferential treatment, the cab drivers they might not tip because traffic was too heavy, or the custodians in their offices who they might not even acknowledge, day in and day out. The educated middle-class lifestyle would not be possible without the dutiful, and at times demeaned and disrespected, efforts of the working class. Anybody who has ever worked in the service sector knows that members of the educated middle-class can be rude, unreasonable, hostile, racist/sexist/whateverist, and generally anti-social as well. And being treated that way can lead to justifiable anger, frustration, hostility, and the like from those who wait on and clean up after the privileged few.

A true "virtual village square" would reflect society as it is, not as intellectual elites might desire it to be. Racism is a reality; an ugly reality, but a reality nonetheless. So is sexism. So is insensitivity toward the aggrieved, unforgiving vitriol toward the privileged, intellectual snobbery, and class-based resentments. Some might argue that those who want to express coarse views or use impolite language can easily find other channels online, which is certainly true, but that argument is shallow and misses the larger point—if news media truly want their feedback forums to be virtual village squares, they should be far more accommodating of views and language that are found in the village squares and town halls of the real world, much of it angry and impolite.

THE MYTH OF 'RESTORING CIVILITY'

Another enduring myth of audience feedback is that, in the past, it was far more "civil" than in modern times. That argument also does not hold up to historic evidence or the realities of modern society. Certainly, the myth evaporates when one considers the fiery rhetoric in which "freedom of the press" was forged and written into law.

The highly selective, heavily edited, and largely sanitized excerpts now found in letters-to-the-editor sections of mainstream news organizations do not have the vibrant egalitarianism of their Enlightenment-era predecessors. Modern letters forums are, for the most part, reserved for polite opinions regarding current events, and many of the larger publications will only publish responses to articles published in their pages previously (thus, modern LTEs also can be viewed as de facto promotions for the publications themselves; that is especially true in modern magazines). What few submissions do get through editors' various filters are not just heavily edited for length and style, but also are confined into distinct spaces, often no more than a fraction of one printed page . A front-page letter to the editor is unheard of today, whereas they were quite common in the 18th century, from James Franklin's *New England Courant* in the 1720s to the *Madras Courier* of the 1790s. News and the discussion of the news were intermixed back then; today, they are strictly segregated. The rhetoric of the Enlightenment could be bombastic, insinuating, hostile, and rude; in the 2010s, comments that are strident and in bad taste are rejected from LTE forums, and that rejection also robs the forums of their ability to accurately reflect the passion and robust disagreements of an otherwise nonviolent public.

That is not the case in all media forums, of course. In the 1980s and 1990s, a few newspapers experimented with anonymous call-in forums, through which readers could leave anonymous voicemails that would later be transcribed and printed verbatim in the newspapers.[16] Some of those forums are still in use; *The Athens News* of Athens, Ohio, launched its own in 2012, and the feature immediately became quite popular—"The Athens VOICE" on August 11, 2014, had nine submissions covering a variety of local, national, and international topics, as well as six online comments in response. Likewise, talkback radio provides a ready forum for opinions from the public that often offends the sensibilities of the educated middle-class. That such forums can, and sometime do, include statements that are undeniably racist, sexist, or otherwise "-ist" often gives the educated elite the examples they need to argue against such forums, but too often those examples are extreme and uncommon. Relying on gut-reactions to extreme examples, critics of anonymous print, online, and broadcast forums too often ignore that the forums also include multiple expressions of opinion that are polite, reasoned, informed, and sincere. They just come from people who, for whatever reason, are not comfortable writing more traditional, signed letters to the editor.

Much of the criticism toward unfettered online forums comes from socio-political elites—academics, high-ranking journalists, policy wonks, special-interest advocates, career politicians, and business executives. Those groups are, not surprisingly, the most frequent targets of anonymous attacks and vitriol via those forums. Evidence suggests that such elitism is not shared by the broader public, who read and participate in those forums.[17]

Media professionals and scholars who are "seeking a return to civility in online comments"[18] seem to pine for a fantasyland dreamed up in an ivory tower, and they wax nostalgic for a "civility" that never existed in reality.

THE MYTH OF AUTHORSHIP

Another popular myth in effete journalism circles is the notion that perceived "incivility" in audience feedback is caused by anonymity. Worse, many have concocted a myth that somehow democracy is built upon the principles of authorship, most often phrased as, "if you don't have the guts to sign your name, you don't deserve to be heard." That was certainly the mantra of the totalitarian governments who have tried to suppress freedom of expression for centuries through the modern era, but the free-speech advocates who fought against such tyranny from the 17th century onward often wrote under pseudonyms (as evidenced in Chapter 3), including many high-ranking elected officials and, in the U.S., several signatories to the Declaration of Independence.

It might be a stretch to argue causation between the increased elitism of the professional news media over the past decades and the decline in public support of those media over the same time, but the correlational data is hard to ignore. Online discussion forums have broad popularity despite—and perhaps because of—the rancorous diversity of comments found in those anonymous forums.[19] Most modern editors become incensed at the very suggestion of publishing anonymous letters to the editor with unwavering zeal,[20] which demonstrates a fundamental and self-defeating blind spot in professional journalism.

The complex origins of "must-sign" policies were discussed in Chapter 4, but to summarize, opinion editors in the mid-20th century sought to professionalize their forums to match the professionalization of journalism itself, and the general consensus was that requiring letter-writers to sign their names would improve the quality of submissions, thus making the editing process easier and more pleasant. That is, it was a very practical consideration, tinged a bit with Red Scare paranoia (requiring names was one way to deter "commies" from expressing their opinions in Western media, it was thought). In the decades since, the journalism community has constructed a mythical philosophy around the practice, elevating it from its practical and political origins to being (incorrectly) identified as a principle of democratic philosophy. (One might just as well argue that citizens should have to sign their ballots on election day so they can be held accountable for their votes.) Over time, most journalists have come to hold strong hostility toward anonymous writers and anonymity itself, particularly with regard to online discussion forums in the early 21st century.[21] Journalists who believe strongly in "must-sign" policies also tend to be dismissive (sometimes hostile) toward research that suggests those policies have a chilling effect on broader participation.[22]

Some editors will withhold the names of writers, but only if the writer has a good reason. Melissa Hale-Spencer, a staunch proponent of "must-sign" policies, said she will consider withholding the name of a letter writer to *The Altamont Enterprise*, her newspaper in upstate New York. But it would have to be for good reason—an example she gave is of a school bus driver writing a critical letter about the school district's budget priorities. "That's very different from anonymous letters," she said. "The editor knows who the writer is."[23] John M. Derby does the same at his five weekly newspapers in Merced and Stanislaus counties in central California. "I will not print the name of the writer if I feel his or her job is at stake or his safety is at stake," Derby wrote in an email in 2013.[24] "This comes up most often when a person works for a public agency or even a place of higher learning. I do not do it often, and I am the one who makes that decision along with my managing editor. To give you an idea of how often, I do not recall withholding the name of a letter signer in the past year, and I publish five weekly community newspapers."

Although few editors will mention any drawbacks to "must-sign" policies, nearly all agree that the policies do create additional work. If writers' names are to be published with comments, then the editors must ensure that the names belong to the writers, especially to ensure that the names do not belong to somebody else. Standard practice is for publications to require that writers include not only their names, but also their home addresses and telephone numbers, and that information in turn is used by editors to contact the writers to verify authorship. Before widespread adoption of the Internet in newsrooms, editors had few tools to triangulate such information—they would call the number on the letter, ask the person who answered if she was the author of the letter, and hope that they hadn't just been duped. Modern search engines, people-search databases, and other online search tools give editors the ability to independently correlate names with addresses and phone numbers. It is still possible, though, for mischievous writers to trick editors into publishing somebody else's name with a letter.

Derby has been sued for printing the wrong name with a letter. "Twice in my career I have been sued because of publishing letters to the editor," Derby recalled in an email.[25] "They were signed, but the first one had a false signature and the second one was a former employee of the person the letter to the editor was about. . . . While neither suit went the full course, the first one was very costly because I had very little money and had to pay for an attorney to defend the paper. I have become a whole lot more careful since." An even more dramatic case of "fake names" was experienced by Andrew Schotz, assistant manger of *The Gazette* in Gaithersburg, Maryland, when he was a reporter for a weekly newspaper in upstate New York. "I was covering an internal squabble within the police department that had become public. At some point, we got a fake letter to the editor, written by someone attacking one particular faction. We ran the letter," Schotz wrote in an email.[26] "It turns out the name and (I think) address were made up. We soon realized that other questionable letters (different names, different handwriting, different attacks, but aligned with the original fake letter's camp) had come in. I think some had made it to print by that time, too." Schotz later worked for a daily newspaper in Maryland that published a "fake-name" letter: "It was signed by someone (a real person), but that person hadn't written the letter. We ran a correction (that might have included a brief apology, too)." Schotz, who is an adamant proponent of "must-sign" policies, said that editors should never cut corners when it comes to verifying authorship.

Journalism's obsession with authorship and dogmatic opposition to anonymity has led to a catch-22 for such highly principled, well-intended, and experienced news workers. It is a phenomenon perhaps best termed "the name game." "Must-sign" editors invest considerable time in verifying the authenticity of the names that are provided as required, time taken away from editing and organizing submissions by content. The accommodation of anonymous submissions would negate the need for any such procedure, allowing editors to make selections based solely on the content of the opinions (including rejection of opinions they deem unsuitable for their forums, whether signed or not). The process has been normalized into newsroom routines since the 1960s, at least, and with it a pseudo-ethical sense of obligation toward requiring and verifying authorship of even the most mundane, harmless submissions.

Consider a case from April 2013. Erika Neldner of *The Cherokee Ledger-News* in Woodstock, Georgia, was verifying the names on letters to the editor in what is usually a straightforward process, but one letter took her several hours to verify. The content of the letter was essentially perfect—it was short, civil in tone, about a newsworthy topic, and essentially free of grammatical errors. The problem was solely related to authorship, and demonstrates the extent to which many editors will go to restrict "outsider" access to their forums.

Here is a rundown, in Neldner's own words,[27] of the efforts she put into verifying authorship of that one letter:

> "When I called to verify the letter, something told me to ask a few questions (more than normal) about the letter. The 'letter-writer' said he

was in a meeting and he would have to call me back. In the meantime, I searched his phone number on the Internet, which yielded an apology letter from an editor in Maryland last year. It said they had been 'hoodwinked.' So, I searched the e-mail address, and it came back to two letters to the editor published in a newspaper in Kingston, N.Y., in April and August of 2011. The names associated with the e-mail address or phone number in other newspapers were different from the name signed to the letter we received this week.

Intrigued, we went a step further and checked for the letter-writer's name in standard 411.com (and similar sites) searches, yielding nothing . . . and took a look at the property tax records in the county, searching for the address. We found that the condominium number provided did not exist.

Lastly, we searched one line of the letter in Google and found the exact letter had been published in numerous newspapers across the country in the last couple of days.

Now, the letter could be fraudulently written or it could be a form letter from a large organization trying to get a message across. The guy called back and left me a message from a 661 area code (his return number was a 312 area code—neither in our local area). . . . Obviously, we are not running the letter—but it did make for a very interesting Friday afternoon!"[28]

Neldner's extra effort was uniformly praised by her colleagues, of course, and even a pro-anonymity critic such as me has to give credit where credit it due—Neldner bent over backwards to enforce her newspaper's must-sign policy, and that suggests she might be just as diligent in upholding the other professional tenets to which she and the vast majority of journalists adhere. She certainly didn't do anything that could be considered "wrong" in terms of professional ethics or professional practice. But in the big scheme of things, it seems like a very large investment of time and effort to address a very small issue.

The profession's obsession with authorship has led to a pronounced blind spot among journalists toward the nature of writing. The distinction between writers and authors was discussed in the introduction of this book, but to rehash, the difference is basically that writing is the practice of expression for expression's sake, whereas authorship is the creation of works that are intended to bring fame and/or financial reward to the author. Professional journalism is a form of authorship—reporters write for paychecks and bylines and professional recognition; editors work with reporters to attract audiences and, by extension, advertisers or sponsors. It's all about the prestige and the paychecks, and that in itself is not ethically wrong. But when the authors create forums for their readers to respond, and then invite that response, they should not look down their noses at what comes in. A garbage-truck driver may be very good at his job, and a cook at the local high school may be very good at her job, and a tax accountant at hers, and a dentist at hers, but that doesn't mean any of them are necessarily gifted writers, trained in the skills of research or the art of persuasive argument. The same could be said of a high-school student, a retired war veteran, an engineering professor, and so forth. Why should their lack of writing talents exclude them from being able to join the public dialogue? There is a serious disconnect between the purpose behind feedback forums and the practices of managing them when the status of "authorship" is considered far more important than the content of a submission.

It is not uncommon for editors to publish an inflammatory, dubiously sourced letter bearing a "real name" while, the very same day, reject an excellent and poignant submission simply because the writer does not want her name to be published in the newspaper. Very few editors would even consider running a "name withheld" letter, and even those who do often require that the writer talk to the editor to explain why the request is being made, with the editor assuming the role of arbiter as to whether the writer has a "good reason" to wish to remain anonymous, and not the writer herself.

CONCLUSION: AUDIENCE FEEDBACK
FOR THE NEW ENLIGHTENMENT

As most news professionals well know, it's quite easy to criticize the performance of journalists, but it is something else entirely to suggest reasonable approaches to improvement. Journalists also are justifiably reluctant to take advice from academics who have never done the work of handling audience feedback and/or who have never been the targets of the sometimes ugly, unfair, and downright cruel rhetoric of 21st-century feedback forums.

This entire book, and especially this concluding chapter, was written with all of that in mind. I was an opinion-page editor myself, and during my time in that role I handled many hundreds, if not thousands, of letters to the editor, several of them testing the limits of my tolerance for fringe ideas and ugly rhetoric. As a public scholar with often controversial opinions, I also have been subjected to the hostility and personal attacks sometimes found in anonymous feedback forums (ironically, some of that hostility has come from journalists and journalism scholars writing anonymously). And although much of what precedes this section may seem highly critical of the evolution of journalism norms and practices regarding audience feedback, it should be said very clearly that I have the utmost respect and admiration for any journalist who spends time seriously thinking about these issues, especially for the journalists who are named herein. Reasonable people can disagree, and although I may disagree with many of the principles most journalists currently apply to audience feedback, I deeply respect their commitment to high standards and to their clear desire to be ethical in their work.

That said, my biggest worry about the immediate future of audience feedback is that it is being bifurcated into two unsustainable extremes. On the one hand is the anything-goes free-for-all of un-moderated, unmanaged online forums, toward which journalists have so much disdain that they basically ignore them until serious problems pop up. On the other are the highly controlled forums that are micromanaged to such a degree that they lose all credibility as virtual village squares. The middle ground is found in those few publications that provide considerable breadth in terms of forum participation, that have staff members actively engaged in the conversation, and that act quickly and decisively to delete comments that are very clearly out of line.

It might be too much to ask media to overthrow decades of "must-sign" precedent, but a softening toward "name withheld" letters may be a reasonable compromise toward the sustainable middle, as demonstrated by some of the editors mentioned earlier. It is a practice justified by many centuries of good results and multiple positive examples from modern times. There are still many editors who will accommodate a "name withheld" request, but only if the editor feels there is a good reason; by giving all writers that option, editors would automatically be signaling they are more willing to accommodate disenfranchised voices, but without surrendering entirely the control over which submissions get published (the basis for selection being the substance of the content, not the act of authorship). At minimum, a more liberal approach to "name withheld" commentary would signal that the editors are willing to give writers the benefit of the doubt as to what they, the writers, believe to be good reason to remain anonymous.

Likewise, editors who want their forums to be accurate reflections of their communities, warts and all, maybe should be less strident in rejecting or deleting submissions that are "offensive" with regard to race, gender, age, or other characteristics. Political correctness is anathema to free expression, especially when the standards for what is considered "correct" is ever changing and increasingly restrictive. The benefit of publishing such comments is to keep conversations about racism, sexism, ageism, and so forth in the public dialogue. Only by allowing an "-ism" to rear its ugly head can society remain on guard against letting such monstrous beliefs reverse social progress.

There are any number of other creative approaches editors could take to make their forums more reflective of society as it is. A radical approach might be to use a lottery system to select each edition's letters—throw all acceptable letters in a pool and randomly select those to be published. Arguably, that would be the most scientific and unbiased approach, but it would certainly increase the likelihood of an "ugly" letter getting published. Another approach might be called the "pillory" approach, through which editors highlight one particularly outrageous opinion each week, with commentary, such as "The Most Racist Letter of the Week," boxed and with an editorial rejoinder explaining why the letter stands as an example of the depths of social dysfunction—that would not only make sure the public is aware of such persistent prejudice, but it also would subject those opinions to the public shaming that most certainly would ensue. The key is for editors to start looking for more ways to say "yes" to submissions that would spark dialogue, and start cutting back on all the ways they say "no" to controversial statements.

Finally, on the issue of "civility," it might be best for modern media professionals to look within their own ranks for improvement rather than to wag fingers and chastise the impolite public sphere. Much of the "uncivil" rhetoric journalists are loath to tolerate in feedback forums is little more than amateurish mimicry of what is said or written by pundits, politicians, talk-show hosts, columnists, and other media performers. The snarky smugness of media professionals on the arrogant left will undeniably be met by strident, "tough" indignation from the insensitive right, and vice versa. Open disrespect toward one another by campaigning politicians, trash-talking by entertainment celebrities and professional athletes, and the blasé disregard for honesty from much of the corporate world, is unlikely to inspire polite and principled discourse from the masses. That's not to say that the news media has created the rancorous lack of decorum found today in the halls of government, commerce, and culture, nor that it should scale back coverage of the conflicts and controversies that increasingly define those aspects of society. But maybe the news professionals of the 21st century should get over themselves, give the public a break, and let people who want to participate in feedback forums boldly and frankly, and once again, speak their minds.

NOTES

1. Pew Research Center for the People & The Press, "Press Widely Criticized, But Trusted More than Other Information Sources: Views of the News Media, 1985–2011," Pew Research Center for the People & The Press [website], Washington, D.C., September 22, 2011. Accessed August 13, 2014, from www.people-press.org/2011/09/22/press-widely-criticized-but-trusted-more-than-other-institutions/.
2. Pew Research Center for the People & The Press, "Press Widely Criticized, But Trusted More than Other Information Sources."
3. *The New York Times*, "To Our Readers," *The New York Times*, August 6, 2007. Accessed April 9, 2013, from www.nytimes.com/2007/08/06/opinion/l06note-web.html?_r=0.
4. David Folkenflik and Mark Memmott, "NPR to Discontinue 'Talk of the Nation," The Two-Way: Breaking News from NPR [website], March 29, 2013. Accessed August 13, 2014, from www.npr.org/blogs/thetwo-way/2013/03/29/175677788/talkofthenation.
5. Folkenflik and Memmott, "NPR to Discontinue 'Talk of the Nation."
6. Suzanne LaBarre, "Why We're Shutting Off Our Comments," *Popular Science*, September 24, 2013. Accessed September 9, 2014, from www.popsci.com/science/article/2013–09/why-were-shutting-our-comments.

7. Rem Rieder, "No Comment," *American Journalism Review*, Washington, D.C., June/July 2010. Accessed September 9, 2014, from http://ajrarchive.org/article.asp?id=4878.
8. Rem Rieder, "Miami Herald Ends Anonymous Comments," USAToday.com, February 15, 2013. Accessed August 13, 2014, from www.usatoday.com/story/money/columnist/2013/02/15/rem-rieder-miami-herald-facebook-commenting/1919555/.
9. Jack Rosenberry,"Users Support Online Anonymity Despite Increasing Negativity," *Newspaper Research Journal* 32, 2 (2011), 6–19.
10. Hans K. Meyer and Michael Clay Carey, "In Moderation: Examining How Journalists' Attitudes Toward Online Comments Affect the Creation of Community," *Journalism Practice* 8, 2 (2014), 213–28.
11. Kalman Seigel, *Talking Back to* The New York Times: *Letters to the Editor, 1851–1971* (New York: Quadrangle Books), 9.
12. Margaret Sullivan, "Seeking a Return to Civility in Online Comments," *The Buffalo News*, Buffalo, N.Y., June 20, 2010. Accessed July 1, 2010, from www.buffalonews.com/2010/06/20/1088283/seeking-a-return-to-civility-in.html.
13. Sokari Ekine, "Africa News Empowers Citizens to Report Online," Mediashift [website]. Accessed August 13, 2014, from www.pbs.org/mediashift/2008/10/africa-news-empowers-citizens-to-report-online287/
14. Siegel, *Talking Back to* The New York Times, 8.
15. Amelia Lester, "Ladylike: Julia Gillard's Misogyny Speech," *The New Yorker*, October 9, 2012. Accessed August 13, 2014, from www.newyorker.com/news/news-desk/ladylike-julia-gillards-misogyny-speech.
16. James Aucoin, "Does Newspaper Call-In Line Expand Public Conversation?" *Newspaper Research Journal* 18, 3&4 (1997), 122–40.
17. Rosenberry, "Users Support Online Anonymity Despite Increasing Negativity"; Hans K. Meyer and Michael Clay Carey, "In Moderation: Examining How Journalists' Attitudes Toward Online Comments Affect the Creation of Community," *Journalism Practice* 8, 2 (2014), 213–28.
18. Sullivan, "Seeking a Return to Civility in Online Comments."
19. Rosenberry, "Users Support Online Anonymity Despite Increasing Negativity."
20. Bill Reader, "An Ethical 'Blind Spot': Problems of Anonymous Letters to the Editor," *Journal of Mass Media Ethics* 20, 1 (2005), 62–76; Bill Reader, "Free Press vs. Free Speech? The Rhetoric of 'Civility' in Regard to Anonymous Online Comments," *Journalism & Mass Communication Quarterly* 89, 3 (2012), 495–513.
21. Reader, "Free Press vs. Free Speech?"
22. Bill Reader, Guido Stempel, and Douglass Daniel, "Age, Wealth, Education Predict Letters to the Editor," *Newspaper Research Journal* 25, 4 (2004), 55–66.
23. Personal communication, March 22, 2013 (telephone interview).
24. Personal communication, March 12, 2013 (email).
25. Personal communication, March 12, 2013 (email).
26. Personal communication, March 11, 2013 (email).
27. The message was posted to the listserv of the International Society of Weekly Newspaper Editors, of which the author of this book is a member.
28. Email to the listserv of the International Society of Weekly Newspaper Editors, April 12, 2013.

Index

For Product Safety Concerns and Information please contact our EU
representative GPSR@taylorandfrancis.com
Taylor & Francis Verlag GmbH, Kaufingerstraße 24, 80331 München, Germany